Praise for *Big Business Marketing for Small Business Budgets*

"Starting with the Internet boom, we seemed to get right back in the habit of sloppy quality, indifferent service, and expensive but vacuous advertising. McMurtry reminds us how to do it right. It's one of the first places I'd turn to systematically review my own, or a client's, selling and marketing activities."

—Robert H. Waterman, Jr.
Coauthor of *In Search of Excellence*

"The real beauty of Jeanette Maw McMurtry's *Big Business Marketing for Small Business Budgets* is that it is practical—full of ideas and insights that small business owners and managers can begin to use immediately, without sorting through a lot of MBA-school theories. And the real value of her book is that it is laser-focused on the precise needs of her audience: people who are trying to make small businesses succeed."

—Kathleen Larey Lewton, APR, Fellow PRSA
2001 National President, Public Relations Society of America

Big Business
Marketing for

SMALL

BUSINESS

BUDGETS

Jeanette Maw McMurtry

McGraw-Hill

*New York   Chicago   San Francisco   Lisbon   London   Madrid   Mexico City
Milan   New Delhi   San Juan   Seoul   Singapore   Sydney   Toronto*

1 2 3 4 5 6 7 8 9 0   AGM/AGM   0 9 8 7 6 5 4 3

ISBN 0-07-140597-6

McGraw-Hill books are available at special quantity discounts to use as premiums and sales promotions, or for use in corporate training programs. For more information, please write to the Director of Special Sales, Professional Publishing, McGraw-Hill, Two Penn Plaza, New York, NY 10121-2298. Or contact your local bookstore.

 This book is printed on recycled, acid-free paper containing a minimum of 50% recycled, de-inked fiber.

Library of Congress Cataloging-in-Publication Data

McMurtry, Jeanette Maw.
   Big business marketing for small business budgets / by Jeanette Maw McMurtry.
      p.   cm.
   ISBN 0-07-140597-6 (Paperback : alk. paper)
1. Marketing—Management. 2. Small business—Marketing. I. Title.

   HF5415.13 .M3694 2003
   658.8—dc21

                                                      2002152444

To John, with deep gratitude, for helping make all my dreams come true.

Contents

Part 1

Understanding the Principles and Value of Lifetime Marketing

Reversing the Telescope—Learn to See Your Business from the
Outside In
*Eight Common Mistakes • Marketing That Gets Results •
Reversing the Telescope • Why Are Relationships Important?
• Getting Started—Lifetime Marketing Checklist •
Worksheet: Is Your Marketing Program Set Up to Fail or
Succeed?*

If Mass Advertising Is So Great, Why Do So Many Advertisers
Go Out of Business?
*The Fallacies of Mass Advertising • Advertising Waste •
The Lifetime Marketing Difference • Getting Started—
Lifetime Marketing Checklist • Worksheet: Is Your
Advertising Generating Results?*

Worksheet: Create a Profile Matrix for Your Most Profitable and Valuable Segments

Part 4

Building Your Lifetime Marketing Plan

Acknowledgments

There are many people who have helped make this book a reality by sharing their knowledge, believing in me, and encouraging me to try. First is my mother, Mildred Maw. There was never a dream she did not believe I could achieve. Next is my father, Grant Maw, whose fierce determination to overcome challenges has and always will be a great inspiration to me. Then there is my husband, John, whose endless confidence, tremendous support, and personal example have given me much strength and courage. Special thanks go to my sisters, Meridee Calder and Cynthia Maw; my mother-in-law, Virginia McMurtry; and my friend, Joanne Grimm, for their undying enthusiasm and support for everything I do. I also thank Charles Graves, whose obstinate encouragement over the years has helped pushed me out of comfort zones into new territory.

Thanks also go to the many accomplished marketing and business professionals who shared with me their time and stories for this book and to all the people with whom I have worked in various capacities who taught me to think beyond boundaries and challenge relentlessly.

Special gratitude goes to Ann Wildman, my editor, who literally made this happen, and to all the wonderful friends who helped me survive writing this book while giving birth to twin daughters, Jenevieve Virginia and Jordan June, and raising their two-year-old sister, Jessica Rose.

Jeanette Maw McMurtry

Introduction

With the advent of customer relationship management (CRM) technology and the Internet, big companies can play by the same rules for personalized communications and customer interaction that traditionally have been reserved for small businesses. As a result, it is imperative that small businesses improve on their own game, find ways to better manage and maintain customer relationships, and rethink their marketing initiatives in order to keep up with and fend off competitors with deeper pockets and greater resources.

Although competing with big business may seem like a losing proposition, it can be done, successfully and affordably, by developing and executing marketing activities that are designed to capture the loyalty and thus lifetime value of your best customers or, in other words, engaging in *lifetime marketing*. Lifetime marketing is about treating customers as if each one of them is your most important customer, offering customers high value in products and services, and rewarding them for their business in order to earn a lifetime of their loyalty.

Many big businesses, such as those ranked in the Fortune 500, have embraced the concept of lifetime marketing and have relied on the principles of lifetime marketing to build brand equity among their most valued customers. They have been able to do this with the use of CRM technology and savvy marketing teams. However, lifetime marketing success does not have to be limited to the big and wealthy; it is achievable by businesses of any size—from independent freelancers or consultants to companies with dozens or thousands of employees. It boils down to changing attitudes and urgencies about marketing and redefining the process altogether.

To succeed in today's environment, businesses of all sizes need to rethink the way they do marketing. The new paradigm—the one that builds lifetime loyalty and thus continuous revenue streams—focuses on the facts that there is no general public, there is no mass market, and there is no single message or promotion that will influence all customers. There are only individuals who want options, service, value, rewards, and recognition.

Since the 1990s we have been operating in what has been dubbed the age of the individual consumer. This is so because consumers have more control over the marketing process than ever before. It used to be that brands could offer customers a single distribution channel, and everyone was happy. This is not true for today's customers. Today's customers want and demand multichannel options—the Internet, catalogs, phone, fax, and in-store shopping. We want to choose how to do business, and we want to choose how we receive marketing messages. We opt in, opt out, tune in, and tune out. And we speak out if we feel that our privacy or trust has been violated. We also reassign our loyalty if we feel that we have not been treated fairly or that a product fails to meet our high expectations.

The consumer of the 2000s is more demanding and expects more than in any other age of marketing. Businesses thus have greater challenges than ever before. The traditional forms of marketing simply do not work now and have not worked for a long time. Consumers are less attentive to mass advertising in this age of diminished leisure time and heightened remote control usage. Consumers are also more informed and educated than in the past. With the Internet, consumers can and do research products, prices, warranties, service plans, and customer service issues and do competitive comparisons. Research shows that a growing number of consumers use the Internet for product research before ever contacting vendors. Consumers armed with information tend to be more selective in the shopping process and expect and demand more from the brands they choose. Businesses of all sizes thus have to market smarter and cater more to individual customers than ever before.

The positive side to this scenario is that customer loyalties tend to run deep. Once a consumer chooses a brand to satisfy a want or need, he will stay loyal to that brand if his experience is positive, if he continues to receive added value, and if he is rewarded and recognized for his patronage. Customer retention does more for a company's bottom line than customer acquisition because it costs far less to generate incremental sales from existing customers than it does to solicit and convert new leads. By keeping customers loyal to their brands for the lifetime of their purchasing cycle, businesses can succeed over the long term and sustain lasting profitability. Small businesses need to be able to offer the same level of customer management as large businesses in order to capture and maintain this new level of loyalty. They can do so by adapting big business marketing principles to their current resources and budgets.

Marketing for a lifetime, or executing programs for capturing the lifetime value of your best customers, is the single most important marketing goal any business can achieve. All marketing efforts and expenditures need to be aimed at this outcome. Virtually anything else is a waste of time, money, and resources.

Big Business Marketing for Small Business Budgets is designed to provide owners and marketing managers of small businesses with the same marketing knowledge, perspective, and tools as their big business counterparts in order to help level the playing field. By reading this book, you will learn how to market for a lifetime, or capture the lifetime value of your most valued customers through personal, relevant, and motivating communications that keep people close to your brand and loyal in their purchases. When you do this successfully, you will build a successful, enduring business.

The end result of properly developed lifetime marketing programs is one of the strongest competitive advantages a business can create. If you can give consumers what they want and need, reward them for their loyalty, and communicate with them in a way that makes them feel as if they are your most valued customers, competing businesses will be wasting their time trying to entice away your customers. If done correctly, lifetime marketing results in customer loyalty, increased sales, and qualified referrals. Achieving these three goals will ensure longevity and profitability for any business. Mass advertising, which I call "advertising roulette" because you never know if you are going to hit the target and score, does little to provide a business with this type of long-term security.

The core value of this book is to discover winning ideas and strategies and learn how to execute them on a smaller level, one that is in line with your company's resources and budgets. My goal is to help businesses achieve a lifetime of success by marketing smarter—from product development and distribution to pricing and promotion. I hope to help readers define their own perspectives about marketing and incorporate ideas from others' successes into their own individualized marketing plans.

Throughout this book I present many examples and draw even more conclusions. These conclusions are based on my experiences, successes, research, and observations while fulfilling numerous roles in marketing, advertising, and public relations. I present several rules for lifetime marketing success.

Big Business Marketing for Small Business Budgets teaches winning principles, shares compelling examples, and provides tools that will enable you to easily assess your current marketing strengths and weaknesses and create successful programs specific to the needs of your business. At the end of each chapter is a worksheet for this purpose. You will find a complete tool kit at my Web site, *www.mcmurtrygroup.com*. You also will find up-to-date examples of successful lifetime marketing programs, sample tools and templates of marketing materials, and a schedule of lifetime marketing seminars and events.

Lifetime marketing works. However, it is not a quick fix. Anything worthwhile takes time. And this is especially so in marketing. Just as most of the relationships you have built personally and professionally took time and effort to build, so too do those involving customers and prospects. If you are looking for a quick fix, you are reading the wrong book. If you are looking for a long-term solution for building a strong customer and prospect base, building brand equity and loyalty among your most valued customers, and achieving steady revenue streams, enjoy!

Part 1

Understanding the Principles and Value of Lifetime Marketing

1 Why So Many Marketing Plans Fail—Eight Primary Reasons

Reversing the Telescope—Learn to See Your Business from the Outside In

Businesses that adhere to the old school of marketing, which involves pushing goods and services toward the masses and waiting for consumers to take them or leave them, are most often the same businesses that struggle to remain competitive. This is because we are living in a new age of business—one in which customers have taken charge of the marketing process rather than the other way around.

In this new marketing paradigm, customers define the products they want, where and when they will purchase the products, and how they want to communicate with the producers of those products. Consumers no longer respond to mass marketing as they did before and refuse to be treated as anything less than a valued individual. Customers are demanding that businesses provide them with the best possible service, the greatest possible number of choices, and the highest level of personalization possible. Customers want to be treated as if they are a brand's most valued customer through individual attention and offerings. They want to be given choices regarding product features, how businesses communicate with them, how they communicate with businesses, and how they are rewarded for their business.

Eight Common Mistakes

The purpose of this book is to provide owners and managers of small businesses and even marketing managers at large businesses with a new perspective on marketing and the tools to achieve unequaled results without spending unprecedented dollars. The first step is to understand why many programs fail and to avoid the common mistakes that both large and small businesses make.

Marketing plans fail often because they are

- Egocentric
- Overreaching
- Overbearing
- Nebulous
- Void of ownership
- Out of site, out of mind
- Budget-oriented
- Immeasurable

Egocentric

Out of either intimidation or incompetence, or both, marketers too often cater their marketing efforts to the business owner (sometimes themselves), CEO, board of directors, or other heads of their business environment. And all too often the reigning business executives have little or no marketing in their résumés and no direct experience in serving the customer. Yet marketers still build strategies and creative campaigns based on what will make management happy or, in other words, what will best prolong their job security and result in a better job evaluation. When these are the influences that drive marketing plans (and in my observation, they often are), marketing has little chance of generating desired returns and thus fails.

Advertisements or any communications activities generated by the preceding motives, typically result in what I call "ego ads" or "board of director ads." They please a small audience for the short term (until the results come in) but fail to have an impact on the bottom line. Copy for ego ads espouses the company mission, making leaders feel proud and self-actualized (as per Maslow's hierarchy of needs), but fail miserably when it comes to appealing to consumers and their decision processes. Making customers feel closer to self-actualization is a far more profitable endeavor than making company executives feel this way, yet this priority has eluded many a marketer.

Overreaching

Marketing failures often can be summed up by the old adage of "trying to be everything to everyone." This approach fails in most areas of life, and it most definitely fails in marketing. Most consumer businesses are not commodities and thus pedal products that appeal to specific customer groups. It is as simple as the fact that all women's clothing does not appeal to all women. Nature-loving women might shop at L.L. Bean or Lands' End for basic, neutral, and comfortable clothing; more flashy women might camp out at Neiman Marcus; and more practical women frequent discounters such as Nordstrom Rack and Ross Dress for Less. In this example, I have just identified three types of shoppers for women's clothing. It is highly unlikely that the same black dress would appeal to representatives of each of these groups.

Tips and Tactics

Identify your customers with the highest propensity to be profitable over the long term, and focus your efforts toward capturing their lifetime value. Do not try to capture every single customer's long-term business. This is not realistic or profitable.

Successful businesses understand that customers have acute differences in shopping preferences and incorporate these differences into their business and marketing plans rather than launch general programs that attempt to appeal to all customer segments simultaneously. On the other hand, some businesses fear that by pursuing a specific market niche they will ostracize potential consumers and thus not achieve high levels of sales. The reality is that in a consumer-driven marketing environment, you risk losing more over the long term by not defining your market position and fulfilling a niche that your business is highly qualified to serve. By focusing your business on fulfilling a lucrative niche, you will increase the chances of achieving long-term stability for your business. You will be able to launch highly targeted product development and marketing programs that allow you to operate your business more efficiently on several levels. Given the product and service demands of today's consumers, niche marketing coupled with relevant and appropriate marketing activities is far more likely to succeed than the "one size fits all" approach, especially for small businesses trying to carve out a market position upon which they can build.

Overbearing

A big mistake many business owners and marketing managers make is trying to do too much given their current resources and circumstances. When this happens, marketing plans become dissertations on what could be done by someone else, maybe even a competitor, with greater resources and deeper pockets. For a marketing plan to succeed, it must be executed, and for a plan to be executed, it must be realistic. As a small business owner, your marketing team might consist of you and a handful of supporting cast members; therefore, you might be better off setting two to three primary objectives and giving yourself a full year to accomplish them. These objectives might be as simple as

1. Creating a strong customer database so that you can record individual transactions, identify key selling opportunities for individuals, sort customers into segments, and so on
2. Adapting your Web site to better collect customer data
3. Executing three or more communications programs for each of your top three customer segments

Companies that define more than they can execute get frustrated and often feel too overwhelmed to even get started. Thus the marketing plan is put in a file folder and left there until the marketing manager changes jobs and throws it in the recycle bin.

Tips and Tactics

Marketing plans need to include a realistic working calendar with due dates and responsibilities. This will help you avoid feeling overwhelmed, pace your efforts, and ensure that your plan gets executed in a timely manner.

Out of Site, Out of Mind

The minute a marketing plan is put away or filed is the minute that it is set up to fail. While many business owners mentally commit to marketing, and know that it is critical to growing their business, they often get sidetracked with projects that have more tangible deadlines, such as production schedules, requests for proposals, and so on. I see this all too often as a consultant. A client of mine actually sidelined the marketing process midstream because she was just too busy concentrating on a single sales opportunity. Months later, she still had not gotten back to her intention to build a strong marketing program. Hopefully for her, that one sale will close and will keep her business profitable for years to come.

To avoid losing focus on your marketing program, keep it visible. I do not mean keep it in your inbox under a plethora of other documents and to-do lists, but keep it visible in an actionable way. This can be done by

- Writing your goals and action items in large print, one goal or action per page, and placing these on bulletin boards where they are frequently noticed.
- Creating a timeline for executing each action item in your plan. Put these items on your calendar in a way that you are reminded of them daily until they are done. Organizational tools such as Microsoft Outlook, personal digital assistants (PDAs), and even bulletin boards offer a great way to keep your action items fresh on your mind.
- Writing action items for each month on a white board in your office and in the conference room so that others can view your goals. Knowing that others are expecting you to fulfill these items often helps ensure that you do.

- Sharing your action items and timelines with other departments. They may be able to share resources with you, and again, knowing that they now expect fulfillment by you helps keep your marketing goals on your A list.

Nebulous

Marketing plans need to be specific to succeed. By setting goals that are ill defined or too general, marketing plans fail to be actionable. Often, companies set goals of becoming the "best of breed" or "most desired" in their industry, which are very broad and poorly defined goals. How does one define best of breed or most desired in measurable terms, how will one know when these goals have been achieved? Will achieving these goals strengthen current customer relationships and attract qualified leads? Broad, general goals are often rooted in claims that anyone can make about their company, whether or not they are true. Marketing goals need to be defined in quantifiable terms and actionable. For example:

- Increase new leads from Web site by 10 percent by providing incentives for visitors to register for future brand communications.
- Acquire at least one new customer per quarter.
- Increase business from existing customers by 20 percent through cross-selling and up-selling efforts.

These are actionable, achievable, and measurable. Goals that do not set forth a benchmark for measurement and a method of accomplishment may be too nebulous for a marketing team and supporting departments to embrace.

Tips and Tactics

A marketing plan should be a learning plan. Integrate activities that will enable you to learn more about your customers, their needs, and which communications vehicles reach them best. By applying your learning to future efforts, you will achieve greater efficiencies and success.

Void of Ownership

My mother has a figurine in her kitchen with the phrase "A mother's work is never done" inscribed on it. This same concept applies to marketing. A program is never complete, an effort never finalized. This is so because marketing does not stop when the ads are placed or the letters are mailed. Lifetime marketing programs continue far beyond a campaign's execution and involve far more than the marketing department. Sales, customer service, operations, administration, and office support staff must embrace the overall marketing goals and take ownership for their success. The actions and abilities of these people to execute their jobs in a way that addresses customers' needs and expectations are critical to making customers want to assign their lifetime loyalty to your brand. Before finalizing any marketing goals or executing any campaigns, get consensus. If your employees, especially those who interact with customers such as sales and support personnel, do not take ownership of helping you achieve these goals and adapt their behavior accordingly, your marketing programs will fail. You need not only to get consensus but also to get commitment. Outline actions that each department must take to ensure that customers' experiences with your brand are consistent, based on individual needs and transactions, and satisfying beyond what they could get from a competitor. Without this, your marketing plan is strictly academic.

Tips and Tactics

Keep your marketing plans simple by setting clear and realistic goals given your time and resources. Do not try to keep up with a competitor's marketing budget. Stay focused on your individual circumstances and realities.

Budget-Oriented

Budget-oriented does not refer to marketing plans with budgets but rather to marketing plans that are driven by budgets rather than by goals. As a consultant, I have too often heard, "I spend money in radio, in newspaper, and in specialty magazines. I don't have the budget to do anything else." This statement is often followed by "This is how I've always done things, even though I can't tell you what works best." Marketers with this mindset spend their time making sure that they get the best deal with their chosen media outlets and invest little or no thought in whether or not this medium will work for their business.

Many marketers buy media space or time just because it seems like the necessary thing to do or because they listen to a specific radio station or read the local paper. They have never kept track of who their customers are, what influences them, and which advertising outlets reach their customers and which do not. As a result, they throw their money away without any indication of a return on their investment.

Before you spend another dime on advertising, no matter how good a deal you may have sitting before you, build a marketing plan based on the lifetime marketing principles set forth in this book. Only engage in advertising opportunities that support and enhance your lifetime marketing efforts. By doing this, chances are pretty high that you will save money and achieve a higher return.

If you stick to the following process, you will spend your resources far more wisely, generate results from your efforts, and increase your long-term profitability.

- Get to know your customers—their needs and purchasing influences
- Set goals according to customer needs and your business's resources
- Develop action items that address these needs as individually as possible.
- Deliver your messages via media and outlets that have proven exposure and credibility among your audiences.

Tips and Tactics

If you are a one-person business, share your marketing goals and action items with owners of similar businesses whom you admire. Getting an outsider's opinion usually helps keep things in perspective and often leads to new ideas.

Immeasurable

If you cannot track the results of your programs, you do not know if you have failed or succeeded in generating more business or accomplishing other business goals. To identify the value of your expenditures, stick to this simple rule: If you cannot measure it, do not do it. To identify the value of your expenditures toward capturing customers' lifetime value, follow this rule: If you cannot measure it down to the individual level, do not do it. Enough said.

The fundamental reason that many marketing plans fail to achieve desired sales results is because they focus on the wants of the business team and not on those of customers. In reality, customers' wants are very simple. Most often it is the little things that bring customers back.

According to various consumer studies, customers want

- **Recognition.** Customers want to be recognized as individuals with unique needs and desires. They like to be called by name.
- **Service.** Customers want thoughtful and consistent service provided by employees at all levels of the organization. They like service that goes beyond what is expected.
- **Options/Diversity.** Customers want a wide variety of products. Businesses face the challenge of satisfying diverse customer requirements.
- **Information.** Customers are more involved in their purchases than ever before. They read labels and research products and functional alternatives on the Internet so that they can make informed decisions.
- **Identification.** We tend to identify our own image with the products we buy—cars, homes, clubs we join, and so on. Companies can build on customers' needs to associate with winning businesses through testimonials and endorsements and by providing customers with an informative business environment.

Marketing That Gets Results

Customers are able to control the marketing process in large part because of the many options available to them and because of the technologies available today that allow them to choose how they shop and demand individualized attention. Businesses that are thriving in this new marketplace are those which view customers as individuals with specific needs, interests, tastes, personalities, and emotional references rather than a statistic within a mass population.

Thriving businesses in this new world of personalization are those which communicate and cater to individual needs and values and offer choices for just about everything—from specific product features and pricing to multichannel purchasing options such as shopping on the Internet, by phone, through catalogs, or the old-fashioned way by actually visiting a bricks-and-mortar store and interacting with a live person in real time. Businesses that do this successfully, such as Eddie Bauer, Barnes & Noble, Target, Circuit City, and Armani Exchange, are among the most successful and stable businesses of our time. These companies get it. They understand who their customers are, what their customers want and expect, and how their customers want to shop and communicate with them.

Knowing who your customers are demographically and psychographically, what they need from products within your category, what they expect in terms of product functionality and customer service, and what types of interactions and relationships they want and expect to have with your brand is the key to entering the new market paradigm of marketing for a lifetime and getting the results you desire for your business. This is the first step to becoming a *lifetime marketer*—one that executes marketing strategies from the outside in versus the inside out in order to capture the lifetime of purchases from their most valuable customers. These are the marketers that achieve greater efficiencies and profitability.

Capturing the lifetime loyalty of your best and most lucrative customers before your competition does is the only way to stay in business in today's customer-oriented business environment. Yet even when faced with this reality, many businesses fail to produce customer-oriented marketing initiatives, and still waste valuable resources and money on developing and executing marketing plans built from the business's perspective rather than that of the customers.

Many businesses, small and large, need to make a significant paradigm shift and instead of developing plans from the perspective of the business, they need to build marketing programs from the perspective of their customers, or what I call *customer-oriented marketing plans* that personalize marketing messages, offers, and even products for a brand's most valued customers and prospects.

Big businesses have long dominated the game of personalized marketing because of the deep pockets they have to purchase sophisticated customer management and database programs, execute deep and extensive direct marketing campaigns, and build strong brand recognition through outrageously expensive advertising programs. Yet small businesses can launch equally effective marketing programs by executing lifetime marketing principles on much smaller budgets. This book sets forth many strategies and ideas that will enable smaller businesses to level the playing field when it comes to personalizing customers' brand experiences and communications.

Tips and Tactics

When gathering input for your marketing plan, talk first to your customers and second to your internal colleagues and management. Doing the reverse may limit your thinking and muddy your ability to hear clearly what your customers are saying.

Reversing the Telescope

Again, lifetime marketing is about learning to block out the internal perspective and see your business, products, and services from the same perspective as your customers. In other words, "learning to think from the outside in" rather than projecting your thinking outward and hoping that there is a customer out there who can relate to it.

Years ago I worked with a woman who was given the responsibility to develop new marketing programs for a specific division of her company. She came to me with preconceived notions of what customers believed about her brand and what their needs were. Her notions were based on her own attitudes and those of her superiors. She had no actual foundation for her conclusions, just her assumptions and those of many others. At my suggestion, we ended up doing a small market research project to confirm her assumptions and found quite abruptly that her customers' needs actually were quite different from what she and her associates had believed them to be. Sadly, this scenario is far too often true among small businesses never having made the effort to survey their customers and valued prospects. Basing marketing decisions on assumptions rarely pays off. More often it wastes valuable time, money, and other resources.

Lifetime marketers develop relevant—and successful—campaigns by first identifying

- Who their most profitable customers are
- What their customers' specific product needs and behavior patterns are
- What emotions drive their decisions and why they make the brand/vendor decisions that they do

Successful marketers also have a clear understanding of the goals that the customer sets for the product involved, such as the notion that "buying this product will enable me to perform better, faster, and get the recognition and promotion I deserve."

Reversing the telescope means taking an in-depth look at what influences your customers, what emotions drive their decisions, and why they seek specific brands. This applies to both business-to-consumer and business-to-business marketing activities. When it comes to business-to-business marketing, it is amazing to me how many business owners really do not know much about the people that drive the decisions to buy their products. They know which businesses buy their products, but businesses are not customers—*people* are. As a result, there is no such thing as business-to-business marketing, just *people-to-people marketing*. If you communicate like a business that is simply an institution, not a concerned individual with knowledge about what other individuals need, then your communications will be sterile, impersonal, and unnoticed. Unlike businesses, people have emotions, fears, and hopeful anticipations that drive their decisions. They have insecurities that influence their behavior, and they deal with internal politics that influence just about everything they do.

People's decisions regarding business issues are not based solely on extrinsic factors such as money, ease of execution, customer service, and so on but rather are largely based on such intrinsic factors as "Will this make me look good to my boss?" "Will it help me accomplish my goals so that I can get a promotion?" and "Will it make my job easier so that I will have more leisure time?" These factors are not job-related, but rather person-related, and they are most often the most critical influencers.

Tips and Tactics

Market to businesses in the same way that you would market to consumers. You are trying to establish relationships with people making business decisions, not institutions or committees.

I was asking a new client questions about her customers in order to develop a strategic plan for an upcoming business event. Partway through the discussion, the client stopped and said to me, "Wow. I never realized how little I understand my customers. This is embarrassing." Not only can it be embarrassing to not understand those who buy your products, it also can be devastating to your bottom line and long-term potential. My client's business had been in operation for more than 20 years and had succeeded by default. She has been lucky enough to have a few good long-term customers. Think of the potential business lost by not understanding more about customers, their associated needs and wants, not only in terms of repeat business but also in terms of acquiring new customers. Unfortunately, many businesses are in the same situation as the one I just described. They survive, but they miss out on the opportunity to build their businesses and secure long-term profitability.

By looking at your business from the customers' perspective, not only will you gain a better understanding of what your marketing activities need to achieve, what messages to communicate to whom, and when and how, you also will be able to build relationships that last a lifetime.

Why Are Relationships Important?

The facts speak for themselves.

- Businesses with a 98 percent customer retention rate are twice as profitable as those with a 94 percent retention rate.
- According to the Pareto principle, 80 percent of a given business's sales come from 20 percent of its customers.
- On average, businesses have a 15 to 20 percent customer turnover each year.
- Businesses retaining 80 percent of their customers keep them 5 years.
- Businesses retaining 90 percent of their customers keep them 10 years.
- Research shows that a company's best customers outspend others by
  - 16 to 1 in retailing
  - 13 to 1 in the restaurant business
  - 12 to 1 in airlines
  - 5 to 1 in the hotel industry

Relationship-building activities help to secure customer loyalty in a highly efficient and economical way. For example, it costs significantly less to keep customers than it does to acquire new ones. Consider the cost differences between acquisition and retention strategies (Figure 1-1):

- The average cost to acquire one customer: $20.00
- The average cost to retain one customer: $4.00

Building long-term relationships with customers not only results in repeat business, it costs significantly less than it does to bring in new customers.

Figure 1-1 *The Cost of Customer Acquisition versus Customer Retention*

Cost to Emphasize Acquisition		Cost to Emphasize Retention	
Acquire 6 customers	$120	Acquire 3 customers	$60
Retain 5 customers	$20	Retain 20 customers	$80
Total cost	$140	Total cost	$140
Total customers	11	Total customers	23

By understanding and practicing lifetime marketing principles, business owners can appeal directly to the right emotions of the right consumer groups and build relationships that last through the purchasing life cycles of its most valuable customers. This is the whole premise of my motto, *marketing for a lifetime.*

Getting Started—Lifetime Marketing Checklist

Before beginning on any marketing program, keep in mind the following points and activities:

1. Marketing plans fail essentially for the following eight reasons:

   - Egocentric
   - Overreaching
   - Overbearing
   - Out of site, out of mind
   - Nebulous
   - Void of ownership
   - Budget-based
   - Void of measurement

2. All goals and actions need to be based on the customers' needs and values, not the company's.
3. The most successful marketing programs are those which focus on a targeted group of consumers and provide relevant needs for that group.
4. Businesses need to build marketing plans that are realistic given their current resources, circumstances, and time for execution.

Action Items

1. Define specific goals and actions for achieving each goal. Make them clear and concise so that all involved parties understand your goals and can embrace them.
2. To maximize your marketing efforts, get consensus at all levels, from top to bottom. Include representatives from sales, customer service, operations, and senior management in planning discussions and goal setting.
3. Develop your goals and then your budget. Do not base decisions on what actions are the cheapest. Spending more to do something right pays off much more quickly than spending a little money many times over.
4. Integrate metrics for each of your goals so that you can clearly determine the success and impact your programs are having on business initiatives, such as lead generation, customer retention, brand equity, and so on.
5. Keep your marketing plan visible, and share it within the organization. Never file it away for completion "in the future."

Worksheet: Is Your Marketing Program Set Up to Fail or Succeed?

Answering the following questions will help you determine if you are set up to fail or succeed before you even get started. Check the box to the right of each question that most appropriately fits your current situation.

	1	2	3	4
Does your company have clearly defined marketing goals? 1. Yes 2. No				
What are your marketing goals based on? 1. Actual consumer data and feedback. 2. Directives from the CEO or top management. 3. Market opportunities defined via market research, analyses, and other scientific methods. 4. Traditional marketing activities from the past.				
How do you measure the success of your marketing activities? 1. Through year-over-year (YOY) comparisons. 2. By dollar amount spent. 3. Through customer feedback and apparent increases in activity. 4. Don't measure in any way.				
How have your marketing efforts been developed? 1. To appeal to customer groups and corresponding needs. 2. To appeal to the mass population. 3. To appeal to a specific demographic. 4. To appeal to top management and direct superiors.				
After completing a marketing plan, what happens next? 1. It is shared with all departments and posted in visible places. 2. It is filed away until needed for accounting purposes.				

	1	2	3	4
3. It is shared within the marketing department and assignments are made. 4. Nothing.				
Who is invited to participate in planning sessions? 1. Department/team leaders. 2. Advertising sales representatives. 3. Marketing team/agency representatives. 4. Just the creator, for example, business owner or marketing vice president.				
How often do you conduct customer surveys? 1. Quarterly. 2. Yearly. 3. Biannually. 4. Never.				
What drives marketing goals? 1. Actual customers needs, values, and expectations. 2. Directives from the CEO and top management. 3. Business goals, for example, revenue growth, margins, and so on. 4. The mood of the marketing team at the time.				
How do you determine the communications channels used for reaching your customers? 1. Identify the best channels for personalized, individual communications. 2. Whichever channels offer the best rates at the time. 3. Whichever channels are most often accessed by customers. 4. Stick to the channels always used.				

Score

Five or more questions, 1. Your business is on the right track, putting customers needs ahead of personal agendas.

Five or more questions, 2. Time to look at marketing from your customers' perspectives instead of that of your business. If you put your customers' needs first, you will be surprised at how easy it is to find affordable ways to reach your goals.

Five or more questions, 3. For the most part, your actions are based on sound principles. However, you need to update your thinking by putting aside the old rules and starting to focus on the new rule: *customers first*.

Five or more questions, 4. The fact that you are reading this book means that all is not lost. Congratulations on realizing that you need to start putting some thought behind your marketing efforts.

2 Mass Advertising versus Lifetime Advertising

If Mass Advertising Is So Great, Why Do So Many Advertisers Go Out of Business?

Few things are as permeating in today's society as advertising. Everywhere we go we are inundated with advertising messages. In elevators; on airplanes; on grocery store carts and even floors; on store receipts; on computer and cell-phone screens; on the sides of trucks and vans; on billboards along our highways; on kiosks along sidewalks; and on hallways in public buildings, we are exposed to some form of advertising. The latest news is that advertisers will soon be able to place their logos on the midriffs of cheerleaders and eventually on the moon. There seems to be no end to the places where advertising is cropping up.

Mass advertising, such as radio, television, newspapers, magazines, and the above-mentioned forms, has its place and can be very effective for established brands, if done correctly. One of the most effective uses of mass advertising is simply *brand maintenance,* or keeping your brand at the forefront of customers' minds. Most of the ads we see during our local news broadcasts and prime-time viewing hours are for brands that we all know and likely have experienced at some point in our consumer lifetimes. Many of the ads do not prompt us to immediate action, for example, to take advantage of a current sale or call for special premiums or discounts, but rather are simply geared toward keeping the brand at the forefront of our minds. The strategy behind these ads is to achieve "mind share" for a given brand of products. These ads are strategically placed to air at a high enough frequency to take mind share away from competitors and secure a top place in the minds of the viewing audience. Many brands have used mass media successfully to do just this. Through years of advertising, Kleenex is the name that comes to most minds for facial tissue, Coke for cola drinks, Band-Aids for sterile adhesive bandages, Xerox for copying, and so on.

The key here is that it took years of very expensive advertising for these brands to achieve the mind share they have, and it takes enormous advertising and business resources to maintain it. *Xerox* is still the term often used in office settings for making a photocopy, yet Canon and Hewlett-Packard have taken over a great deal of the market share. Xerox brand's longevity and very existence have been in question as its sales and stock value have hit historic lows. Currently, competitor Canon's stock is nearly four times as valuable, yet you do not often hear business executives ask their assistants to "Canon" a copy of a document. Coca-Cola is running a very tight race for the top soft-drink distributor in the world against Pepsi, yet more often we ask for a Coke when we would accept a Pepsi just as readily. These consumer idiosyncrasies resulted from a great deal of advertising and a great deal of money spent.

However, just because a brand has the top-of-mind share in a certain category does not guarantee its success over the long term. Subsequently, just because you outspend your competitors in advertising does not guarantee sales success, long-term profitability, or market dominance. More important in today's market place is achieving brand equity and loyalty. This is achieved through lifetime marketing activities that build lasting sales with customers according to their personal needs and experience with the brand. Marketers are learning that brand awareness or exposure through mass advertising is simply not enough to maintain a competitive edge and long-term customer loyalty. Thus many large consumer brands are integrating mass advertising and relationship marketing strategies. Lifetime marketers realize the many fallacies of mass advertising alone and are making the paradigm shift to lifetime marketing.

The Fallacies of Mass Advertising
Entertainment versus Strategic Value

In many cases, advertising has become another form of entertainment rather than a strategic business initiative. Every year, America's TV viewers are presented with a series of new and often unusual advertisements, especially around Super Bowl time. For the most part, Super Bowl advertisements are competing to be the most entertaining and different. Many focus very little on the products they are supposed to be promoting, and many are quickly forgotten after their very expensive debut, which reaches thousands, if not millions, of consumers with little or no interest in the product. Yet each 30-second spot still costs more than $1 million and in most cases several more millions to produce. Most Super Bowl ads have a very short lifespan, and as we saw with the Super Bowls in 1999 and 2000, so did many of the advertising companies, which were dot-com businesses. In fact, the majority of the dot-com companies that ran ads during the 1999 Super Bowl were shortly out of business.

Many of the advertisements that debuted during recent Super Bowls support my argument that advertising, specifically TV advertising, has became an exercise in creating entertaining vignettes more than an exercise in moving inventory through customer acquisition and retention. You may recall seeing ads about the Wild West "cat herders" or the great "squirrel run" mimicking the famous annual run with the bulls in Spain. These were clever and attention-getting, but do you recall the brand associated with these ads? And do you recall the specific message?

In most cases, the millions of dollars spent on producing television ads for Super Bowl Sunday and the millions more to air them generated little impact on the corresponding brands' business success and viability. According to a report by the *Wall Street Journal,* advertisers during the 2001 Super Bowl paid an average of $2 million per 30-second spot. Unfortunately for the advertisers, only two of the seven top advertisers finished the year with positive gains in market share. The other five lost significant ground (Figure 2-1).

How has mass advertising evolved into such an expensive yet ineffective practice? In many cases it is a result of clients allowing advertising agencies to take charge of their marketing efforts rather than the other way around. The focus of numerous advertising campaigns for both large and small businesses has shifted from sound business plans and objectives to personal agendas of achieving recognition for creative brilliance.

Figure 2-1 *Market Share Results for 2001 Super Bowl Advertisers*

Brand	Agency	Percent of Market Share	Share Points Gained or Lost
MasterCard	McCann-Erickson	27.0	+1.4
Dentyne Ice	BatesWorldwide	14.9	+0.6
Doritos	BBDO Worldwide	37.6	−0.1
Visa	BBDO Worldwide	50.5	−0.2
Pepsi-Cola	BBDO Worldwide	14.4	−0.4
Budweiser	Various	12.1	−0.5
Cingular	BBDO Worldwide	17.0	−3.0

Sources: Agency estimates; Nielsen Monitor Plus; Information Resources, Inc., survey of stores excluding Wal-Mart; Beverage Digest;Yankee Group estimates third quarter 2001.

The Award Factor

One of the biggest frustrations I have had when working with advertising agencies is what I call the *award factor*. Many creative teams focus so heavily on lining their walls with plaques and trophies from the Addy, CLIO, Mobius, Cannes Lions, and other prestigious industry award programs that they forget clients' objectives of selling more products and building brand equity. They typically present very clever, fresh advertising ideas to clients who quite often get so caught up in the unusual creative presentation that they too forget their objective and their target customers' frame of reference. As a result, we see a lot of clever, entertaining ads that do little more than just that—entertain.

For many of the expensive ads we have seen debuted during recent Super Bowl broadcasts, the only gain was to the ad agency in the form of another trophy, unfortunately, at the client's expense. In fact, EDS's "cat herders" ad from the Super Bowl in 2000 made it on *Adweek*'s list of top spots for 2000. The ad review talks about the clever, unique creative execution yet mentions nothing about results. In fact, EDS launched the "cat herders" ad during the Super Bowl in 2000 and the "squirrel run" ad during the Super Bowl in 2001 with plans to launch the third part of this campaign during the Super Bowl in 2002. However, the company decided to forgo the third ad, forgo the Super Bowl altogether, and instead create four new ads that ran a total of 58 times during the 17 days of the

2002 Olympic Winter Games in Salt Lake City, Utah. Instead of paying the $1.9 million per 30-second spot during the Super Bowl, it paid roughly a mere $600,000 per 30-second spot during the Olympics, and the ads were more message-oriented than entertainment-oriented like those of its previous campaign. Several other companies that traditionally advertised during the Super Bowl pulled their campaigns in 2002 and sought to use their money in ways that would build more market share rather than more entertainment for the masses.

Tips and Tactics

When developing advertisements, make sure that your creative team follows a clearly defined marketing plan and addresses real customer needs and emotions. Be careful not to let the art of creativity override the science of strategic marketing.

Apple's famous and trend-setting "1984" ad illustrates the power of creative passion versus the drive for results. Agency Chiat/Day was given the charge to create an ad that would delay the sales of IBM's newly released PCjr for at least 30 days when the new Macintosh was expected to be on the shelves. The creative team was attempting to create a memorable ad based on George Orwell's famous novel *1984* that would make its debut at the Super Bowl in 1984. The ad's production process took on a movielike approach with passionate creative minds calling the shots, not the client. In fact, the copywriter assigned to the project went ahead and produced the ad without getting final approval from the client. His justification was that the client was dragging its feet, and he could always get another job if his decision backfired. When the ad debuted for the company's board of directors, several were very unhappy with the ad, and the company ended up trying to cancel its contract for Super Bowl advertising. This is a classic example of what happens when agencies put creativity before a client's needs. Unfortunately, in my experience, this has become an all too common practice.

Another example of the misdirected impact of creative ads comes from Pets.com. You may remember the series of TV ads featuring a spotted sock-puppet dog. These clever ads became very popular and even had a cultlike following. While they were successful at creating laughs and winning awards and ad industry recognition, they failed in the most critical area of all: generating sales for Pets.com. Shortly after the campaign's execution, Pets.com was added to the dot-com casualty list and is now a URL for bricks-and-mortar competitor PetSmart.

The lesson here is for marketing managers to set definite marketing goals and to take control of their ad campaign development to ensure that it supports these goals rather than just creative objectives. When executing according to customers' values and needs, advertising agencies can produce effective advertisements that support lifetime marketing efforts. This occurs when the ads are based on actual customer data and research and are developed according to the values of the brand's most valued customers.

Saturn produced a series of advertisements that illustrate how mass media can support lifetime marketing efforts. Instead of producing typical car advertisements showing a car's rugged or precise performance capabilities, Saturn's agency, Hal Riney and Partners, created ads that promoted a different kind of car-buying experience for consumers, the kind for which customers had expressed a desire. Saturn was an immediate success. People flocked to Saturn dealerships in pursuit of a pleasant, no-hype car-buying experience. These ads were based on the emotional issues and concerns of car buyers and addressed them in a very effective way.

Through its brand-defining marketing, Saturn was able to establish a cult-like following of consumers and achieve stellar sales results in a very short amount of time. Remarkably, the ads did not focus on products; they focused on consumers and their real needs and concerns. By doing so, Saturn produced a highly successful advertising campaign that had a significant impact on its bottom line and supported the company's lifetime marketing efforts, or those activities that provide personal interaction and communications with customers based on their transaction histories. Saturn engages in many lifetime marketing activities. For example, registered owners can go to Saturn's Web site and take advantage of many added-value offerings, all of which provide a true benefit while at the same time endearing owners to the brand. These include service reminders, travel assistance, an events calendar, retailer programs with partners such as Lands' End and Carlson Wagonlit Travel, an online magazine, company and product news, e-cards, and games such as Saturn trivia. In 1994, Saturn held a homecoming bash at one of its plants that drew more than 40,000 Saturn fans.

Marketing materials do not have to be boring and full of coupons or slashed prices to get attention. You can still produce clever marketing programs, but you need to do so with a strategy in mind, one that encompasses solid information about your target customers and their extrinsic and intrinsic needs and decision-making factors and supports all your other lifetime marketing activities. Mass advertising needs to be a support function, not the primary means of marketing.

Lack of Measurement

Another reason that a great deal of mass advertising fails is because no one knows if it succeeds. Given the billions of dollars that are spent on TV advertising alone each year, it is mind-boggling that few companies can produce valid data showing that their investments produced positive returns.

While I was working in international marketing for American Express, the marketing team of which I was a part was given the charge to prove that advertising had a direct impact on sales. Harvey Golub, then CEO, froze the team's international advertising budget until this could be proven. No other division of American Express had ever been given this task, nor had our agency, Ogilvy & Mather, New York City. Additionally, we could not find another Fortune 100 company that had measured its advertising programs in such a way. We found ourselves in uncharted territory, a surprising situation given the huge advertising budgets spent each year by America's largest companies.

No business can sustain ad budgets of millions to hundreds of millions of dollars for the long term without sales accountability and maintain a competitive market position, especially in the face of a slowing economy. Companies that use mass advertising to sustain their brands' exposure or support lifetime marketing efforts must incorporate methods for learning which messages and media vehicles generate the most response among specific customer segments. Otherwise, advertising purchases will continue to be an expensive guessing game.

Even with metrics in place, it is difficult to precisely measure the results of mass-media campaigns. Too often consumers will reply "they saw it on the radio." In other words, they do not always remember where they saw or heard a marketing message, nor do they always want to admit it. Many people are reluctant to review their media habits, nor do they want to admit that they were influenced by advertising. At the same time, businesses need to be able to determine the return on their advertising dollars in order to build sales and profitability efficiently and allocate resources wisely. Businesses need to put in place the most reliable methods of measurement possible so that they may measure with some certainty the messages and vehicles that generate the most response and which consumer groups have the highest propensity to purchase. By doing so, they will be better able to properly allocate future resources and develop successful campaigns. If businesses are not able to do this, advertising dollars will continue to go to waste.

Advertising Waste

Many mass advertising campaigns result in high rates of "advertising waste" by reaching many consumers that will never have a need for or interest in the given products. Media outlets such as television, radio, and print base their rates on viewership and circulation regardless of how many of those people fit your specific customer profiles and have a need for your products or services. You pay to reach a large number of people that have no propensity to buy your products and likely never will, while hoping to reach those that are qualified leads. As a result, you end up wasting a great deal of money. Lifetime marketing efforts help you focus on reaching just the customers you need to reach and eliminate advertising waste by reaching each customer in a relevant and meaningful way. Think of the return on your investment when every person you reach has a high propensity to respond. Think of the reverse scenario associated with many television advertising purchases.

Let's say that $200,000 buys a 30-second spot on national TV to reach 1 million people. This sounds impressive. It costs just $0.20 to reach each person. However, you are only interested in reaching females aged 25 to 45 with young children aged 1 to 5. For the show you purchase, the viewership consists of only 100,000 consumers in this segment. So now your cost per relevant impression is up to $2 each. Of those 100,000 people who fit your target, only 10 percent are in a position to purchase your product within the next 3 to 6 months. Now you are spending $20 to reach each person who is a qualified candidate for purchasing your products in the imminent future. Additionally, you have just spent $200,000 to reach 10,000 likely candidates and 990,000 unlikely candidates. Suddenly this TV buy does not seem so attractive.

One of my clients had the attitude that in order to outgun the competition, he needed to advertise in every possible media outlet that covered his local market area. He ran spots on all the local radio stations and ads in every newspaper, specialty guide, and phone book. He loved to hear his jingles and see his business name in print. He justified his overly abundant media buying strategy by negotiating the lowest rates possible with every ad representative. When I met him, he had been doing this for years, yet he could not tell me what medium or what advertising messages were successful. He just knew he had to advertise, especially with the same outlets that carried his competitors' ads.

Unfortunately, many business owners make this same mistake. They get nervous when they see a competitor in the local paper and they are not there. Chances are your competitor is there because you are and could not tell you the return on his or her ad budgets either. Rather than throwing your money toward every sales rep in town, adhering to lifetime marketing principles will help you to focus your efforts and make every dollar count. While it is important to have visibility in your local market areas, and mass media provides this opportunity, it needs to be done strategically and in a way that supports more targeted, focused, and measurable activities rather than the other way around. Successful marketers realize that using valuable advertising dollars to generate repeat business from existing customers is far more productive than using mass media to solicit new inquiries.

Tips and Tactics

When collecting data for customer profiles, ask which media outlets are used most often, for example, TV, radio, daily newspapers, and so on. Knowing this will enable you to purchase targeted and appropriate media to support your lifetime marketing efforts.

Mass media should be used as reinforcement for your lifetime marketing efforts—those which target customers in the most personal, individual way possible. Public visibility will keep your brand fresh in the minds of customers and assure prospects that your brand is alive and strong. Seeing your logo or brand in targeted, appropriate media outlets also helps to reinforce recent decisions to purchase from you. This is an integral part of the consumer decision process that will be discussed later. However, it needs to be used in a way that minimizes waste and maximizes your overall marketing program.

The Lifetime Marketing Difference

As discussed earlier, lifetime marketing has many advantages over mass marketing. One key distinction is the ability to reward customers according to their individual relationship with your brand and their expressed needs. Lifetime marketing rewards customers for loyalty, whereas mass marketing cannot recognize individual customers, let alone their transaction histories.

Lifetime marketing pays off over the long term by generating steady revenue streams and acquiring new customers via referrals from valued customers. For many retailers, mass advertising typically pays off the most when promoting deep discounts and other types of sales designed to move inventory quickly. This does not result in long-term sales generated by repeat business or referrals. Thus companies who emphasize strictly mass media fall short when it comes to long-term profitability, and in today's business environment, this often leads to failure.

Again, lifetime marketing involves getting to know who your customers are as individuals rather than demographics or businesses. It requires understanding the emotions they attach to your product or service and how these emotions influence purchasing patterns and choices, brand selection, and more. It means communicating with customers on a level that makes them feel noticed and valued and makes them want to do business with you again. Lifetime marketing also means rewarding customers for their business and their loyalty.

Smart lifetime marketers find ways to reward customers that build equity in their brands and make it costly for customers to switch to a competitor, and these marketers put their advertising dollars toward promoting these value-offering programs. MCI has done a great job in offering programs that create brand equity and make brand switching complicated and costly. Most recently, the company offered points for every call made, redeemable for Delta Airlines Frequent Flyer miles. In the early 1990s, MCI launched the Friends and Family program, which asked customers to identify up to 20 phone numbers of people they called frequently. If they could get those 20 people to also enroll in the program, they would receive a 20 percent discount whenever they called one another. This program is a brilliant example of lifetime marketing for many reasons.

- First, it rewarded customers with a discount for using their service.
- Second, it motivated customers to do MCI's sales work for them. Customers recruited new customers and were paid far less to do so than any salesperson ever would be. This method is certainly far cheaper and consumer-friendly than hiring a staff to interrupt people's dinner hours and stumble through scripted sales pitches in an attempt to get them to switch carriers for long-distance telephone service.
- Third, it built brand equity that would be hard for any competitor to touch. Customers enrolled in the program invested personal time in preparing the list of 20 friends or family members and had openly

endorsed the MCI brand. As a result, it would be a waste of time, and for many people personally embarrassing, to switch brands. And by doing so, they also would lose the discounts they had earned.

Frequent purchaser programs are another successful method for building brand equity. Airlines have been very successful at maintaining brand loyalty in order to get that free trip. When given a choice, many business and leisure airline travelers choose the airline for which they have the most Frequent Flyer points. Phone and credit card companies have done a good job of capitalizing on this success by offering points for specific airlines. Personally, one of the main reasons I chose my current long-distance carrier is because I get Delta Frequent Flyer points for each dollar I spend. Since I am a frequent Delta flyer, I am motivated to add miles to my account so that I can get more rewards quickly. I am not interested in starting over with another airline because it takes years to accumulate enough points to get a free airline ticket. The other long-distance carriers do not even interest me with promises of lower rates because I would lose this distinct value. Building this type of brand equity among your most valued customers is a critical aspect of successful lifetime marketing. It does not take big business budgets to achieve strong levels of brand equity among customers. It simply takes knowing what your customers value and providing it to them in a way that is convenient and relevant.

Tips and Tactics

Find ways to reward customers that are relevant to your business, your customers, and your relationship with each other. Rewards can be as simple as discounts on purchases or free gifts or service packages. Whatever you offer, make sure that it is relevant to your customers' needs, makes them feel valued, and supports your desired brand image.

Getting Started—Lifetime Marketing Checklist

Mass media can play a role in your lifetime marketing plan if executed strategically as a means to support more personalized, relevant communications rather than a means to stimulate long-term sales. Your resources will be best used if you carefully select only those outlets which have proven exposure among current customers and prospects to whom you want to market for a lifetime.

Action Items

1. Take charge of your mass-marketing programs by defining clear goals and directing your agency toward these goals.
2. Be accountable and make your advertising agency accountable. Clearly define how you will measure the success of your advertising, and link that success to your lifetime marketing efforts.
3. Survey customers to find out which media vehicles they use most often.
4. Set your priorities. Pinpoint publications or broadcast stations that are designed to appeal to your most valuable segments and hence prospects.
5. Purchase media that will reach your core customer and prospect groups. Do not waste money trying to reach customers who represent the least gain to you. Avoid the temptation to purchase an outlet just because it offers a low price.
6. If you choose to engage in mass marketing to help solicit new customers, develop your ads in a way that will appeal to your most valued customers. By doing so, you will appeal to your most valued prospects.
7. Develop advertisements that motivate first and amuse second.
8. Create marketing programs that allow you to learn. Learning objectives might be to determine which message has the most pull for specific customer groups, which media generates the most response, which types of media outlets generate the most response, and what level of emotional appeal generates the most result. Using mass media to learn about your customers' media viewing or media believability trends will better enable you to market to them in a personalized way.

Worksheet: Is Your Advertising Generating Results?

Questions to Ask Yourself	1	2
What do I hope to accomplish by using mass-media outlets? 1. Generate prospects. 2. Increase sales.		
What have I learned from past mass-media purchases? 1. Which outlets get the most response. 2. Nothing.		
What type of results have I achieved in the past? 1. Increase in inquiries via phone or the Web. 2. Don't know.		
What drives the creative development of my ads? 1. Customer data/research. 2. Advertising agency.		
I use separate ads to deliver different messages to different audiences via appropriate media vehicles rather than one message to all. 1. True. 2. False.		
I selected my advertising agency according to 1. Results generated and strategic strengths. 2. Creative output.		
Questions to Ask Your Advertising Agency		
Do you measure the impact of your campaigns? 1. Yes. 2. No.		

	1	2
If yes, please describe methods used. 1. Different metrics per medium or message. 2. Phone calls to clients.		
Describe the campaign of which you are most proud? 1. Emphasis is on results. 2. Emphasis is on creative product.		
Do you have an experienced media planner on your team? 1. Yes. 2. No.		
How do you use mass advertising to support relationship marketing? 1. Reference values of core customers to drive consumers to Web site for data collection. 2. Do not integrate the two approaches.		

Score

Questions Asked of Yourself

Three or more questions, 1. You are on the right track. Stay focused on using mass advertising to solicit new prospects and convert to lifetime marketing candidates.

Three or more questions, 2. Time to rethink how you are spending your money and your use of mass-media outlets.

Questions Asked of Your Agency

Three or more questions, 1. Your agency is on the right track. Work together to further refine your mass-media efforts according to specific customer profiles and needs.

Three or more questions, 2. Hire a new agency. You need a team that will help you maximize your advertising efforts and achieve lifetime marketing success.

3 The Principles of Lifetime Marketing

Why Market for a Lifetime When You Need Revenue Today?

Many marketing programs and even businesses fail simply because of vision problems. Business managers often cannot see beyond the current quarter's sales goals and instead focus all their energy on the here and now rather than on building a solid base of qualified customers that will generate current and future sales. The rise and fall of the dot-com businesses in the late 1990s is a great example of what happens when myopia guides business decisions. For the first known time in Wall Street's history, investors threw out all the rules and were investing millions in companies that had no proven success, revenue stream, or solid business plans defining a vision for long-term success. They saw quick profits based on a few lucky initial public offerings (IPOs) and threw themselves into the IPO frenzy. Unfortunately, many if not most of the dot-coms that made their investors rich overnight are gone today. The owners and managers of many failed dot-coms focused on one thing—a quick return. As a result, many failed to focus on building a lasting business and value proposition. Their goal was to get operating as quickly as possible, to window dress the business by hiring a lot of employees and producing exciting ads, and then to conduct an IPO and retire—all within 2 to 3 years. Most of these businesses never reached their IPO goals. For each one that did, thousands did not. The companies that achieved successful IPOs and are still in operation today are those which focused on being in business for the long term and thus attempted to build solid relationships with their direct and channel customers.

Like the thousands of failed dot-coms, businesses that focus on their current market environment only are quickly left behind and often fail to make a comeback. In the end, millions of dollars and valuable resources are wasted, and potentially good ideas are dead in the water.

Why Lifetime Marketing?

In order to succeed for the long term, you must keep one eye on your current business and the other on your future business. If your marketing efforts stop at generating sales for the current quarter or fiscal year, so will your business. Lifetime marketing is simply the strategy of marketing to current customers and qualified prospects in a way that builds personal equity in and passion for a brand. Passion? Yes, as overstated as it may seem, you need to instill passion for your brand because passion does not die or change with the wind. Passion rules behavior. Synonyms for passion include *fervor, craze, obsession, delight, enthusiasm,* and *excitement*. These words describe exactly how all businesses want their customers to feel about their brands. Think of the consequences if you could make your customers obsessed with your brand to the point that they could not get enough of what you offer or so enthusiastic that they would tell everyone they know about your brand or so delighted with their brand experience they would never think of switching to the competition even if your price were higher. My grandfather used to get in very heated debates with his neighbor about Chevy versus Ford trucks. His temper flared at every insult about a Chevy truck's quality and performance, whereas his neighbor reacted the same way about his comments about Ford. This kind of passionate loyalty lasts a lifetime, passes through generations, and results in great word-of-mouth marketing. In my grandfather's case, it also resulted in stressful relations between neighbors.

Even if a brand's quality starts to slip, passionate customers remain loyal, have faith that the brand will correct its problems, and defend it to critics. A great example of this is Harley Davidson. For a period of years, Harley's quality suffered to the degree that the saying on the street was, "You need to buy two Harleys at the same time, one for riding and the other for parts." Despite their joke-generating product quality, Harley bikes continued to sell among a core group of passionate riders. Harley, which has since turned its quality around through aggressive total quality management efforts, has successfully capitalized on the customer passion associated with its brand by creating innovative marketing programs, one of which is the Harley Owners Group (H.O.G.). The H.O.G. program organizes adventurous activities that bring owners together periodically to ride, to have fun, and most importantly, to talk about their enthusiasm for and obsession with their Harleys. As a result, the passion gets stronger and the loyalty more secure. The H.O.G. program started in 1983 and grew to more than 650,000 members and around 1200 chapters worldwide.

Passionate customers

- Talk positively and frequently about your brand (the most valuable marketing of all)
- Look forward to their next interaction with your brand
- Look forward to their next purchase of your products
- Are the first to try your new products and services
- Are understanding if at first you do not get all products features working right
- Defend your brand and products to critics and users of competing products

So how do you instill passion among your customers? This is what lifetime marketing is all about. Lifetime marketers create passion for a brand by

- Making customers feel important
- Standing behind their promises and perceived promises (even when the customer is wrong)
- Getting to know customers inside and out
- Offering customers exactly what they need when they need it
- Providing exceptional customer service and convenience-based services
- Educating customers about a particular product category so that they can make informed decisions
- Treating customers like partners rather than revenue streams
- Communicating to customers through appropriate channels and messages

When customers become passionate, they become lifetime loyalists and your best "on the street" marketers. As silly as it may sound, you need to think of your job as driving people to commit "purchases of passion" rather than "crimes of passion."

If you can perform these activities consistently, you will have a business that will weather the most threatening storms, minimize the competition, and profit for the long term. Your business will thrive because you

- Know who your most profitable customers are
- Know who your most valuable prospects are
- Learn to listen to customers' specific needs and develop products, services, and marketing programs accordingly
- Have highly satisfied customers who will stand behind your brand even if your product's quality or service falters temporarily
- Use your resources wisely—targeting customers and prospects most likely to purchase rather than wasting money shouting your brand's messages to the world
- Offer customers relevant promotions and incentives for additional purchases and thus achieve higher response rates
- Reward customers appropriately for their business and referrals
- Gain highly qualified leads through personal referrals from happy customers
- Have loyal customers that are passionate about your brand and likely never to switch to a competitor
- Retain customers and secure repeat sales for the long term

The benefits associated with having passionate, loyal customers are the reasons to market for a lifetime rather than to focus on getting revenue today. If your business cannot succeed after accomplishing the preceding, you need to take a much deeper look at how you do business internally and externally, far beyond your marketing and sales activities.

When you commit to *marketing for a lifetime*, you become a lifetime business—one that keeps customers for their purchasing lifetimes and lengthens its own lifetime through enhanced and steady revenue streams. If your goal is to build a business that will last more than a few years and increase in profitability, you must commit yourself and everyone involved with your business to lifetime marketing. Everyone must focus on the long-term potential that every transaction has rather than short-term individual, department, or business goals.

Shortly after the September 2001 terrorist attacks on the United States, the automobile industry engaged in what I call near-sighted marketing activities. Top executives rightly anticipated an economic slowdown. As predictions of an economic crumble mounted, most automobile manufacturers rushed to offer unprecedented deals to consumers in order to move inventory and avoid devastating sales loses for fourth quarter 2001. They did this by offering huge discounts and 0 to 2.9 percent interest rates for up to 60 months. During this time, the U.S. Commerce Department showed a record 0.3 percent surge in retail sales for October 2001 and attributed much of the gain to the low financing offered by automakers. This tactic was very successful and resulted in many dealers nationwide posting significant gains over similar sales periods of previous years. However, at the same time, the manufacturers set the stage for bleak sales immediately afterwards and a prolonged need to offer profit-slimming discounts. Consumers who would likely have purchased in the spring of 2002 instead made purchases in the fourth quarter of 2001.

When small businesses make near-sighted sales and marketing decisions, the consequences are often more devastating. Instead of securing a steady revenue stream, they experience a revenue roller coaster that can put any business at risk of failing. Successful businesses realize this and instead focus on creating promotions that offer long-term value and build brand equity for customers and hence themselves.

Tips and Tactics

To get the most out of your marketing dollars, your first priority should be to keep your brand alive among existing customers through relevant correspondence and promotions. Second, introduce your brand to prospects that resemble your best customers.

Research shows that marketing to your existing customers is far more lucrative than spending money and resources on cold calls to prospects. A marketing consultant in the United Kingdom claimed that once his financial services client started marketing to existing customers in lieu of prospects, new business increased by 650 percent. On average, businesses that focus on marketing to existing customers can expect a 10 percent increase in new business over cold-call marketing.

A report prepared by The Aberdeen Group on the value of customer relationship management (CRM) software showed a 30 percent increase in business for Comshare, a provider of financial services applications, after implementing a CRM software program. Much of this boost was attributed to improvements in lead generation and customer service. After implementing CRM technology, the company also realized a reduction of about 7000 calls per month to its help line and a 40 percent increase in inquiries from customers and prospects. Siebel, a leading manufacturer of CRM software, claims that through its programs, client Quick & Reilly generated increases of 15 percent in productivity, 50 percent in lead conversions, 10 percent in customer retention, and 5 percent in cross-selling.

Becoming a Lifetime Business

Marketing to existing customers is only successful if customers are served and managed properly. No amount of marketing, regardless of how brilliant or compelling an offer may be, will overcome a business's failure to provide quality products and service. The owner of a property management and maintenance company I had used for years decided to implement a "high-price strategy" to boost his company's image as the highest-quality provider—and ultimately increase his profits. To do this, he increased his prices by nearly 50 percent. Unfortunately for him, this strategy had the potential to bankrupt his business, as several of his customers quickly started shopping for other providers once they discovered his new prices. His strategy was flawed for two key reasons. First, he had not surveyed his current customers to assess their satisfaction with his company's quality, and second, he had not offered customers any added-value services to justify the higher prices. As a result, customers who were not happy with the existing quality and those who wanted more value or extra services for their money took their business elsewhere.

To be a lifetime business, you must keep abreast of customers' attitudes toward your business, product category, and most important, satisfaction with your product and service. Customers with low satisfaction levels need to be identified and addressed in a different way than those with high satisfaction levels. Businesses that are able to satisfy and retain a high percentage of their customers tend to keep them for a longer period of time. This is likely a result of knowing and fulfilling customers' needs and expectations. Consider the following market research statistics:

- Businesses retaining 80 percent of their customers keep them 5 years.
- Businesses retaining 90 percent of their customers keep them 10 years.

Tips and Tactics

Conduct regular surveys, formal or informal, among your best customers to assess their satisfaction, product usage needs, purchasing behaviors, and overall attitude toward your brand. Doing so will enable you to address real and valid needs in your marketing messages.

The foundation of lifetime marketing is to identify who your best customers are and collect information about their needs and transactions with your brand so that you can market to them as individually as possible.

Components of Lifetime Marketing

Commitment at Every Level

Customer data collection is only one part of the lifetime marketing equation. Businesses have to have a deep-rooted commitment to lifetime marketing that goes far beyond collecting customer data. Lifetime marketers use customer data to identify needs and wants, build relationships founded on trust, and communicate relevant messages and offer appropriate promotions. Later chapters discuss how to segment customers according to their purchase patterns, needs, life cycle, and product orientation so that you can send groups of customers personal, individual messages and promotions. Being able to communicate as personally as possible is the key to lifetime marketing success and the reason for spending time, money, and energy on collecting key customer data.

Before embarking on a mission to make your company a lifetime business, you must have 100 percent commitment—not only from yourself but also from all your employees. Lifetime businesses not only engage in relationship-building marketing activities and personalized communications, but they also engage in exceptional customer service and product development. Inconsistencies and discrepancies in customer service, product quality, communication, and marketing promises will defeat lifetime marketing efforts and could cause serious, irreparable damage to your brand. Customer service personnel must practice customer service for a lifetime, product development managers must develop product quality that lasts a lifetime, and marketing leaders must create relevant programs that capture customers' lifetime value.

Tips and Tactics

If you are a freelancer, make sure that you practice lifetime marketing in all aspects—account administration to product quality and delivery. Uphold the highest possible levels of professionalism and responsiveness, and only hire other freelancers who will uphold the standards expected by your customers.

Getting employee support for lifetime marketing activities is critical to growing your brand and achieving core business goals. Melinda Gladitsch, cofounder of one of the first Web development companies to go public in the 1990s, attributes much of her business's rapid success to being able to get commitment to extraordinary customer service and production quality from employees. Gladitsch claims that she was able to do this by hiring the most talented employees she could find, including them in the development of product and customer service initiatives, and then trusting them to do their jobs and serve customers with little interference from management. As a result, Gladitsch and her partners were able to grow Eagle River Interactive from a small company in a Colorado resort town to an international company with seven offices throughout the United States and Europe, conduct a successful IPO, and sell out in just 3 years.

Continuity is part of commitment. To succeed, finish what you start. It is amazing how much time and money businesses spend contemplating "out of the box" ideas, listening to recommendations, and even developing new programs just to quickly resort back to "in the box" thinking and activities. If you want to become a lifetime business that uses its marketing resources wisely, build a plan, get consensus companywide, secure commitment at every level, and then execute without looking back.

Lifetime businesses are committed to

- Putting the customers' needs first
- Listening to customers

- Recording each customer transaction
- Reviewing customer data periodically to identify trends
- Creating and maintaining customer profiles
- Speaking to customers in their own language
- Rewarding customers for past and present business
- Rewarding customers for referrals
- Creating equity in their brands through individualized promotions and rewards

Trust—The Foundation of Lifetime Marketing

By communicating to customers on a highly personal level, you are able to build trust, which is perhaps the most important brand variable for success. American Express has built a large empire of personal travel and financial services largely on its reputation of standing behind its customers or card members. Many people choose to use their American Express cards, even if it means paying an annual fee not charged by other card companies, because they know they can trust American Express to take care of them in a satisfactory way should their card get lost or in the hands of fraudulent users. They have built a $20 billion-plus travelers' check business on this reputation alone.

Building trust between a business and its customers, whether consumers or resellers, is the foundation of successful lifetime marketing—and any type of marketing for that matter. Consumers seek to do business with providers whom they trust to stand behind their products, deliver on their promises, serve their individual needs, and more than ever, reward them for their business. Businesses that are able to establish trust with all customer groups—direct purchasers, end users, and resellers—are those which not only achieve market longevity but also market dominance. If trust is not maintained, businesses quickly lose their competitive edge and much more.

Novell, the one-time world leader in computer networks, provides a good example of the power of trust. The network company can attribute much of its tremendous success in the 1980s and early 1990s to its ability to establish trust among its network of resellers. The company also can attribute its rapid downward spiral to its breaking the trust with the market channel that had helped to secure its dominance of the computer network business. In the early 1980s, Novell virtually closed the door to all competition by first offering the best product in its category and then building an unbreakable market channel loyal to selling its products worldwide. According to one of the team members responsible for

Novell's channel management during its rapid growth days, these relationships were hugely successful because they were based on honor. Resellers were told that they could trust Novell not to undersell them internally or engage in other activities that jeopardized their ability to sell and make a profit. Rules were established internally to make sure that this promise was never broken. Top executives at Novell presented the promise to channel representatives and backed up their words with signed contracts. They also made sure that employees at all levels throughout the company upheld the promises made to channel sales partners. Novell created dealer counsels that brought together a sample of dealers throughout the world each year to discuss key issues, concerns, and needs. Top executives listened and then acted on expressed needs and concerns. The company's commitment to resellers was executed not only by maintaining its promises but also by offering valuable services such as educational programs, marketing development funds for reseller promotions, and sound business advice to resellers to help ensure their business longevity.

As the trust grew stronger between Novell and its channel customers, so did the company's bottom line. Novell quickly owned the network category and amassed millions in profits for the company and executives. However, all this was quickly lost when the promises to resellers were broken and the trust destroyed. When this happened, Novell saw its stock plummet from a high of $35 per share in March of 1993 to a low of $3.10 in September of 2001. The door then opened for significant competitors to enter the market, most notably Microsoft.

The power of trust between a business and its customers has far-reaching implications. Not only does it build sales, but it also builds goodwill and brand strength within a company's markets and core communities. For many organizations, particularly those having to answer to community interests, such as nonprofit and health care organizations, it can mean millions of dollars saved in managing public issues that have an impact on profitability and business goals.

Tips and Tactics

Build trust for your business and brand by standing behind your products, honoring your commitments, helping associates and partners succeed, and treating customers and employees with dignity and respect.

For example, Intermountain Health Care (IHC), a large network of hospitals, clinics, and managed health care plans in the intermountain west, is the leader in its market. The price of leadership is continual public scrutiny and criticism from competitors and others with various agendas. IHC has dealt successfully with a host of issues through the years, not the least of which was a battle to maintain the historic tax exemptions of its nonprofit hospitals.

Under the direction of John Taylor, vice president of public relations and advertising, and Tom Vitelli, senior director, the company has developed a highly successful program for building valuable alliances and third-party support throughout the community. Through the company's "Opinion Leader Visit Program," top-ranking executives and trustees from company hospitals and headquarters visit annually with community officials such as city and county council representatives, mayors, and county commissioners to give what they call "stewardship reports." These reports outline the services and contributions the company has made, such as $150 million in annual charitable services and other benefits to the community. The visits provide a forum for sharing valuable facts and data and for gathering information from constituents and customers. The visits also build personal relationships and trust among individuals who have the potential to influence groups of valuable customers. As a result, IHC has many supporters even among those who are not affiliated with the company in a business sense.

In one instance, a state legislator launched into a criticism with the question, "What are we going to do about IHC?" Immediately, one of the opinion leaders who was familiar with the organization stood up in defense of IHC and shared some valuable facts that quickly silenced the critic. This is the kind of trustworthiness that lifetime marketing seeks to establish with customers. Imagine if every time a prospect considered purchasing a competitor's product, an existing customer jumped through hoops to convince him or her to purchase your product. This is the kind of customer loyalty of which most businesses can only dream.

Building lifetime trust involves delivering not only on your word but also on customers' expectations. When I was setting up my home office, I purchased some filing cabinets from OfficeMax. When the items arrived, they did not have all the parts I believed they would have. My sales representative checked into the items and called me back to confirm that the parts were not included with the cabinets I had purchased. She then went a step further. She gave me the phone number of the manufacturer to call so that I could purchase the missing parts and then assured me that she would reimburse the expense because the order had not met my expectations. The cost to reimburse me equaled the cost of one of the items. The OfficeMax sales representative quickly earned my loyalty. I also learned to trust that OfficeMax could provide me with what I need and would stand behind my expectations, even if it meant a loss to the company.

Lifetime businesses build trust starting at the first customer transaction, use that trust to capture lifetime sales, and generate referrals from their most valued customers. Customer trust is based on

- Standing behind products
- A high level of customer service
- Providing information so that customers can make informed decisions and purchases
- Offering customers rewards for business
- Offering consistency in service and product quality
- Meeting and exceeding customer expectations

When companies put customer trust and issues before their own, the trust and support are often reciprocated in ways that no other form of marketing can even touch. A good example is the Odwalla beverage case. In 1996, several *E. coli* cases in Washington State were traced to Odwalla's fresh apple juice products. As a result of drinking contaminated apple juice, a young girl died. This tragedy easily could have folded the company, which had positioned itself as the provider of natural, healthy bottled fruit juices and smoothies for whole-body nourishment. Instead of skirting the issue or waiting to point blame at someone else, Odwalla immediately pulled all its products and established open, honest lines of communication with consumers, the media, and financial analysts. It also communicated frequently all its activities, investigation results, and plans to the public at large and to its distributors. The goal was to assure the public and its distributors that it was doing everything possible to find the source of the problem and to prevent any further *E. coli* cases no matter the cost to the company. Its willingness to restore safety and confidence in its brand at all costs maintained trust in the brand during a very critical period. In time, distributors restocked their shelves with Odwalla products, and consumers continued consuming.

In contrast to Odwalla's positive comeback from a negative situation, Hudson Foods, a large supplier of beef products, was forced to sell assets to one of its fiercest competitors for a fraction of its original worth as a result of an *E. coli* outbreak traced to one of its meat-processing plants. In response to the outbreak, the company first stonewalled federal officials about how much product was potentially contaminated. Additionally, the company was accused of incorrectly sourcing the outbreak and failing to report all the product that was potentially affected. News of these instances sent an alarming message to its customer chain that company interests outweighed their interests, and many of their large accounts took their business elsewhere. Shortly afterward, the company was forced to close down.

The irony of these two *E. coli* cases is that the company whose contaminated product resulted in one known death quickly recovered its losses, from sales to stock valuation, and is now a thriving business. The company with the very same crisis yet no reported attributed deaths was quickly out of business because its customers had lost all trust in its products and communications.

Trust built on open communications and putting customers' interests before company profitability can overcome the most serious brand crises.

Focus

The key to making your business a lifetime business is to stay focused on building lasting customer relationships that result in current and long-term sales. Each customer represents a lifetime of sales for specific products. Successful businesses capture not only a customer's immediate sale but also each subsequent sale for their category for their entire purchasing life cycle. For example, if the average consumer purchases five cars over his or her lifetime, then car dealers and manufacturers need to focus on capturing each of those five sales among existing customers.

Focus involves identifying who your best customers are and learning to look at these customers individually first and collectively second. It means taking the time to understand what matters most to your most valuable customers in terms of product sales, customer service, and support and then exceeding their expectations in these categories. It means creating marketing programs that cater to your most valuable customers, making them feel valued, and giving them additional reasons to stay loyal to your brand. Focus is about knowing who makes your company profitable and then directing targeted, meaningful communication to these individuals and customer groups. This should be your top marketing priority.

Tips and Tactics

Focus on your most valuable customers first. By prioritizing your efforts and spending the most resources on those most likely to have an impact on your bottom line, you will have greater chances of increasing your long-term profitability. Learn to look at your business from the perspective of your most valuable customers to identify future strategic moves, initiatives, and product ideas.

Referral Marketing

A very valuable by-product of lifetime marketing is *referral marketing.* Once you have identified your best customers, you also have identified your best prospects. By offering customers rewards and incentives to refer your business to potential consumers that resemble themselves, you are building a strong base of highly qualified prospects and leads for your sales team. Again, MCI's Friends and Family program, which rewarded customers for signing up new customers, is an excellent example of the power of referral marketing. It is far cheaper to offer customers rewards for referrals than to spend money on cold advertising that may or may not reach qualified prospects. It is also far more effective. Marketing to cold direct mail lists typically results in a 1 percent or less response rate.

Lifetime marketing helps to generate new referrals via the cheapest possible form—word of mouth. A study conducted in the United Kingdom for the automobile insurance industry showed that word of mouth provided more name awareness for specific brands of insurance than TV, print, and direct mail advertising combined—as much as 27 percent more. Word-of-mouth marketing is often generated by providing satisfied customers with incentives for signing up or referring friends. At one time, AOL offered members $50 for each new customer they were able to get signed up.

No matter how big or small your business is, you can affordably and easily strengthen equity in your brand by rewarding customers for referrals. It all depends on what you are willing to offer and how that offer will be perceived by customers. In some cases, rewards for new business referrals might seem inappropriate, such as a lawyer offering a percentage of any new business acquired through a referral. If this is the case, find some other way to show customers that you appreciate their word-of-mouth support. Just make it relevant to your customers' needs and your business in general.

The power of referral marketing is compounded when you consider the referral rate potential of each satisfied customer. If each customer refers on average three customers, then that customer is worth not only his or her lifetime value but also that of three other customers. The value continues to add up. Marketing programs thus need to motivate referrals. Successful incentives include discounts, added-value services, membership reward programs, and so on.

Customer Retention

Given that acquiring new customers is significantly more costly than generating repeat business from existing customers, lifetime marketing is essential to running an efficient and profitable business. Marketing to existing customers results in a shorter sales conversion cycle because they already know and trust your brand. Typically, response rates generated by campaigns to existing customers are far higher than those aimed at prospective customers. Yesmail, a provider of e-mail marketing services, conducted an e-mail campaign that targeted a travel site's existing clients and achieved a 56 percent click-through rate from the e-mail text to the designated Web site. The company also achieved a 35 percent conversion rate, meaning that 35 percent of the e-mail recipients (the most valuable customers) responded positively to the promotion's offer. These results are unheard of when using mass marketing or cold marketing. The campaign also encouraged customers to forward the specific offer to friends and colleagues. For doing so, members were rewarded with a free upgrade to their membership status. Because the promotion was forwarded to new prospects by a trusted source and not a marketing or sales representative, the campaign was successful. The company's membership increased by 79 percent as a result of just one carefully planned and executed campaign. This campaign succeeded because it built on existing relationships and past transactions, focused on the company's best customers, and offered something of value in return for qualified referrals.

The following example demonstrates how retained customers add up to increased business and value.

1. If your typical customer spends an average of $50 a month on your products, this adds up to $600 each year in new revenue.
2. If you have 300 loyal customers, you have $180,000 in potential revenues per year.
3. Subtract your costs per sale (direct and indirect), and multiply by a discount rate to compensate for the future value of money to determine the annual lifetime value (LTV) per customer. (This calculation will be explored further later in this chapter.)
4. If your average customer's net value or profit to you is $300 per year, you will experience $90,000 in profit from those 300 loyal customers.
5. If each customer refers two new customers and you gain another 100 new customers on your own for a given year and retain their annual purchases, you will have 700 new customers that represent an annual profit of $210,000.

Now take calculations and determine your business's potential for 5, 10, and 15 years. Capturing the LTV of existing and new customers will enable you to grow your business far beyond your current sales cycle.

Up-selling, cross-selling, and reselling customers is the key to achieving a lasting profit stream, as just illustrated. However, it must be done very carefully. As Charles Graves of Charles Graves & Associates so correctly states, "Customers don't want to be sold or told, they would rather be involved."

Lifetime marketing is sensitive to these important customer needs. Successful campaigns do not communicate in a way that abruptly hustles new business but rather inform customers of new options and alternatives and help them achieve personal goals. When businesses offer customers promotions such as rewards or discounts on future purchases, customers feel valued and appreciated. By doing so, businesses become partners, not just another source of needed goods or services.

Rewarding customers for their business and loyalty is one of the best ways to retain them.

Individualized Promotions

Instead of offering the mass public the same incentives and promotional deals, lifetime businesses review their customer data and categorize customers according to like purchasing patterns and cycles, identified needs, and so on. For example, a marketer might select a database of customers whose purchase cycles will renew in the near future. A *purchase cycle* refers to the average time span between purchases for a specific category. Let's say, for example, that the purchase cycle for an automobile is 5 years. Automobile dealers or manufacturers would then sort for all customers who purchased a car between 4 and 5 years ago. These customers would then be sent an offer to trade in their old vehicles for new ones and get 0 percent financing as a reward for past and future business or some other motivating offer. Additional rewards could include free floor mats for sedan customers or free bed liners for truck owners.

By including information about past purchases, you are reassuring your customers that their business with you did not go unnoticed and that you understand their individual needs. Nissan has done this effectively with its customer satisfaction program implemented by its Canada division to help determine the level of satisfaction among customers and develop programs that increase overall satisfaction. Customers are sent a questionnaire once a year to assess satisfaction. Subsequent marketing materials are sent according to what was answered; that is, those complaining about leg space would get a letter about the enhanced leg space in the Altima. This program helps identify problems so that they can be corrected and satisfaction restored. A toll-free number is also engraved in all cars so that customers can call the company directly with problems rather than rely solely on the dealer. All conversations are recorded, and a complete record is kept in order to keep current on customer needs and wants.

Responding to individual needs is what lifetime marketing is all about and what makes businesses profitable for their lifetimes. By offering current customers exclusive deals, you are building brand equity and increasing perceived relationship value. Marketing to customers at the peak of their purchase cycle also will help to even out the sales cycles so that you do not achieve all your sales at once and then starve for the next several months.

Efficiency

Direct marketers have been using LTV calculations for years to help refine mailing lists in order to better ensure that businesses reach their best customers and minimize waste. The goal is to retain customers who have a high LTV because they are frequent and/or high-dollar purchasers and to remove customers or prospects from marketing databases who have shown little or no profit potential. By doing this, marketers spend money on reaching customers and consumer groups with the highest propensity to respond to specific offers and avoid spending money on those least likely to respond.

LTV calculations help businesses quickly identify who their best customers are and who their weakest ones are so that they can use resources wisely and maximize the return on their marketing investments.

Tips and Tactics

Determine the customers most likely to generate a positive return by sorting customers into revealing categories such as recency and frequency of purchases, monetary value per purchase, incidence of upgrades, returns, ancillary purchases, life-cycle phase (for example, years left likely to purchase), purchase renewal date, and so on.

LTV is calculated by determining the worth of each customer's net profit over that customer's lifetime of purchases. To determine this accurately, you need to know how many years customers are likely to purchase products in your category, or their life cycle, the average purchase per customer, purchase frequency, direct and overhead costs, retention rate, acquisition cost, and so on. The key to maximizing each customer's lifetime value is obviously to retain that person as a customer as long as possible throughout his or her purchasing lifetime. Marketing activities thus should focus on adding value and other services that motivate customers to stick with your brand rather than switch to another.

Calculating Lifetime Value (LTV)

LTV represents the future profits computed in today's dollars using net present value or the net present value of the profit that you will realize on the average new customer during a given number of years. It is calculated by forecasting the discounted profit stream from a lifetime of patronage from one customer. In simpler terms, it is the net present value of each customer's average transaction times the number of transactions per year multiplied by the number of years that purchases are likely to be made. For example, if the average net present value per customer transaction for your business is $20, and the average customer makes three purchases a year, you have a $60 annual value per customer. If a customer's purchase lifetime expectancy is 10 years, that customer represents a profit of $600 over his or her lifetime.

To determine LTV, you must understand

- Purchase cycle—the time span between purchases (one car every 5 years)
- Life cycle—the frequency of purchase per customer lifetime (5 cars over 45 years or 9 car purchases)
- Average value of each purchase per customer
- Cost to acquire each customer
- Cost to maintain each customer
- Costs per sale—direct and indirect

To determine a customer's annual value, subtract all costs from revenue generated per customer transaction to determine the net present value (NPV) of each purchase. Multiply the NPV by the number of transactions per year. Take the customer's annual NPV and multiply it by the number of years a customer is expected to purchase your product, or the purchase life expectancy, which is also referred to as *life cycle*. You will then know a customer's projected annual and lifetime value. Knowing this will help you to determine which customers you should spend your valuable resources on and which are not worth your time.

You can set up a simple spreadsheet to calculate a customer's lifetime value. First, of course, you must know what your customers spend—hence the importance of recording customer transactions down to the individual level. Figure 3-1 can be used to calculate each individual customer's worth and each customer category's worth. A customer category for a pet supply store may be all customers who own dogs versus cats.

Figure 3-1 *Sample Calculation for Determining Annual Profit per Customer*

Average sale value	$100
Cost of goods sold (50%)	$50
Revenue	$50
Administrative costs (credit charges, percent discounted for risk management, and so on)	$5
Promotional costs (discounts, coupons, advertising per unit sold)	$6
NPV or profit per transaction	$39

A customer who spends an average of $100 per transaction represents $39 in profit per transaction. Customers who purchase twice a year and likely will purchase for 10 years represent $78 in annual profits and an LTV of $780.

To determine a customer segment's worth, this formula is slightly modified. Let's say that dog owners spend an average of $100 for each transaction with a specific pet supply store and that the store has 50 customers in the dog owner segment. The LTV of this customer segment would then be determined as shown in Figure 3-2.

Retaining customers and their value over time is the primary purpose of lifetime marketing. Figures 3-3 and 3-4 show the potential returns achieved through customer retention for a group of 1000 customers.

Figure 3-2 *Sample Calculation for Determining Annual Profit per Customer Segment*

Average sale value (individual value × number in segment)	$5000
Cost of goods sold (50%)	$2500
Revenue	$2500
Administrative costs (credit charges, percent discounted for risk management—10% total)	$250
Promotional costs (discounts, coupons, advertising per unit sold—3% of sales)	$150
NPV	$2100

Figure 3-3 *Cumulative Customer LTV (Before Lifetime Marketing)*

	Year 1	Year 2	Year 3	Year 4
Customers	1000	400	180	90
Retention rate (%)	40	45	50	55
Purchases per year	1	1	1	1
Average purchase value	$150	$150	$150	$150
Total revenue	$150,000	$60,000	$27,000	$13,500
Cost percentage	50	50	50	50
Total costs*	$75,000	$30,000	$13,500	$6,750
Profits				
Gross profits	$75,000	$30,000	$13,500	$6,750
Discount rate	1	1.2	1.44	1.73
NPV profit	$75,000	$25,000	$9,375	$3,902
Cumulative NPV	$75,000	$100,000	$109,375	$113,277
LTV per customer	$75.00	$100.00	$109.38	$113.28

*Total costs include direct costs, overhead, promotional costs, acquisition costs. Discount-rate calculation: [(1 + interest rate) × (risk factor)]year + AR/365 (AR = accounts receivable and refers to the number of days for payment. This typically ranges from 30 to 90 days depending on the customer's history. For established customers, 90 days is often used.)

Figure 3-4 *Cumulative Customer LTV (After Lifetime Marketing)*

	Year 1	Year 2	Year 3	Year 4
Referral rate (%)	5	5	5	5
Referred customers		50	28	17
Customers	1000	550	331	216
Retention (%)	50	55	60	65
Average sales	$180	$200	$220	$240
Total revenue	$180,000	$110,000	$72,820	$51,840
Cost percentage	50	50	50	50
Total costs*	$100,000	$60,500	$39,720	$28,080
Gross profits	$80,000	$49,500	$33,100	$23,760
Discount rate	1	1.2	1.44	1.73
NPV profit	$80,000	$41,250	$22,986	$13,734
Cumulative NPV	$80,000	$121,250	$144,236	$157,970
LTV per customer	$80.00	$121.52	$144.24	$157.97

*Total costs include direct costs, overhead, promotional costs, acquisition costs. Discount-rate calculation: [(1 + interest rate) × (risk factor)]year + AR/365 (AR = accounts receivable and refers to the number of days for payment. This typically ranges from 30 to 90 days depending on the customer's history. For established customers, 90 days is often used.)

Retention rate refers to number of customers continuing to make purchases on an annual basis. To determine LTV rates for customers making purchases on a nonannual basis, for example, every 5 years for automobiles, the retention rate is determined as follows:

$$RR = (\text{repurchase rate})^{1/y}$$

where y represents the purchase cycle or time interval for new purchases, for example, automobile purchases every 5 years.

The total number of customers reflects the retention rate from the previous year. For example, in Figure 3-4, the 550 customers in year 2 represent a 50 percent retention rate of the first year's 1000 customers plus the 50 referred customers. Year 3 shows the total number of customers retained from the previous year plus referred customers, and so on. Revenues are based on sales from the original 1000 customers. Profits equal revenue minus total costs. Discount rate is to compensate for changes in the value of money over time. The discount rate equals $(1 + i)^n$, where i is the interest rate and n is the number of years.

The Power of Lifetime Marketing

Companies that do not engage in lifetime marketing practices have few ways of knowing the value of their marketing investments and specific customer needs and purchasing patterns. These same companies are likely to fail in today's environment because more and more customers are expecting businesses to know their purchase histories and specific needs and to treat them accordingly. With the vast amount of customer data-management technology available today, they should.

Lifetime marketing offers many inherent benefits:

- By calculating the LTV potential for various consumer groups, you can determine the potential of marketing campaigns before executing them on a broad scale.
- You are better able to determine how best to spend your marketing resources by identifying prospects with the greatest profit potential.
- LTV calculations help to identify customers who make you the most money versus those who actually cost you money to maintain.
- Understanding who your best customers are helps you to identify your best prospects and communicate to them in a personal and meaningful manner.
- By learning to think like your customers, you can market to them wisely and appropriately, thus achieving higher response and sales conversion rates.

The Steadman Hawkins Sports Medicine Foundation in Vail, Colorado, provides a good example of how powerful the payoff from good customer relationships and positive brand experiences can be. Started by world-renowned orthopedic surgeons J. Richard Steadman and Richard Hawkins, the foundation raises money to conduct research on new procedures for treating bone and joint injuries. Drs. Steadman and Hawkins have pioneered many new orthopedic procedures and are credited with saving the careers of hundreds of professional athletes from Olympic-medalist skiers to Hall of Fame NFL players, golfers, and tennis champions. Beyond professional athletes, the Steadman Hawkins Clinic has treated thousands of active adults determined to ski, play tennis, hike, bike—you name it—into their late eighties. These are the doctors' most important customers, yet they are not household names, as are many of their patients, such as Greg Norman, Terrell Davis, Bruce Smith, Chris Evert, Jane Fonda, and others. Patients whose active lifestyles have been restored by the doctors' legendary medical skills and service not only sing their praises to others and generate numerous referrals but also donate millions of dollars for the foundation's ongoing research programs, expecting nothing in return.

The foundation has a very high rate of repeat donors, most of whom are satisfied patients. The foundation's success is based not only on excellent care but also on its ability to maintain strong relationships with a core group of satisfied customers. This is done through regular mailings to keep them informed about the achievements and programs of the foundation and through biannual events that allow donors to mingle with the doctors and foundation staff in a relaxed and fun atmosphere. These events include an annual ski classic where individuals can race on a ski team along with former U.S. Ski Team and Olympic champions and learn from the pros how to perfect their own skills. The 3-day event allows many opportunities for personal interaction through various social events such as dinner parties and private concerts for the event attendees performed by the likes of Judy Collins and Mandy Patinkin. The foundation also hosts a summer fund-raising event that offers numerous opportunities for personal relationship development. These events actually have created an elite core of loyalists by bringing together people with common experiences, values, and commitments. When brought together twice a year, their friendships, many of which have resulted from these events, are strengthened, and so is their loyalty to the foundation because most compare notes about their own health care experience and relationships with the doctors and foundation staff. In a sense, these events are the fund-raising world's version of Harley Davidson's H.O.G. rallies.

The foundation's fund-raising efforts have been tremendously successful. From 1993 to 2000, the number of donors increased from 33 to 831, and direct mail campaigns during 2000–2001 achieved 14.68 and 12.63 percent response rates from recent and current donors. Figure 3-5 shows that results from the foundation's 2000–2001 direct mail campaign also are significantly different between donors or customers and prospects.

Figure 3-5 *Direct Marketing Results from the Steadman Hawkins Sports Media Foundation: Donors versus Prospects*

Audience	Sample	Number of Respondents	Percent of Respondents	Dollars Received
Donors (past or current year)	1826	268	14.68	$71,993
Current (last 60 days)	760	96	12.63	$15,508
Prospects	2311	36	1.56	$5,130

These data reinforce the lifetime principle that marketing to satisfied customers generates a far greater return and response than marketing to prospects. By maintaining strong relationships and communications with current and recent donors, the foundation is able to use its fund-raising resources efficiently and achieve very high response rates to its solicitation campaigns. This same principle applies to businesses in any industry: By building strong relationships with customers through quality service, information sharing, and reinforcement events (activities that create opportunities for nonselling personal interaction), customers are retained and transaction values increased.

Getting Started—Lifetime Marketing Checklist

Lifetime marketing pays off in many ways and is limited only by the creativity and time you choose to put into it. Remember,

- It costs less to retain customers than to acquire new ones.
- Your best customers outspend other customers significantly.
- Loyal and satisfied customers generate qualified referrals.
- By building brand equity through rewards and added services, you will keep customers closer to your brand longer.

Market for a lifetime if you want to be able to

- Know who your customers are and what influences their decisions
- Execute highly appropriate and efficient marketing programs
- Retain customers
- Increase the revenue stream of each individual customer
- Be in your business for the long term
- Market smarter than ever before

Action Items

1. Identify ways to address the following aspects of lifetime marketing:
   - Commitment at all levels
   - Trust
   - Focus
   - Referral marketing
   - Customer retention practices
   - Individualized promotions
   - Efficiency
2. Focus on both short- and long-term sales and revenues at all times.
3. Instill passion for your brand by offering the best, the different, and the excellent.
4. Listen to your customers so that you can learn to think like them and offer what they want, not what you want or think they want.
5. Work first to satisfy and retain customers and second to get new ones.
6. Build trust by being trustworthy in all areas of business—product quality, service, and support.
7. Motivate customers to refer new customers by offering rewards.
8. Offer individual promotions based on customers' past transactions and future needs.

Worksheet: How Close Are You to Becoming a *Lifetime* Business?

Ask yourself the following questions to determine if you have what it takes to market for a lifetime.

	Yes, No, or Don't Know
My current marketing programs are measurable, have paid for themselves, and have generated new business.	
I can measure the impact of my marketing programs and the return on my expenditures.	
My marketing programs focus on generating long-term sales and visibility versus meeting short-term goals.	
My customers are passionate about my brand because of the product quality, service, and rewards I offer.	
I listen to customers' needs and issues and develop marketing programs accordingly.	
My communications appeal directly to the emotions of my customers rather than my own.	
My communications educate rather than just sell products.	
Customers feel appreciated when they do business with me.	
I know who my most satisfied and most lucrative customers are.	
My most satisfied and most lucrative customers are one and the same.	
Customers trust my brand, my service, and my employees.	

	Yes, No, or Don't Know
I give my customers reasons and rewards for referring friends and family members.	
I am set up to keep track of my customers' transactions so that I can market to them individually.	

Score

Five or more questions, yes. You are already on your way to becoming a lifetime business. Use this book to guide your current thinking and further develop your strategic planning.

Five or more questions, no. It is time to wake up and pay attention to how you are managing and marketing your business and how you are interacting with your customers.

Five or more questions, don't know. Who is minding the farm? If you are responsible for making this business successful, you need to take the time to learn about your customers and how to make them happy.

For those in the "no" and "don't know" ranks, get your glasses on and start looking at your business from your customers' perspectives. This is the only way to succeed in business for the long term.

Part 2

Getting to Know Your Customers— Inside and Out

First Things First

Learn to Think Like Your Best Customers before Spending a Single Marketing Dollar

I f you were to ask a roomful of people what they believe is the most important feature to look for when purchasing a new car, you likely would get as many answers as there were people. This holds true if the room were full of people with diverse demographics or people with similar, nearly identical demographics.

Decision processes vary by individual, thus strengthening the notion that there is no "general public" and that mass advertising is really a game of marketing roulette whereby companies randomly throw out marketing messages and hope that they hit a target.

One of the biggest mistakes many business owners make is marketing according to demographics only. Demographics represent a very small aspect of your customer. In the 1970s, a marketing article asked the question, "Are Grace Slick and Tricia Nixon Cox the same person?" Grace, a rock singer, and Tricia, the daughter of President Nixon, had the exact same demographics: urban, working women, college graduates, aged 25 to 35, similar income levels, and a household of three—including one child. Yet, from what we know about these two individuals, their lifestyles, needs, personal tastes, and political viewpoints are very different. As a result, their purchase preferences and decision processes are likely to be very different as well. An individual's decision process is based on his or her unique set of emotions, needs, and experiences, not on the demographic cluster to which he or she belongs.

Lifetime businesses look beyond customer or consumer demographics. Such businesses have learned what emotional influencers are behind customer purchase decisions, how lifestyles and values affect decisions, who and what influence their customers and prospects, and what a brand needs to offer and do to keep a customer's business for a lifetime. By learning the various factors that influence and motivate people to select brands within your product category, you can create effective and efficient marketing programs.

Analyzing Current Customers

As simple as it sounds, the first step to learning to think like your customers is to discover who your current customers are. You may know them demographically, but do you really know them in terms of lifestyle, needs and concerns, product usage, and so on? Do you know which customers are valuable to you and which are not?

Your marketing efforts should focus primarily on customers and customer groups that represent the greatest profit potential to your business over the long term—or the greatest *lifetime value*. It may be tempting to try to capture the lifetime value of every person who walks in your door, but how realistic is this? Some customers may only need your product once, and no amount of superior marketing will bring them back; others may be growing out of their need for your category or approaching the end of their purchasing life cycle; and others simply may have solid relationships with other vendors. Knowing the circumstances of your customers is critical to knowing who is worthy of most of your resources.

Beyond knowing to whom you are marketing, you must know to what influences you are trying to appeal. Collecting customer information enables you to market effectively on both an individual and a group basis. Once you understand who your best customers are, you can sort your customers into groups according to product usage, needs, purchasing behavior, influencers, and so on and communicate to groups in a way that is relevant, personal, and *individualized*. Without these data, your communication efforts simply will be a guessing game and, most often, an exercise in futility.

Tips and Tactics

The first step to becoming a lifetime marketer is to set up a system for recording customer transactions. For small businesses serving a small group of clientele, this can be as simple as an Excel spreadsheet program or paper-based customer files. For larger businesses, more complex database management systems are available that allow for the management of hundreds and thousands of customer data files. The important thing is to create an appropriate system for the size and nature of your business, use it continuously, and review the data often.

Following are some critical steps for identifying and getting to know your best customers and prospects.

Step 1: Identify Your Most Valuable Customers

To identify your most valuable customers, those worthy of the bulk of your marketing resources, you need to do an analysis that indicates which customers purchased most *recently* and most *frequently* and spent the most *money*—an RFM analysis. These customers are the ones who are most likely to purchase from you again and generate the greatest revenue stream.

Tracking and recording customer transactions does not have to be an expensive and complicated process. There are numerous customer relationship management (CRM) programs that can help you store and manage data. You can go the expensive route by purchasing sophisticated software programs from leading CRM vendors such as Siebel and Oracle, or you can create you own databases using such programs as Excel, Access, Blackbaud, and even Outlook. More important than the program you use is the information you store. Customer analysis for lifetime marketing goes far beyond transaction history and demographics. You need to create a custom database that contains data points reflecting demographics and transaction history such as products purchased, average dollar value per transaction, purchase frequency, known decision influences (for example, price and convenience), special requests or needs, reasons for purchase (gifts, self, holidays), and specific characteristics, values, lifestyle issues, and so on that will help you understand how your customers think and make buying decisions. Once you collect this kind of information, you can then build customer profiles that will guide your marketing efforts and help you to identify your best prospects.

Step 2: Build Customer Profiles

After identifying the customer groups most worthy of your marketing resources, you need to develop profiles for each. Customer profiles should be as comprehensive as possible, containing a broad spectrum of information, such as

- Demographics
- Geodemographics
- Consumer orientation
- Generational influences
- Category cycle
- Market adaptation cycle

Demographics

Demographics are simply social classifications, such as

- Age
- Gender
- Marital status
- Race
- Income
- Education

These data typically are used for selecting communications vehicles and are a guide for media buyers and planners. Print and broadcast media are sold largely on demographics. Media buyers and planners have large data files of demographics for specific regions of the country, affinity and ethnic groups, and so on. This information provides a general parameter for customer segments, such as adults aged 18 to 49, which constitutes the most sought after demographic among advertisers because they are the heaviest spenders in many consumer categories.

U.S. Census data detail demographics down to specific communities, ZIP Codes, and neighborhoods, helping marketers pinpoint consumer groups most likely to need and purchase specific products or brands or support particular political issues. Demographics about specific geographic clusters are especially helpful for direct marketers, market research experts, and those compiling mailing lists.

Figure 4-1 presents a summary of national statistics from the U.S. Census 2000. U.S. Census data for the nation as a whole and on a state-by-state basis can be found at *www.census.gov* and *www.factfinder.census.gov*. You can easily view data tables and graphs for the nation as a whole or specific states.

Figure 4-1 *National Statistics from U.S. Census 2000*

Subject	Number	Percent
Total population	281,421,906	100.0
Sex		
Male	138,053,563	49.1
Female	143,368,343	50.9
Age		
<5 years	19,175,798	6.8
5–9 years	20,549,505	7.3
10–14 years	20,528,072	7.3
15–19 years	20,219,890	7.2
20–24 years	18,964,001	6.7
25–34 years	39,891,724	14.2
35–44 years	45,148,527	16.0
45–54 years	37,677,952	13.4
55–59 years	13,469,237	4.8
60–64 years	10,805,447	3.8
65–74 years	18,390,986	6.5
75–84 years	12,361,180	4.4
≥85 years	4,239,587	1.5
Median age (years)	35.3	(X)

(continues)

Figure 4-1 *continued*

18 years and over	209,128,094	74.3
Male	100,994,367	35.9
Female	108,133,727	38.4
21 years and over	196,899,193	70.0
62 years and over	41,256,029	14.7
65 years and over	34,991,753	12.4
Male	14,409,625	5.1
Female	20,582,128	7.3
Race		
One race	274,595,678	97.6
White	211,460,626	75.1
Black or African American	34,658,190	12.3
American Indian and Alaska Native	2,475,956	0.9
Asian	10,242,998	3.6
Asian Indian	1,678,765	0.6
Chinese	2,432,585	0.9
Filipino	1,850,314	0.7
Japanese	796,700	0.3
Korean	1,076,872	0.4
Vietnamese	1,122,528	0.4
Other Asian	1,285,234	0.5
Native Hawaiian and other Pacific Islander	398,835	0.1
Native Hawaiian	140,652	0.0
Guamanian or Chamorro	58,240	0.0
Samoan	91,029	0.0
Other Pacific Islander	108,914	0.0
Some other race	15,359,073	5.5
Two or more races	6,826,228	2.4

Source: U.S. Census, 2000.

Tips and Tactics

You can find valuable information about your target customer groups by reading state-of-the-industry reports compiled by industry associations and magazines. You also can purchase reports from research firms or commission them to conduct original research specific to your needs.

This U.S. Census information may be interesting and does shed some light on the U.S. population according to race, housing, family, age, and sex, but it tells you nothing about the emotional makeup of your specific target group. You may now know that there are more females in the United States than males, that the median age is 35.3, and that 51.7 percent of all U.S. households are those of married couples with children. These data can be encouraging by letting you know that people within your desired demographic exist, but that is as far as they go.

You need demographics, but you also need to consider the following other influences.

Geodemographics

Geodemographics help to shed light on customers within a specific community or neighborhood as defined by the U.S. Census data. While multiple communities may share similar demographics, they may have very different values. Towns with similar patterns may support very different industries, even when in close proximity. I live in Eagle, Colorado, a small mountain town between Vail and Aspen ski resorts. The Vail Valley, of which Eagle is a part, consists of little towns along Interstate 70, the nation's primary artery from west to east. While these towns are all along a 30-mile corridor and share similar demographics, the values have been surprisingly different over the years. Eagle, on the west end of the valley, was rooted in ranching and until the late 1990s boasted one gas station, one small grocery store, a handful of saloons, no traffic lights, and lots of wide open spaces. As the Vail Valley developed, people in Eagle worked their land, rode their horses, and branded their cattle. At the same time, just 20 miles east in the town of Avon, the primary focus was on golfing and skiing. The largest housing divisions were centered around golf courses and contained several vacation homes for out-of-towners. Both towns had similar median ages, percentages of males versus females, and family households, yet the community values were different. On paper, it appeared that one marketing program would have succeeded in both communities, especially because of their proximity to each other. In reality, this is not so true. If you based your marketing decisions on just demographics and developed advertising to appeal to a median-income or median-age consumer, you likely would have gained some ground in one town but wasted a lot of money in the other.

Tips and Tactics

An excellent way to learn about your customers is simply to ask them. While in the process of completing a transaction, informally ask them about their interests, why they chose your brand, their intended product usage, and so on. Make the most of "customer chatter" by getting your customers to talk about themselves rather than always talking about your brand or products.

Consumer Orientation

Consumer orientation refers to a customer's personal psychology, or web of attitudes, behaviors, and decision-making patterns. As consumers, our life experiences, environment, upbringing, insecurities, and confidences influence what we purchase and why.

Understanding consumer orientations provides valuable insight on physical, emotional, and psychological factors that influence purchases. Different models exist to help you determine the various factors affecting your customers' decisions. There are numerous consumer data companies that peddle mailing lists built to specific ZIP Codes, demographics, and geodemographics. You can buy mailing lists built according to almost any demographic. However, until you have an in-depth understanding of why your customers chose your product and brand in the first place, you likely will waste a great deal of money second-guessing which lists to purchase and which messages to deliver.

Several years ago, SRI International, a nonprofit research organization, developed the VALS™ system for categorizing customers according to their self-orientation and available resources. VALS, which is currently run by SRI Consulting Business Intelligence, identifies three core orientations into which all U.S. consumers fall: principle, status, and action. Consumers who are principle-driven make choices based on abstract ideas rather than feelings or events or a need to be accepted by others. Those with a status orientation seek products and services that make them look successful to others, whereas action-oriented consumers desire social and physical activity and even risk.

The VALS network provides excellent insights into the values that influence consumers' purchasing decisions. Even though it was developed several years ago, I still refer to this model because human behavior and needs have not changed. It does an excellent job of incorporating complex psychological issues that most consumer segmentation programs do not address at all. The VALS network helps marketers determine decision-influencing preferences, for example, control or freedom, tradition or novelty, information or stimulation, hands-on activities or intellectual abstractions.

VALS categories resulted from an extensive development effort spanning 5 years of research and were based largely on several large national surveys covering consumer opinion. You actually can take the survey yourself to see which category you fall into by going to the group's Web site, *www.sric-bi.com.*

VALS uses psychographics, a combination of psychology and demographics, to understand and predict consumer behavior. As a business owner or manager, you need to identify which psychographic category represents your most valuable customers. Your marketing, product mix, customer service, and interaction should then reflect the associated values and fill the corresponding needs. You can determine where your customers fall by surveying them, analyzing current customer trends and information, and then identifying the underlying psychology that motivates your customers to buy what they do. After surveying your customers and studying past trends, you may identify some classifications that are all your own. If you do create your own customer segments, just make sure that your assessments are accurate and that your audiences are reachable.

VALS segments consumers according to self-orientation and resources. *Self-orientation* refers to the underlying psychology that drives a person's attitudes, activities, and consumer behavior. *Resources* refer to a person's age, education, income, energy level, and self-confidence—all of which drive levels of consumerism, or influence one's propensity to purchase. Each group has different perspectives on life and varying priorities and resource constraints. Individuals

Figure 4-2 *VALS Categories of Consumers*

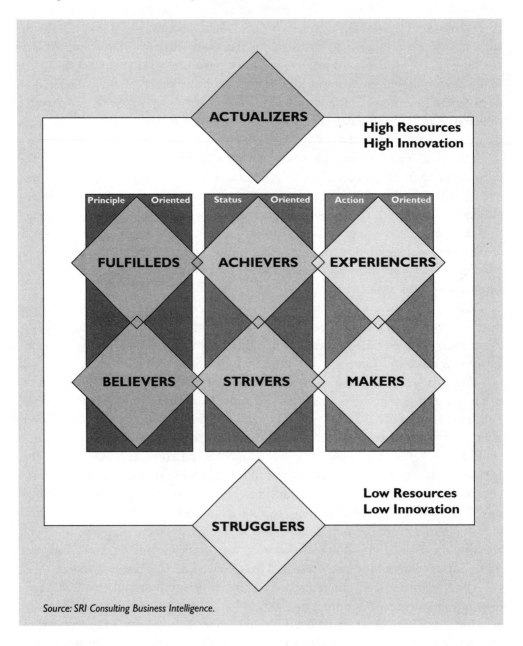

Source: SRI Consulting Business Intelligence.

within these groups are influenced by marketing messages in different ways. If you used these values as a guide for your marketing messages, you would approach various consumer groups in very different ways. One message might be highly effective among "strivers" and be insulting to "actualizers" at the same time. This is why it is so important to know the values and mind sets of your customers.

Figure 4-2 maps out the various self-orientations and consumer profiles defined by the VALS network. Figures 4-3 through 4-10 present message suggestions for marketing to the specific groups listed.

Figure 4-3 *Strugglers*

People with limited interests and activities who are focused on meeting the urgent needs of the present moment

Key Influencers/Messages

• Reliable	• Friendly	• Trust
• Discount	• Easy to use	• All-American
• Brand name	• Traditional	• Free gift/offer

Avoid

• Authority	• Broad-scale thinking	• Fast, pushy sales approaches
• Technical information	• Upscale	

Figure 4-4 *Makers*

Practical people who have constructive skills and value self-sufficiency

Key Influencers/Messages

• Free trial	• Practicality	• Reputation
• Local brand	• Durable	• Guarantee

Avoid

• Extravagance	• Intellectualism	
• Infringement of rights	• Status	

Figure 4-5 *Experiencers*

Enthusiastic, impulsive people who seek variety and excitement and savor the new, off-beat, and risky

Key Influencers/Messages

• Successful	• Variety	• Performance
• Individualistic	• New	• Status
• Unique	• Immediate	

Avoid

• Inactivity	• Boring images
• Typical ideas	• Status quo

Figure 4-6 *Strivers*

People who seek motivation, self-definition, and approval from the world around them and are striving to find a secure and valid place in life

Key Influencers/Messages

• Affordable price	• Approval of others	• Perceived quality
• Power	• Status	

Avoid

• Authority	• Broad concept
• High risk	• Detailed/technical information

Figure 4-7 *Achievers*

Successful career- and work-oriented people who care about image

Key Influencers/Messages

• Success/achievement	• Predictable
• Prestige	• Status

Avoid

• High risk	• Change
• Different	• Boring

Figure 4-8 *Believers*

Conservative, conventional people with concrete beliefs based on traditional, established values and codes

Key Influencers/Messages

• Reliable	• Low price	• Future planning
• Improved	• Guarantee	• Established brand
• Trusted		

Avoid

• Innovative ideas	• Novelty
• Technical information	• Trendy, off-the-wall humor

Figure 4-9 *Fulfilled*

Mature, satisfied, comfortable people who are content with their careers, families, and station in life

Key Influencers/Messages

• Reasonable	• Guarantee
• Durable	• Established brand

Avoid

• Radical approach	• Pushy sales approaches

Figure 4-10 *Actualizers*

Successful, sophisticated, active people with high self-esteem whose possessions and recreation reflect a cultivated taste for finer things

Key Influencers/Messages

• Excellence	• High quality
• Product superiority	• Leading information

Avoid

• Inferiority	• Lack of control, choice

The only way to be sure of your customers' VALS types is to have them take the VALS survey, which is administered by SRI Consulting Business Intelligence. However, using your intuition to sort individual customers and prospects into segments such as those mapped out in the preceding figures can help you deliver relevant and motivating messages and promotions more efficiently than ever.

Generational Influences

A customer's generation has many influences on purchasing behavior. Knowing how to market to each generation's specific needs can have a significant impact on the success of a marketing program. Following are brief descriptions of key generations and their corresponding needs, values, and behavior or attitudinal patterns.

Older Americans
- More than 60 million noninstitutionalized Americans over age 50
- Respond to personal, sensitive messages that provide technical detail
- Hungry for information that will help in their senior years
- Need help coping with and enjoying many life changes
- Free time goes to increased personal care, housekeeping, reading, and TV

Baby boomers
- Approximately 80 million strong
- Born between 1950 and 1963
- Individualists who think for themselves
- Goals focus on self-interests, self-actualization, and upward mobility
- Want products that are convenient, quick, easy, and flexible
- Need help managing many choices in today's market
- Increased tendency toward frugality and savings
- Concerned about preserving health, environment, and financial assets
- Want goods and services delivered in their contemporary forms

Generation Xers
- More than 44 million
- Born between 1965 and 1976
- Next generation of primary customers for many businesses
- Skeptical outlook: 20 percent believe that their chances of a desired career and lifestyle are fair
- Extremely sensitive to authenticity of messages
- Expected demographics include higher poverty rate, decreased home ownership, skimpier health benefits

Millennial generation
- Approximately 30 million teenagers
- Future customers for today's businesses
- Absorbed with their own needs
- Savvy, optimistic, resent being talked down to
- Images and attitudes formed today likely will influence the next phase of life
- Distinguish between honest and whitewashed advertising messages

Category Cycles

Knowing a customer's attitude toward and perceived value regarding a specific category will enable you to prioritize your customers, better allocate your marketing resources, and identify proper messages for your one-on-one correspondence.

For example, consumers tend to fall into broad categories according to their emotional attitudes toward specific products or attitudinal patterns. Following are examples of extrinsic (physical, social) and intrinsic (emotional, psychological) factors that influence purchases of health care plans.

Extrinsic factors
- Young and carefree
- Family-focused
- People with specific health problems
- People with high need and little choice

Intrinsic factors
- Those willing to pay premium for highest possible quality
- Those with the perception that no quality differences exist
- Active sports- and nutrition-focused people who have no immediate need
- Naturalists, holistic people who seek alternative health care methods

Travel service providers have identified several categories for travelers, such as

- Budget-conscious
- Worriers or "Nervous Nellies"
- Business travelers
- Ever-ready or impulsive travelers
- Family-focused
- Globe trotters

Tips and Tactics

To determine customer categories for your business, study industry research on consumer attitudes and trends, talk to your sales force, and study usage patterns. Publications such as *American Demographics* also can be very helpful in determining purchasing trends, consumer influencers, and other general issues that can then be refined according to your specific business and customer profiles.

By identifying groups of customers with whom you do business, you can identify customers most likely to respond to given marketing messages and thus maximize your marketing efforts. You can then develop individual messages that apply to entire customer segments rather than to just one customer. Although these messages may be sent en masse to a given segment, they will have individual appeal and relevance. For example, you could send the statement shown in Figure 4-11 to an entire segment of customers who purchased large-screen TVs.

Figure 4-11 *Sample Communication for Specific Customer Segment*

Dear Joe,

We hope you are enjoying your new large-screen TV. You might be interested to know that we have a new line of DVD players that are the perfect complement to your system. Because you are a valued customer, we will give you 20 percent off any DVD player purchase within the next 30 days. Just reference this e-mail and customer code number 555. We look forward to seeing you soon.

Sincerely,

Customer Service Manager

ABC Store

P.S.: We just got a shipment of recently released movies on DVD. Be sure to pick up a few of your favorites when purchasing your new DVD.

We also can classify customers according to purchase cycle. Every category of products has a purchase cycle associated with it. For example, consumers typically purchase a new car every 5.6 years. Many automobile marketers keep a database of all purchasers and market heavily to them just before they are due to purchase a new car. This method, called *just-in-time marketing,* is highly effective. No matter what product or service you sell, just-in-time marketing should be a key focus of your marketing efforts.

Market Adaptation Sequence

Another influence on customers' decision processes is where they fit in the *market adaptation sequence,* or their readiness to accept and purchase specific products. This is especially important for new inventions and new products. The high-tech industry provides a good example of how consumers vary in the category readiness with the advent of PCs. When PCs were first introduced to mainstream America, only a few people scrambled to purchase them immediately despite the steep prices. Today, only a few years later, millions of U.S. homes have at least one PC. The same pattern applied to the acceptance and frequent use of the Internet. At first, consumers were to slow to adapt, but now the usage rates are exploding. Marketers need to identify where their prime customers fit and tailor their messages accordingly.

Figure 4-12, created by marketing veteran Regis McKenna, describes the market adaptation cycle discussed in his book, *Relationship Marketing.*

In most cases, your most effective marketing will be to early adapters and innovators. Laggards represent the most difficult group to reach and typically do not generate a worthwhile return.

Figure 4-12 *The Market Adaptation Cycle*

	Innovators	Early Adapters	Late Adapters	Laggards
Product acceptance	Fascinated with technology	Want the latest products	Obvious solutions to problems	Absolute need
Motivation	Want to implement new ideas	Want to gain an edge on competition	Competitive or social pressure, fear of obsolescence	Extreme competition, social pressure

(continues)

Figure 4-12 *continued*

	Innovators	Early Adapters	Late Adapters	Laggards
Confidence level	Willing to experiment, take risks, high confidence	Willing to try new things, take reasonable risks	Avoid risk, slow to change, need references before purchase	Reluctant to change, need strong justification to purchase
Education/ attitude	Self-taught, independent	Will attend night school to learn	Will attend seminar, wants to buy a proven product, needs lots of hand-holding	Will send someone to seminar, needs proof, and ease of use
Acceptance criteria	Latest technology, new feature, high performance	Innovation, better way to do job, selective	Brand is important, pay for only needed features, terms and conditions important	Lowest cost, competitive terms and conditions, brand is very important
Selling strategy	Self-sold once turned on to a product, word of mouth	Benefits, references, word of mouth	Address cost, technical support, needs examples, demonstration	Productivity gains, fear of result without product

Source: Regis McKenna, Relationship Marketing *(Boston: Addison-Wesley, 1991).*

Identify where your customers are in their market adaptation sequence. This will help you to prioritize your customers, refine your customer profile, and most important, develop messages that appeal directly to the emotions attached to your product.

Step 3: Drill Down to the Least Common Denominator

Don't just stop after sorting customers into broad categories. Keep drilling down to specific traits and behaviors directly linked to purchasing behavior that are present among your top customer groups. By doing this, you will be able to further personalize your messages and thus strengthen customer relationships. For example, if you operate a pet supply business, you can easily classify your customers according to dog owner, cat owner, reptile owner, bird owner, or fish owner. Yet, you also can categorize each group. Dog owners could be classified as those who believe that

- Dogs are children in fur coats.
- Dogs are hunting aids and companions.
- Dogs are sports companions.

Of these groups, those who perceive dogs to be children in fur coats might represent the greatest revenue potential because they most often purchase accessories such as dog clothing, fancy treats, expensive beds and toys, and grooming services that other groups might deem to be unnecessary. This could still hold true even if there are more individuals in other categories, such as those who see dogs as sports companions, because these customers tend to purchase only basic items and thus represent lower frequency and volume rates. You need to carefully analyze each segment against all variables so that you can pinpoint your efforts and achieve greater efficiencies.

You decide how far to refine your customer segments. The key is to learn to look at customers in every possible way and from every angle that can influence purchase decisions. Then use your results to identify customers who present the greatest opportunity for your business over the long term.

After identifying customer characteristics, how do you set the course for lifetime marketing?

1. List the characteristics most prevalent among your best customers.
2. Create your own customer segments according to these characteristics, for example, dog owners who view dogs as children in fur coats, past shoulder surgery patients, frequent gift purchasers versus self-use purchasers, and so on.
3. Prepare customer profiles for each customer and customer segment you identify as valuable to your business. Your profiles should include demographics, geodemographics, VALS categories, product usage, purchase frequency, dollar value, and so on.
4. Assign customers to appropriate clusters—those of your own definition and those defined by market research, for example, fulfilleds or makers, laggards, or early adapters. Each customer likely will fall into more

than one category. By creating segments and assigning customers appropriately, you also will be able to identify where most of your valuable customers fit, thus enabling you to better target your marketing programs.

5. Assess these groups according to sales revenue, volume, and growth potential to identify customer segments with the greatest lifetime revenue potential. Set priorities to help you determine resource and time allocation.

With detailed customer knowledge, you can then identify worthwhile prospects by looking at market segments with values and lifestyles similar to your most profitable customers. This information will enable you to develop smart and effective direct-marketing lists as well.

Having in-depth customer profiles will enable you to create a customer-oriented marketing plan that

- Positions your product to appeal directly to customers' needs
- Addresses customers' needs and desires for purchasing your products, such as expanding your channels to include online, mail order, and so on
- Prices your product according to customers' values and price thresholds
- Uses your resources wisely and efficiently
- Promotes your product in a way that appeals directly to the emotions and psychology behind the decision process

In order to categorize customers accurately, you must be able to first collect accurate and useful information about them. There are many options, all at differing prices. Market research does not have to be expensive to be revealing. You can pay a lot of money to have a scientifically validated study, or you can do some simple activities yourself that will not pass the Marketing Research Association's tests for scientific validation but nonetheless will help you gain valuable insight.

Following are some simple and affordable methods for "getting to know your customers inside and out."

Conducting Affordable Market Research

Focus Groups

Advertisers frequently use focus groups to test new product ideas and advertising campaigns before launching them on a broad scale. Usually a handful of consumers who meet defined criteria are brought together to discuss a specific issue and are given a free meal as an incentive to participate. A third-party facilitator is hired to ask the group leading questions and manage feedback from participants. Clients usually sit behind a one-way mirror to view the group discussion and take copious notes.

Focus groups are great for letting you hear unaided comments, responses, and detailed opinions from participants. However, the information you get can be somewhat biased as well. If there is a dominant personality in the group, a person who speaks up too often, you tend to get "group think" and soon find other people changing their opinions or failing to contribute altogether.

Using a third-party facilitator is key to getting accurate information. If you or someone from your organization tried to facilitate a focus group yourself, you likely would not get honest, uninhibited feedback. This is especially critical if you want to learn how your company can improve its service or products, not just all the things your customers like about you now. However, market research firms can be expensive.

If money is an issue and you want to host your own discussion with customers, just be careful about what types of questions you ask and how you use the information. If you sit down with a group of customers representing a specific customer segment of yours, for example, dog owners who see dogs as children in fur coats, be sure to discuss only questions that involve their needs and wants. Do not ask questions about your brand, your service, your competition, and so on. Let them talk objectively about their values. If you get into discussing brand, competitive, or customer service issues, you likely will get misleading information. Also, keep in mind that information from this type of discussion should serve as a general guideline, not as a definitive direction. It is not truly valid information because it was not obtained in an objective manner. Be sure to track all the comments from each participating customer and include them in each customer file so that you can better market to them individually.

Tips and Tactics

Market research can be as simple as picking up the phone and calling customers to find out what their most recent needs or issues are regarding your business category. If you are a sole proprietor or freelancer, take customers to lunch to find out more about their decision influencers and current and anticipated needs.

The advantages of conducting discussions with multiple customers at one time include

- Saving time in collecting customer information
- Face-to-face interaction with customers in a nonsales environment
- Bringing happy customers together, which usually results in positive discussions about your brand, which leads, in turn, to decision reinforcement and enhanced equity

Surveys

Surveys are a simple and very affordable way to get information from customers. You can survey customers and prospects at the point of sale, on your Web site, at trade shows, on the street, or in a mall. The difficult part is getting them to take the time to complete your survey. The quicker and more convenient you make it for them, the higher your response rate will be. Ironically, I am terrible at completing market surveys because I am always feeling pressed for time, even when I am supposed to be relaxing. The best survey effort I gave in the past few years actually was on a ski lift. Representatives of a Swiss chocolate company were in Vail trying to get reactions from Americans on a new product. They hired market researchers to hand out sample chocolate in lift lines and ride up the lifts with skiers to ask them questions about the product's taste and their purchase likelihood. It was great. I got free chocolate and an interesting ride up the lift without having to give up any of my own time—and they got a valid survey response.

The other critical factor in getting good data from survey tools is brevity. Few people will take the time to complete a multipage questionnaire. Many will answer a few questions, especially if they are satisfied customers. No matter what your method of delivery, keep it brief. Make sure that you only ask questions that will truly help you better serve your customers' needs, and avoid any that touch on privacy issues. Ask yourself, "Is it really necessary for me to know their income range (or other variable) in order to serve them?" Invasive questions are a great way to get people to throw your survey away.

For best results, reward people for their time spent answering your questions. Incentives can include a discount off their next purchase, free gifts (for example, a ski pass at the local resort), discounts off products of interest, or free brand merchandise, such as T-shirts, coffee mugs, or pens. Just make sure that the incentive is appropriate and of value to those you are targeting for the survey.

Figure 4-13 is an example of a survey designed to initiate customer profiles. You can access this and other survey suggestions at *www.mcmurtrygroup.com*.

Figure 4-13 *Customer Profile Survey*

We'll Give You $5 for 5 Minutes

Just take 5 minutes to fill out the following information, which helps us learn more about your individual needs, and we'll give you $5 off your current purchase of $30 or more.

Name: _____

Address: _____

Daytime phone number: _____

e-Mail: _____

Reasons for choosing our business: _____

Most important shopping influence (please circle one):

   Price   Service

   Quality   Other

Best way to communicate with you (please circle one):

   Phone   Radio advertisement   e-Mail

   Mail   Newspaper advertisement   Other

Pet profile:

Animal and breed: _____

Name: _____

Age: _____

(continues)

Figure 4-13 *continued*

Products most often purchased: _____

Toy preferences: _____

Special needs: _____

Other items shopped for: _____

Frequency of purchases: _____

Animal and breed (2d pet): _____

Name: _____

Age: _____

Products most often purchased: _____

Toy preferences: _____

Special needs: _____

Other items shopped for: _____

Frequency of purchases: _____

Suggestions for improvement: _____

_____

Overall comments: _____

_____

You usually can access valuable information about customers in your marketplace, such as trends, issues, and so on, from trade associations. Most trade associations produce state-of-the-industry reports that give detailed information about spending levels, purchase intentions, budgets, and so on. These kinds of reports will give you a good understanding of the issues facing your customers and what to expect in the near future.

Research Firms/Brokers

Reports from research firms and industry analysts such as the Gartner Group, IDC, Forrester Research, The Aberdeen Group, Thomas Weisel Partners, and WR Hambrecht also provide great insights into trends and marketplace issues. Typically, you can access press releases and report summaries for no charge on their Web sites. Otherwise, it can be expensive to purchase such reports.

Hoovers.com is also a good source if you want to learn about a business in general. It also provides industry information to help keep you informed about current issues and trends. It is an excellent source when you are trying to collect information about business customers and prospects.

Secondary Research/Periodicals

Secondary research is information that has been published by another party. It covers everything from formal research reports to newspaper articles. Information that has been published recently can be very valuable in helping you to determine issues and trends that affect your customers and target consumer groups. Secondary research includes journals, periodicals, Web pages, government reports, and so on.

Most city and national publications have Web sites that allow you to access their archives. You typically can go to these sites and conduct searches for articles that cover the consumer group or issue you are researching. Some sites provide articles for free, whereas others charge a minimal fee. Some news groups will even e-mail you summaries of stories on topics you request. *The Denver Post* sends me daily e-mails summarizing news for the day on topics of my choice.

Newspapers are a good source for learning about environmental issues that may affect your marketing programs. Reviewing the letters to the editors can give you some insight as to how people feel about specific issues. Again, do not weigh any one opinion too heavily because it likely is not a valid representative of the population you are researching.

The Web

Living in the information age is truly an advantage for marketers today. With the Internet, you can access information on just about any topic anytime, anywhere.

The Internet provides an endless source for learning about customer groups in general terms. Typically, you can find information sites that will guide you to current research and data about a specific consumer group. For example, I recently did a search on AOL for sites pertaining to baby boomers. The search resulted in 133,295 sites. The list of URLs I received included chat sites, date sites, news sites, and association sites. By going to these sites, I can get an understanding of the personal issues many baby boomers face. For example, *www.babyboomers.com* and *www.babyboomers.org* are both sites for associations designed to provide this vast group of consumers with direction and assistance in key issues such as health, insurance, housing, and family in much the same way the American Association of Retired Persons (AARP) does for consumers over age 50. By reviewing the articles on these sites, marketers will gain a current understanding of concerns and problems this target audience is looking to resolve.

Mystery Shopping

Spend some time surfing your competitors' Web sites, shopping at their places of business, if possible, and reading their ads and marketing collateral. You can learn a lot about your customers' needs by paying attention to the messages delivered by your successful competitors. Chances are that their messages are based on their own research and learning over the years.

Intuition

Use your instinct. Your own judgment is based on valuable experience in your industry. While it is never a good idea to base business decisions on assumptions, your instincts will give you general direction. Try to find facts from secondary research or customer interactions to back up your hunches.

Once you've collected customer information, you need a sound software program to help you manage, track, and sort your data. Again, this does not need to be expensive. You can go the high-priced route and purchase sophisticated data-analysis programs, or you can create you own database on programs as simple as an electronic spreadsheet.

Learning from Relevant Reward Programs

Membership programs such as Frequent Flyer Miles and other types of reward programs are not just designed to keep customers committed to a brand; they are also just as much designed as tools for collecting valuable information. Notice that when you sign up for a new program, you answer many questions about your purchasing habits, needs, preferences, media habits, and so on. One such reward program is *e-rewards,* which is an innovative program rewarding consumers for reading e-mails that market products and services offered by a host of partners such as hotels, airlines, and so on. Participants earn points for reading promotional e-mails and can redeem the points for free skiing, hotel stays, and so on. When you sign up to be rewarded for reading promotional e-mails (a bright gesture on its own), you give the company a lot of valuable information about yourself—what you do with your time and your money, which brands you prefer, and what influences your purchase decisions. The survey is quite extensive; therefore, participants are given a gift of their choice for completing it. They can choose a discount voucher for airline travel, automatic points in their account, or a coupon for a free video rental.

No matter how large or small your business may be, customers always appreciate rewards for brand loyalty. Coming up with a reward program that makes your customers feel appreciated, valued, and committed—*and* gives you valuable information—is one of the best actions you can take toward lifetime marketing. Remember, rewards do not have to be expensive, just meaningful.

Hosting Win-Win Special Events

Special events have many purposes in lifetime marketing. Besides strengthening personal relationships, they are a great tool for collecting customer data. As customers and prospects register to attend an event, they give you valuable information about themselves.

High-tech companies often hold user conferences to familiarize customers with product changes, train or retrain customers on product use, or review implementation issues, product training, industry trends, new product plans, and so on. These are highly effective means for identifying customer issues directly. A user conference might include breakout sessions where company representatives discuss specific issues with participants, roundtable discussions where participants are encouraged to speak their minds freely in an informal setting, panel presentations where product representatives field questions, and of course, social mingling where some of the most valuable information is shared through off-hours conversations. Hosts of user conferences and similar events can collect consumer data and glean valuable insight as to concerns, issues, and likes and dislikes through formal and informal presentations and meetings.

Customer events are valuable and appropriate for any sized business that needs to train and update customers about its products' new features, benefits, developments, implementation, or installment. The most important thing is that you listen. Listen to what customers are telling you directly at your organized event, listen to what they tell you in the survey they complete to register, and listen to what they say after hours.

Tracking Customer Information

With the rapid growth in CRM software, several data-tracking programs are available. CRM software can help track each customer transaction, manage customer data electronically, conduct strategic analyses, identify trends, distinguish profitable versus nonprofitable customers, and evaluate the effectiveness of specific promotions and marketing programs. However, such sophisticated technology is not enough. Implementing the latest programs offered by Siebel, Oracle, PeopleSoft, or SAP does not automatically result in customer loyalty and lifetime value. In fact, many vendors of CRM software cannot tell you if their products provide a positive return on business for customers or how they affect the bottom line, primarily because using companies does not adequately measure the impact of their CRM implementations. Businesses using these programs must enact relationship-building strategies systemwide, integrate their own measurement devices, and manage the data in a way that provides valuable information on which marketers can build actionable strategies. Having a sound strategy is critical for any business regardless of size or type of CRM system used. A strong CRM tool or database management system will not compensate for a weak overall strategy or lack of follow-through.

Getting Started—Lifetime Marketing Checklist

Understanding customers' usage patterns, needs, and emotional and physical influencers is critical to successful marketing and to using your resources efficiently and wisely.

Action Items

1. Set up a process for recording customer interaction and history. Make sure that your system will allow you to easily sort for specific variables so that you can identify patterns and thus define customer segments.

2. Create a brief survey to send to current customers that will help you determine their value orientations (VALS status), and gain permission to send them future marketing materials that apply directly to them.

3. Create a brief survey to use at the point of sale to capture data on new customers. Get their permission to send them future marketing materials.

4. Find out as precisely as possible why your current customers chose your brand in the first place.

5. Determine which emotions are behind decisions affecting your category.

6. Identify trade associations that publish industry reports, conduct consumer research, and make this information available to members. Next step: Join the association.

7. Identify sources of secondary information, for example, trade publications or business news outlets, that will help you gain a better understanding of your customers and the market environment that affects their decisions.

8. Identify customer groups that represent the greatest recency, frequency, and monetary (RFM) value to you. Assign a name to each group, and assign customers accordingly.

9. Create in-depth profiles about your most valued customer groups that indicate self-orientation, resources, demographics, generational influences, and so on. Share these profiles with everyone in your organization—not just those employees in sales and marketing.

Worksheet: Getting to Know Your Customers

Answering these questions will help you complete the consumer decision-making process, life-cycle, and customer-profile worksheets in other chapters. A digital copy of this worksheet and all others can be found at *www.mcmurtrygroup.com*.

Customer Characteristics

1. List the average demographics that represent the majority of your customers.

   - Age
   - Gender
   - Income
   - Occupation
   - Education
   - Geographic factors

2. List consumer characteristics that apply to your best customers.

   - Generation
   - Self-orientation
   - Social status
   - Category cycle or perception
   - Market adaptation sequence

3. Which groups of customers represent the highest purchase frequency?
4. Which groups of customers represent the highest dollar amount per transaction, on average?

Customer Motivation

5. What is the average purchase cycle per customer for your product? For example, are purchases most often made weekly, monthly, quarterly, yearly, or more?
6. What are the primary motivators for each customer group purchasing your product? List per customer group. Consider

   - Status
   - Leisure

- Convenience
- Advancement
- Pleasure
- Comfort
- Security
- Basic need, for example, food
- Self-reliance

7. What types of rewards or recognition are most likely to appeal to your key customer groups?
8. What physical need does your product fill?
9. What emotional need does your product fill?
10. What social need does your product fill?
11. What are the primary decision factors associated with your brand? With your category (for example, price, quality, convenience, and so on)?
12. What lifestyle issues affect consumer attitudes about your category, for example, extrinsic versus intrinsic influences?
13. What market adaptation sequence applies to each customer group?

Communications

14. What are the most frequently used and influential information and reference sources among your key customer groups?

    - List communications vehicles (mail, radio, newspaper, magazines, newsletters, and so on) referenced by your key customer groups
    - List reference sources (friends, family, industry leaders or professionals, and so on)

15. Which key messages have had the greatest appeal to core customer groups in the past?
16. List key messages most likely to resonate with each customer group identified.

5 Understanding Consumer Decision Processes

What Influences Purchase Decisions and How to Channel Them in Your Direction

Understanding how consumers make decisions is just as important as understanding why. Years of in-depth research have been conducted to determine the decision process associated with consumers' choices of specific products and brands. This information is revealing as to how decisions are made generally. Marketers need to learn how the process applies to purchases in their business categories and then determine how best to influence the process in their favor.

Consumer Decision Process

Market research reveals that consumers go through a five-step process (Figure 5-1) when making involved decisions. These steps are

1. Recognition of problem or need
2. Image and fact matching

3. Trial purchase
4. Postpurchase evaluation
5. Assignment of loyalty

Figure 5-1 *Consumer Decision Tree*

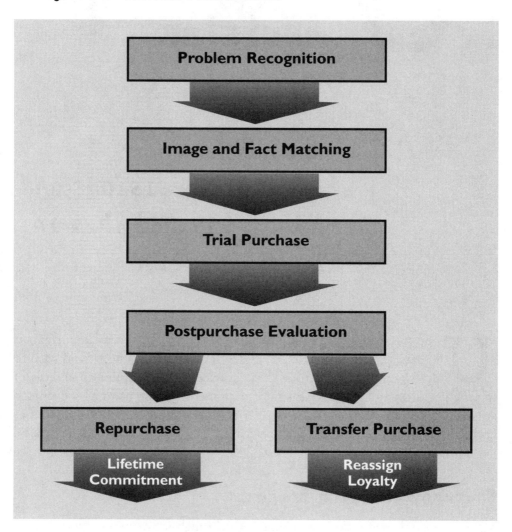

Lifetime marketers learn how their most valued customers apply this process to their decision making and then learn how to market to them in a way that results in the desired decision and behavior. This chapter explores each of these steps and discusses how you can channel the decision process in your favor.

Decision Involvement Levels

An important part of any purchase process that marketers need to address is the level of involvement associated with the decision. Decision involvement includes

High involvement. Personal high-involvement decisions include car and home purchases, whereas professional high-involvement decisions might include extensive, enterprisewide software programs, business equipment, and so on. Consumers are typically highly involved in decisions that result in a long-term commitment or high financial output. These decisions typically involve a great deal of information gathering, such as product referrals and product-brand comparisons.

Low involvement. Low-involvement decisions typically are associated with spontaneous, frequent decisions that result in short-term or low commitment to the product purchased. Price is usually not a factor as products are typically low-cost items and can be replaced inexpensively if they are not satisfactory. Low-involvement purchases include soda, movie tickets, toothpaste, and so on.

High risk. High-risk decisions typically are associated with high-involvement decisions. Risks involve financial loss, safety, value, or a high opportunity cost. Cars and homes are high-risk purchases. For businesses, anything that constitutes a large capital or human resource investment, such as CRM, knowledge management, the Internet, and security systems, is a high-risk decision.

Low risk. These are decisions where the money spent is of little or no consequence to the buyer and few, if any, sacrifices are made to obtain the product or service. If products fail to perform as expected, little is usually lost that cannot be recovered easily. Inexpensive advertising space, community sponsorships, and food items all may fall into this category.

Once you know the various influencers and involvement and risk levels associated with purchasing your business's products, you can develop compelling communications that speak directly to your customers' physical and emotional needs, ease the decision anxiety, and move them to the desired behavior.

Influencing the Decision Process in Your Favor
Problem Recognition

Products typically are designed to fulfill an existing need or to create demand by creating a perceived need. Consumers make purchases to resolve a problem, minor or major. The problems that consumers are looking to resolve can be social, physical, psychological, functional, or personal. Before purchases are made, consumers have to first recognize that they have a problem that must be resolved or a need that must be filled. Problems and needs can be as simple as realizing you need gas in your car or a new tube of toothpaste and as complex as needing a new car or an extensive software program for a global enterprise.

The purpose of brand marketing is to achieve top-of-mind awareness among targeted consumers so that when they recognize that they have a need, they first think of a specific brand's ability to fill it. This is why big brands spend millions of dollars just getting their logos out. Nike is a prime example. Virtually every National Football League and college football uniform bears the Nike swoosh. Nike's logo has such a strong identity that the company's ads need no words, just the swoosh and a compelling photograph to remind people that they have a need to be athletic and that products with the swoosh can address problems associated with performance, for example, help you run farther, jump higher, or swim faster. Nike's logo recognition efforts have cost millions of dollars and many years—two things that most businesses cannot give up as freely in today's market.

While big brands can create subliminal reminders of needs and problems through logo-recognition media campaigns, most businesses will never have even a fraction of the advertising budget it takes to do this. However, smaller brands can still be effective in channeling problem-resolution/need-fulfillment decisions in their direction. Small businesses have many opportunities for less expensive means of brand and logo awareness. For example, consider sponsoring a community theater's performance or a local charity group's fund raiser.

By learning how customers think, lifetime marketers can identify the influences associated with the decision process. Again, each customer cluster or segment approaches the decision process a bit differently. By analyzing the trends and histories of these customer segments, you will be able to get inside your customers' minds and pinpoint the issues influencing the decision process. When you understand these issues, you can build credibility and customer equity for your brand that are far more valuable than having your logo all over the television networks, sports stadiums, newspapers, and the like.

The best way to learn the factors involved with your customers' decisions is simple: Ask them. If you are in retail and have numerous customers, give people a discount at the cash register if they take a few minutes to complete a very brief survey on how they made the decision to shop at your store or buy the products they did. If you are in a business with a small number of customers, take your customers to lunch and ask them personally to define how they chose your brand and what factors influenced their decision. You also can send out a brief survey with your invoices or other regular customer correspondence.

A brief survey could ask the following questions:

1. When shopping for (list product or service), what is the greatest influence in your decision?

   - Price
   - Convenience
   - Product selection
   - Brand selection
   - Multiple shopping options—Internet, catalog, in store
   - Other

2. How did you hear about our brand?
3. What do you like about our brand that influenced your decision to purchase from us?
4. Please rate your experience with us on a scale of 1 to 5, with 1 being very negative and 5 being very positive.

Common decision factors include

- Price
- Quality
- Convenience
- Referral
- Customer service

- Experience with sales and service representatives
- Purchase benefits—Frequent Flyer points and so on
- Brand commitment

Image and Fact Matching

Consumers have never been savvier, nor have they ever had so much information at their disposal to help them make decisions. With the Internet, consumers spend hours researching products, variants among brands, different stores' return policies, product availability, and so on and, of course, looking for the best price and service. Never before have consumers been so well armed with information when going through the decision process.

Providing consumers with detailed and valuable information is one of the most important aspects of lifetime marketing. Strong, lasting relationships are built on mutual respect, trust, and understanding. Consumers who do their homework before making a purchase tend to feel more secure about their choices, have fewer returns, and have a better shopping experience. Informed consumers not only are picky about the products they purchase; they are also picky about the vendors they choose. These same consumers want to feel like a partner in the shopping process, not just a quick sale. They tend to trust the vendors that provide them with information so that they can make better decisions, even if that decision is not always in their best interest. Progressive Insurance goes as far as providing customers with numerous price quotes—theirs and their competitors'—even if their quote is higher than a competitor's. This is their way of letting customers know that they are there to provide the information customers need to make the best decision and that customers' needs come first. This is what partners do. By providing valuable information before the sale is made, businesses gain the trust and respect of many consumers and position their brands as trusted resources for decision-making information. Often this strategy results in the sale, subsequent sales, and referrals.

Consumers not only search for information about products during the information-gathering stage; they also search for information about convenience and customer service issues such as return policies. Most consumers want to be able to choose which channel to use when doing business with your brand—Internet, catalog, phone, mail, fax, or in person at store locations. When you do not offer multiple channels, you may lose the business to a competitor that does. Multichannel options are becoming more and more critical to consumers who demand options and convenience specific to their lifestyles.

Educational Marketing

Educational programs are a very effective way to initiate and build relationships for a lifetime, no matter what industry you are in or the size of the business you operate. And they typically are not as expensive as traditional advertising methods. You can educate customers and consumers one-to-one or en masse about category issues, technology benefits, cost analysis, shopping tips, and political, social, and environmental implications, anything that will help consumers better understand key category issues and thus enable them to make sound decisions. You should find topics that your company is uniquely qualified to address and narrow your themes accordingly. Taking on an entire category can be very cumbersome and expensive. If your category is not well understood by target consumers, you may want to seek support and help from trade associations, vertical vendors, and even competing brands so that your efforts will go further, cost less, and have more impact in less time. When competitors work together to promote an entire category, all brands can benefit because having a strong category is essential to any brand's long-term profitability.

Some of the most successful education programs are those which result in dialogue between consumers and vendors, or the information providers. In the 1980s, the Aspirin Foundation of America sponsored research indicating the effects of aspirin in preventing stroke and heart attack and its impact on the immune system. To help customers get this information in a meaningful and interactive way, their public relations agency set up a toll-free hotline one day each year whereby consumers could get free information and advice directly from cardiologists and general physicians. A mental health system in Utah conducted a similar program for depression. They invited consumers to call a toll-free phone number to speak directly to an experienced psychiatrist or psychologist about issues involving depression. Both hotlines were promoted through press releases rather than expensive paid advertising. The results were phenomenal. The Aspirin Foundation got the word out about the miracle of aspirin, and the mental health facility initiated many new relationships, many of which resulted in referrals to doctors within their system. Both organizations positioned themselves as a leading resource of valuable information and educated consumers in a way that enabled them to make informed decisions. Typically, the source for valuable and helpful information becomes the source for products and services. Thus everybody wins.

Web sites provide consumers with the opportunity to ask businesses questions virtually anytime. However, the answers are not always so quick to come back. People still need interaction with people, no matter how sophisticated technology becomes. Hotlines are a good method for creating this interaction and giving consumers the immediacy they desire.

Beyond helping consumers become more informed about issues surrounding your business category, information-providing activities such as conferences and workshops are ideal for collecting data from qualified leads and getting permission for future marketing. They also create a forum that allows you to get to know your prospects better by briefly surveying those who call your hotline or attend your event. Since you are giving these people free valuable information, they are more likely to answer your questions. You can ask qualifying questions that will help guide your imminent discussion and questions that will enable you to add these people to your lifetime marketing database and sort them into appropriate categories.

Tips and Tactics

Create real-time interactive events that provide customers with valuable information and you with data about qualified leads. Real-time interactions can include hotlines, seminars, product demonstrations, or trade show meetings. The key is to engage in discussions with prospects, qualify them, collect their data, and provide them with valuable information that will initiate a brand relationship.

Educational approaches often cause consumers to perceive that they have a problem or need and therefore must purchase a solution. This approach is typical among high-tech companies launching a new invention. Rob Griggs, a venture capitalist and entrepreneur, has built numerous successful high-tech companies by creating solutions and perceived needs among target consumer groups and then educating consumers accordingly. His success is founded largely on his ability to create new market opportunities and then educate appropriate audiences—end users, resellers, investors, and so on—about the corresponding value proposition. Educational marketing, according to Griggs, ". . . helps with very broad solutions that answer questions yet to be asked."

The key to using educational marketing to build relationships and lifetime value is to provide something of real and lasting value to a large population. Just recently, companies have been coming forward with technology that allows consumers to view e-mail and the Internet from a pair of glasses. A microphone attached to the side of the glasses allows them to give voice commands in response to e-mails or for Web surfing. The solution: in-your-face Internet access, literally. The problem: too busy or technology-obsessed to walk down a sidewalk, go for a run, or ride a train without being productive or responsive to something or someone or too busy to see the scenery around you or interact with people actually in the same place you are. This is a problem I hope to never solve for myself, and no amount of education will ever convince me to live my life in this manner. If your company is peddling a solution and needs to convince consumers that they have a specific problem, make sure that your solution is a realistic one that applies to a valid consumer market and has lasting value. Your product needs to be relevant throughout the lifetime of your consumers and flexible enough to adapt to new audiences or changes in your marketplace.

Education in the high-tech for business markets is critical because usually prices are steep and decision processes are highly involved, long, and tedious. For a new software program, it is not uncommon for the sales cycle to be 9 months to 1 year or even more. Those responsible for purchasing enterprise software programs have a lot at stake. The decisions they make are usually very costly, take a great deal of internal resources to implement, and thus have to pay off for the long term. Unfortunately, many e-business applications have not yet been proven to generate a positive return on investment (ROI). Thus the risk is even greater to the purchaser. Not only do purchasers have budgets to worry about, but they also have their own credibility on the line as well. If they spend hundreds of thousands or even millions of dollars on a product that does not meet management's expectations, their influence and even jobs are at risk. Once a vendor is chosen, it is very difficult to change if you are not happy with the product or service because of time-intensive integration and implementation issues.

One of the biggest complaints I heard when I served as a director of marketing for a high-tech company is that the product did not do what company representatives said it would or what the purchaser expected it to do. If this is the case, purchasers often spend many hours working with program developers to try to fix the problem because it is very timely, costly, and personally embarrassing to start over. The result is a lot of lost productivity and a project that has far exceeded its allocated budget. Neither of these events results in good customer relations. Businesses can reduce the risks for purchasers by first producing products that work as promised, meeting customer quality expectations, accurately promoting a product's functionality and capabilities, and educating consumers in a way that results in realistic expectations for the category and technologies involved.

Smart marketers realize the stakes involved in purchasing products in their category and create programs to help minimize the risks and eliminate the anxiety associated with making a decision. Educating consumers making highly involved decisions is an important step in helping to increase their comfort level, expedite the sales cycle, and ensure that expectations are realistic and appropriate for the products and associated service programs.

Consumers making highly involved decisions tend to seek such information as

- Realistic outcomes of product use
- Comparisons with functional alternatives
- Comparisons with competing brands
- Case studies of other businesses' success with a given product
- ROI expectations
- Complications associated with use
- Costs—both direct and indirect
- Installation time and costs
- Payback schedule
- What to look for in a vendor or technology partner
- Types of service programs to accept or avoid

As the educator or provider of key information being sought by prospects and customers, you will immediately establish credibility as an expert in your field and a valid resource for your category. This is one of the most valuable market positions you can achieve. If members of your marketplace deem you as the authority on a specific product area—benefits, use, development, trends, future projections, and so on—they likely also will associate your brand with quality, longevity, and success and will be comfortable with you and your advice. You cannot *buy* the market position of most knowledgeable and valued resources; you have to *earn* it by educating your customers and prospects on topics relevant to them, not to you or your business.

Educational programs can be serious and factual or fun and inviting. As my friend Rennie J. Truitt, a marketing communications consultant, asserts, "It's not just what you educate consumers about that counts, it's how you deliver the message."

Rennie was involved in one of the most successful product education programs ever—the "dancing raisins" campaign for the California Raisin Advisory Board (CALRAB), which took place in the 1980s. CALRAB needed to find a way to reposition raisins as "cool food" for kids and healthy snacks for moms in an attempt to boost market share for raisins in general and the California brand. The "dancing raisins" were first launched as a claymation television commercial created by advertising agency Foote Cone Belding and then elevated into a highly successful public relations and marketing campaign. Live dancing raisins traveled to schools, shopping malls, state and county fairs, and the like to entertain children and educate moms. The results were phenomenal. Not only did they sell raisins, but they also became an entity in and of themselves. The "dancing raisins" became part of the President's Council on Physical Fitness and several educational efforts such as literacy programs in conjunction with the American Library Association and the White House.

While I am not advocating that you take dance lessons and create an animated mascot for your company, I am advocating that you find a clever way to reach the end user of your product, in this example kids, and a credible way to teach the influencers about the benefits, in this example moms. If you can get attention for your business team as advocates on local issues, you likely will get the attention of various civic group leaders and media representatives, both of whom have significant influence on consumers' decision processes. Again, it does not have to take a lot of money and resources to create fun events that educate and increase brand awareness. Take a good idea and hone it down to the community level. Instead of focusing on the whole United States or even your entire marketplace, focus on reaching consumers at a specific shopping mall or similar environment.

Educational marketing can help you open up new markets and teach new customer segments about the value of your category. For example, when the advertising recession hit in late 2000, many media outlets lost thousands of dollars in advertising contracts overnight. Many large advertisers reduced their budgets drastically, whereas others, such as Montgomery Ward, went out of business altogether. Unfortunately, these events had devastating effects on several newspapers that had carried their ads for years.

An article in the *Wall Street Journal* profiled how the *Modesto Bee,* a local paper in Modesto, California, overcame this challenge through educational marketing. With the loss of two anchor accounts, the publisher of the *Modesto Bee,* was forced to pursue advertising dollars from area small businesses, a market that had been alienated by the local newspaper industry for years because of high prices that only their large competitors could afford. The paper's advertising staff succeeded in securing many new contracts among this target audience not only by offering special programs and prices for this new market but also by educating them about the benefits of newspaper advertising.

To launch the new program developed for small advertisers, the *Bee* held a seminar for business owners on the importance of frequency and other critical issues surrounding newspaper advertising. The seminar drew a crowd of 300 potential customers and resulted in numerous new advertisers. Overall, the program was highly successful. A subsequent promotion offered to the *Bee*'s new small business clients resulted in more than $820,000 in revenue. Their cost to educate new prospects? Very little. The return? Tremendous. The *Bee* overcame a serious environmental threat to its revenue stream and created a very lucrative new source of income.

Educational marketing can be executed in numerous ways—from a simple handout at the point of sale to in-depth seminars. Following are some ideas for successful educational activities.

Shopping Tips

Give consumers a list of questions to ask vendors when shopping for a particular product. This information is very valuable when the decision is highly involved, such as those involving high-tech software, business equipment, and commercial and residential real estate. You usually can find shopping tips already prepared for your product category from trade associations or publications. If you use materials prepared by third parties, make sure that your product meets the criteria defined in these articles. You also can prepare your own material. If you do so, you will need to create it in a manner that is informational not promotional. You will automatically lose credibility by having your name on the document, so keep it newsy in your execution. If you can get a third party such as an industry consultant to put his or her name on it and deliver it on his or her letterhead, even better.

Following are samples of shopping tips for shoppers of enterprisewide software solutions:

1. **Define your objectives.** Determine in advance what your needs are now and what they are likely to be in the future. This will help you to ensure that you purchase a system that meets your current needs and likely will grow to meet your future needs. It also will help you to avoid over-purchasing, or paying for functions you will never use.
2. **Do your homework.** Call appropriate trade associations to get a list of vendors that produce the type of system for which you are looking. Use

the Web to research their products and to download product demos, if available.

3. **Call references.** Once you have identified the top three to five vendors that meet your needs, call their clients. Do not get a list of references from a salesperson because those contacts likely will be prescreened. Call clients listed on the vendors' Web sites to find out about reliability, implementation, and service issues.

The e-learning industry bumped along for several years, hoping that someday the category would get noticed and take off as analysts had predicted. However, when e-learning tools, such as learning management systems, first started getting the attention of high-tech managers and training administrators, they were met with more confusion than excitement. Manufacturers of the tools promised to help organizations train employees on a global basis with more efficiency and lower costs than traditional training methods, such as classroom instruction, offered. The problem was that all the vendors were making the same claims, yet the scope of functionality for various products varied significantly, and the technology kept changing. Another problem was that the vendors could not prove that their products were successful in meeting defined organizational goals. As a result, purchasers were very confused as to what they should purchase immediately that would fit current needs and grow to meet their future needs. Eventually, industry analysts and technology leaders started producing white papers and writing news columns on how to shop for e-learning systems and tools so that purchasers' budgets could be spent more efficiently and wisely.

Tips and Tactics

Preparing shopping tips that relate directly to your customers' decision processes is an excellent way to initiate trust and respect with prospects. The best shopping tips are those which cover all the issues involved, not just the ones that involve your business. Help customers learn how to choose appropriate service programs, compare brands, identify necessary technology versus frills likely to get little use, set up ROI measurements, compare functional alternatives, and so on.

When preparing shopping tips, do your homework. Find out the issues that present the most confusion to customers, and then provide them with the answers. Doing this not only will help you position your company as a valuable information resource, but it also will help you to identify what your customers want and what your company needs to offer.

Customer Events

With word of mouth being the most effective form of marketing, the best use of marketing resources is to create a forum for this to happen. Many companies have done this very successfully by bringing together customers and prospects at organized events. These events can range from formal galas to educational conferences. Lexus hosts spectacular dinner and entertainment events in its key markets. Invited to these events are the top 200 to 300 prime prospects identified for that market and an equal number of satisfied users. After mingling together over fine food and entertainment, during which owners freely discuss their satisfaction with Lexus and its cars, all participants are treated to a viewing of the latest Lexus cars. This type of event serves several purposes: Owners are rewarded for their loyalty with a special night out, and prospects are introduced to satisfied users and hear personal testimonials of positive product use. Both groups are introduced to Lexus' latest cars, and the foundation of future sales is established.

Generation21 Learning Systems, a developer of automated total knowledge management and e-learning solutions, hosts an annual user conference that has been highly effective in strengthening relationships with existing customers and introducing prospects to the company's products and competitive advantages. With about 100 people attending, each conference provides an intimate setting for educating attendees about key trends in the industry and Generation21's technology. A small crowd also ensures that proper attention is given to each attendee. The purpose of the conference is to provide further information on benefits, uses, and technological issues such as implementation to users; introduce the products to prospects; and enable word-of-mouth marketing through fun social events and interactive sessions with company leaders. An industry keynote speaker is brought in each year to discuss the e-learning industry in general and attract interest. Clients present case studies highlighting various benefits from using Generation21's technology, and three tracks of courses at varying levels of sophistication are designed to ensure that the conference meets the specific needs of all attending. Sessions cover basic product features and capabilities, specific functionality of advanced tools, and in-depth technical issues for programmers and developers.

As a result of these user conferences, Generation21 has deeper relationships with existing customers and highly qualified leads.

Cooperative Campaigns

Association marketing, that which involves conducting joint marketing or public relations programs with a vendor in a related or vertical market, is one of the easiest ways to establish your brand in a new marketplace. If your brand is associated with a brand that a consumer respects and trusts through direct experience, it will automatically be perceived as equal in quality, innovation, and strength. Association marketing activities include

- Seminars on your product category conducted and hosted by you and your partner company
- Joint media interviews where reporters interview and quote both parties
- Road shows in which both partners present to and meet with selected customer groups
- Joint trade show booth exhibits
- Joint advertisements that reference key partners

Large companies often have created networks of partners to help them develop and launch new products. Cisco Systems has several partner programs in which it works with third-party vendors to provide a wide range of services to their customers in order to round out their offerings and help position Cisco as a single source for all Internet network solutions. Vendors eligible to become a Cisco partner scramble to be selected in order to be associated with a powerhouse such as Cisco that would add instant credibility for their brand. Selection, in many people's minds, is an automatic endorsement of innovation and excellence. As a small business owner, you should seek association with large brands in your industry that can boost your credibility and provide you with valuable leads. You also can create your own network of companies to band together to educate a marketplace or increase general awareness of a category and members' products.

Community Networking

Learn to speak! Credibility is as much a part of marketing as pasta is a part of Italian food. You must become a visible expert in your field. If you are not an expert already, make a continuous effort to remain up to date on industry trends, needs, projections, limitations, customers, consumer demands, needs, and so on. Then seek opportunities to share your expertise in your community and professional environment. By presenting information on current issues, you will position yourself and your company as knowledgeable leaders on the cutting edge of your field. This type of credibility goes a long way toward reinforcing customers' decisions and acquiring new qualified leads. Speaking outlets include

- Local chapters of trade associations, such as the American Marketing Association, the American Management Association, the Professional Carpet and Upholstery Cleaners Association, and so on
- Service clubs such the Rotary Club, the Lions Club, and the Elks Club
- Chamber of Commerce meetings
- Trade shows and conferences—both local and national. Make sure that you get requests for proposals and submit speaking ideas as appropriate. If you have a new approach to an old solution or a clever way of addressing current trends, you will get an audience.

If you need help with your presentation skills, join a local Toastmasters club.

News Releases

As you develop educational programs for your customer audiences, spread the word. Send out press releases to your local and trade media about your programs. These releases can communicate announcements of the event that serve as a public invitation to attend. Press releases should contain interesting data about consumer and market trends in an area, research results, or a local twist on a national story. By sending out press releases, you are positioning yourself as a media resource for interviews on your topic of expertise, and should you get published, you are delivering important messages to your audiences in a credible and inexpensive manner. Sample press releases can be found at *www.mcmurtry-group.com*.

Community Events

When I worked for a health care system, my job was to help educate consumers about various mental health issues, such as depression, substance abuse and dependency, and family relations issues. Rather than spend money on expensive ads detailing the nature of these diseases or issues, I developed educational programs that helped people in need gain a broader understanding of the causes and cures for complex issues and interact with care providers associated with my brand. My company held free community seminars on a wide variety of issues and used its in-house professionals as the speakers. The response was fabulous. In many cases, the seminars had standing room only. These seminars were a successful marketing tool for many reasons.

- They provided a valuable and relevant service and information to consumers and, as a result, initiated positive new relationships.
- They produced a group of informed customers who were better prepared to make decisions regarding solutions to their individual problems.
- They showcased the personalities and expertise of the company's counselors and positioned the team as a valid, approachable resource for answers and help.
- They provided a forum for direct interaction with customers and providers.
- They allowed the company to collect valuable information about customers and permission to follow up with them.
- They generated new business leads and allowed the company to acquire new customers.

Third-Party Education

In some cases, education might be the best approach, but your business might not be the best resource. This usually occurs when the educator stands to gain too much from a particular outcome. This is especially true when you literally need an act of congress or some other legislative act to enable you to better operate, expand, or market your business. Take the case of Bristol-Myers Squibb (BMS).

In the 1990s, BMS was testing some potential homeopathic products. One such product relied on the bark of the Pacific yew tree, which grows primarily in the coastal northwestern states. The tree grows slowly and was not considered worthwhile for wood products. Yet reviews of traditional medicinal herbs by the U.S. government indicated that the yew tree might have some health benefits. BMS explored these tests and discovered that a by-product of the tree that the company called Taxol was effective in treating ovarian cancer and possibly even breast cancer. However, it took large quantities to treat one patient.

BMS had two problems. First, it could not get enough trees to produce sufficient quantities, largely because the yew trees were scarce already and those around were being harvested by individuals on government lands. Second, the research, development, and testing of large quantities of the drug were very costly. In order to make this a sound business endeavor, BMS needed patent protection for the process and secure access to the yew trees so that it could produce worthwhile quantities of the cancer treatment. Their solution was to petition the U.S. Congress to pass legislation to protect the yew tree resources and get company access to federal lands with yew trees.

However, BMS also knew that if company educators were to educate members of Congress about this issue, its message would come across as too commercial, and the company would risk failing to acquire the protection it needed. Instead, BMS was able to get nurses and cancer survivors to speak to Congress about the power of the yew tree and its ability to treat cancer effectively and save lives. Nurses and patients were quoted in the local papers, thus helping to gain public support as well. As a result, BMS was successful in getting protection of the source of the trees and was able to get the trees it needed for drug development.

The critical factor here is that BMS won this case through the voices of credible third parties—nurses and patients—not its own. When dealing with controversial or difficult cases, consider aligning yourself with others who are passionate about your cause and enable them to speak for you. Also, feed information to your allies that will enable them to further your cause through informal means.

Tips and Tactics

Educate your employees and partners about your critical and pressing business issues so that each one can be an informed and accurate spokesperson for your cause, not just your brand's features and benefits.

Public Events

Hosting educational and inspiring events for the public is a very effective means to get attention for your product category and to position your brand as a contributing member of your community. Tampax, the leading provider of feminine hygiene products, had the challenge of breaking down a cultural barrier that diminished use of its product. It needed to dispel a myth among African American women about the safety of using tampons. To do this, the company, with the help of its public relations agency, Ketchum Communications, organized a special event on women's wellness issues that included discussions about the safety and use of feminine hygiene products, specifically tampons. This event was taken to 22 target cities and created a comfortable and engaging forum for Tampax representatives to have dialogue with this important customer group. The primary goals included reinforcing and initiating relationships between consumers and the brand and dispelling any myths or confusion regarding the use of its category, or tampons.

The event was cosponsored by Black Entertainment Television and consisted of two main activities: an educational forum and an exposition. The forum involved presentations by leading experts on mind, spirit, and health issues pertaining to African American women and included a panel discussion with audience members to allow for valuable consumer dialogue. Entertainment also was included with this event. The second part of the program, the exposition, allowed for one-on-one interactions with participants by providing free manicures, massages, facials, haircuts, fitness demonstrations, workouts, and of course, product samples. The celebrity panelists from the forum were on hand to mingle and interact personally with the participants. A 3-day version of this event was conducted at college campuses to allow Tampax to reach a broader mix of women in their targeted demographic.

The results from this campaign were tremendous. All attendees completing comment cards gave positive feedback, and 80 percent said that they would not have changed anything about the event. Tampax distributed nearly 25,000 samples of its product, thus generating valuable product trial. The company also was able to achieve 180,000 user sessions on the Web site established for this campaign and maintained an average length of visit of 8 minutes.

Not only was Tampax successful at creating new relationships with customers and inducing product trial, but the company also was able to generate a high level of exposure for its brand and educational messages. Nearly 20 million consumer impressions were generated through media coverage of the events.

While this particular campaign may have cost upwards of $1 million to execute, smaller versions can be conducted on local levels. Small businesses can host seminars or after-hour workshops on topics related to their products and market through public relations activities. Hosting events for 30 people is more affordable than events for 300 or 300,000 people. Cohosting an event with partners offering products or services that complement yours is a good way to add appeal and share the costs at the same time.

Webinars

One of the most economical means for educating consumers is through *Webinars*, which are essentially seminars conducted over the Internet rather than at a convention center or other meeting place. Webinars are a highly efficient way to educate people because their impact can be great and the cost low, not only for the host but also for the participants. Everything but the technology is very simple. People from around the world can log onto a specific Web site at a specified time to participate in a seminar or just view the presentation slides and content. The audio portion of Webinars can come either via the computer or over a phone line.

There are many advantages to this type of educational technology. First and foremost is the convenience. With the escalating costs of business travel, coupled with the diminishing sense of travel security worldwide, attendance at conventions and business gatherings continues to taper off. It is also more difficult for employees at any level to justify time away from the office for training purposes, even if it is mandatory, such as training for regulatory requirements. There just is not enough time, money, or interest to attend elective types of training on the same scale as in the past. Webinars make it easy for anyone to listen to your message and interact in real time. Participants can log on during the workday from their desks—learn something new, listen to your message, and still be available for urgent interruptions, signatures, and even instant messages.

Businesses use Webinars to present information on industry trends, introduce new products, report business accomplishments, and so on. For marketing purposes, they are best used as vehicles to educate consumers about current technology, changes, developments, and business strategy within an industry. The most successful approach is to invite outside experts on the topic you want to promote to present information during your Webinar. Their comments can be followed or supported by in-house representatives. If your Webinar is strictly promotional, you will be disappointed in the number of people logging on and the overall response.

Webinars such as those hosted by Placeware, a leading supplier of Web event software, allow a broad range of interactive technology, including

- Personalized viewing of presentation slides
- The ability to back up and look at past slides at any time during a presentation
- Real-time questions and answers. Participants click on a field on their screen to send a question to the presenter during the conference. The presenter can either choose to answer the questions as they come in or defer answers to a later time in the presentation. Questions also can be taken by telephone, depending on the technology in use.
- Live chats with other participants during the seminar

Webinars are good tools for companies

- Whose customers and targeted prospects have easy and prolonged access to computers
- With the ability to demonstrate their products via computers or online
- Targeting customers and prospects worldwide or over a wide geographic area
- Needing to communicate new news quickly in order to stay competitive and keep supply chains and resellers current on new technology and products
- That communicate regularly with customers and resellers over the Internet

Tips and Tactics

Successful Webinars are those that provide

- Relevant information pertaining directly to the target audience's decision process
- Insight from industry leaders, not just vendors' sales representatives
- Current, timely data and information that can be used immediately on the job

Remember, participants are usually on the job. Thus your presentation must be highly relevant to justify participants' time.

To have a successful Webinar, you must market it heavily to those you want to participate. Getting awareness for the event and creating a perception of immediate value are both essential to getting enough attendees to make this effort and cost worthwhile. An efficient way to do this is to maintain e-mail addresses of customers, prospects, partners, and so on and to send them digital invitations to your event. Promoting your event on your Web site and through press releases also will help to increase participation.

The disadvantage of Webinars is the lack of face-to-face interaction. However, with the strong interactive tools offered by Web-conferencing companies, participants can still be communicated with in a personal manner.

Educational events can have significant payoffs for businesses of all sizes. Small businesses can host educational events that reach members within a single community, state, or region. The payoff of educational events is multifaceted. For example:

- You create a forum for one-on-one interaction with customers in which you can listen and learn their direct concerns and needs.
- You are able to reinforce your brand to current customers by further educating them on the benefits and value of your product.
- You are able to disperse valuable information about your product category and brand and dispel any myths or inaccurate perceptions.
- You are able to generate media coverage for your brand through promotional efforts.
- You help to establish your brand as a valuable source for information.
- You are able to generate exposure for your brand that is far more credible than any resulting from paid advertising.
- You gain valuable exposure for less money. Typically public relations activities are less expensive to execute than paid advertising.

Trial Purchase

You can motivate trial for your product and take the anxiety out of the decision process by providing prospects with brand reinforcers—product trials, testimonials, lenient return policies, money-back guarantees, references, and so on. Many first-time purchases are considered trial purchases by users. This is especially so for low-priced items associated with low-involvement decisions. If users are not happy with the brand they chose, they can easily switch brands without incurring too much personal loss. However, with high-priced products, such as automobiles, real estate, and business equipment, that are associated with high-involvement decisions, consumers know that they have to live with their decision for some time to come and cannot switch brands without great monetary or other personal loss. This is what makes many purchase decisions so slow in coming. Typically, people spend months evaluating high-priced items such as large appliances and computer technology before making a purchase.

If you want to shorten the sales cycle and secure a prospect's business before your competitors do, make it easy for your prospect to try your product without a significant commitment by offering a free pilot program or a 30-day trial free of charge. You see 30-day free trial offers all the time on small appliances, new products, books, magazines, and so on. This tactic is successful because it eliminates the risk to the consumer and often secures the sale for the vendor.

Tips and Tactics

Expedite the sales process by offering incentives based on the time it takes to make a decision. For example, if a consumer makes a purchase in 3 months, offer 30 percent off; 6 months, 20 percent; and 9 months, 10 percent. Instead of monetary discounts, the reward could include added-value services or complementary products.

Providing customer references is another good way to create comfort among prospective buyers. Either you can set up a program that enables prospects to talk directly to customers and ask questions, or you can provide prospects with several testimonials about the various benefits of your product. Conversations will go further in terms of building credibility, but both methods help to assure prospects that your product works and is worth purchasing.

Tips and Tactics

To get current customers to serve as references or to supply testimonials, provide them with the utmost quality in products and service. Giving them monetary rewards automatically discredits the endorsement.

Postpurchase Evaluation

Once a purchase is made, consumers making highly involved decisions evaluate the product according to the information they gathered and the criteria they set to determine its effectiveness. If their expectations are not met right away, they will be disenchanted with the product and your brand and either return it or assign their loyalty elsewhere for repeat purchases. Immediately after a purchase, customers should be contacted to make sure that they are happy with the product and that their expectations have been met. A high level of customer service during this period is also critical.

Customers can be contacted in several simple ways:

- **Phone calls.** If appropriate, sales reps should call customers to discuss their satisfaction directly. This is most effective. In the case of my choosing a veterinarian for my dogs, a phone call helped assign my loyalty. I had taken one of my dogs to the vet to evaluate an existing condition. The vet was attentive and called me three times to discuss my pet's condition and treatment options and how I could avoid further treatments that would be long in recovery and expensive. The quality of the calls and the time the vet spent answering my questions resulted in my assigning my future business to him.
- **e-Mail.** e-Mail is a great way to contact customers. You can prepare a form e-mail thanking customers for their business and letting them know who to contact if there is a problem. Although this is a form letter, it will be a personal statement to each customer and make him or her feel valued. When ordering products online, I almost always get an

immediate confirmation, and often these encourage me to reply or call a phone number if I have any customer service issues.

- **Letters.** Consumers still respond to old-fashioned letters asking them for feedback about the sales process and their satisfaction with the product. If you include coupons for subsequent purchases or some other reward, you likely will get a better response. Ask for both positive and negative feedback.
- **On-site visits.** Sales representatives can stop by customers' homes or businesses to ensure that product expectations are being met. Face-to-face visits help to strengthen a personal, one-to-one relationship better than any other form of communication.

Following is a list of topics you may want to address with your customers to more fully assess their satisfaction with your products and customer service:

1. **Product function.** Is the product performing as expected?
2. **Installation or assembly.** Was the product easy to install or assemble?
3. **Customer service.** Ask your customers to rate their overall experience working with your sales team on a scale of maybe 1 to 5.
4. **Customer service.** Did you receive prompt responses from sales representatives? Were you given adequate information for making informed and confident decisions?
5. **Value.** Do you feel that you received good value for your investment?
6. **Loyalty.** Now that the product is installed, would you purchase this same product again? Would you recommend the product or service to others?
7. **Feedback.** What suggestions do you have for the product or customer service?

Assignment of Loyalty

Acquiring a customer is a bit like a dating relationship. You can never take loyalty for granted. You must continue to provide the quality, service, and solutions customers expect from your brand. If these conditions change, so too will their loyalty.

The jewelry business is one that thrives on customer loyalty. Helzberg Diamonds, a nationwide jewelry store chain, keeps customers loyal through seemingly small activities that build relationships and thus customer loyalty between sales associates and their most valuable customers. The company keeps an extensive database of all customers that tracks the nature of their purchases, recency, amount of money spent, type of product, and what times of year the purchases were made. Sale associates then send personal handwritten notes to selected customers that coincide with their purchase patterns. They also send personalized Christmas cards.

Helzberg is able to capture customer contact data largely through its purchase guarantee program that promises to replace any diamond or gem lost from one of its settings. When customers register for this guarantee, they provide valuable marketing data in exchange for the comfort that their investment will never be lost. The company's customers are sorted into more than 50 clusters depending on value to the store's profitability. Top customers receive top resources and promotions such as invitations to special showings, free music CDs, gift certificates for nearby restaurants, newsletters, and so on, all of which help to reinforce their decision to purchase from Helzberg.

Personalized notes to customers work very well for businesses of all sizes when it comes to reinforcing brand alliances. Ann Cathcart, founder and owner of The Learning Camp, has built a strong seasonal business largely on customer loyalty. Each summer, children with learning challenges from around the world attend her camp to help them maintain their academic skills. Her program blends academics and recreation to give children a well-rounded experience. The children attend a 3-week session, which involves a fairly significant time and monetary investment for many families. The program has been highly successful, achieving high satisfaction rates among attendees. Children have a memorable experience living in yurts, riding horses, backpacking, and hiking, but most important, they have a life-changing experience by learning to believe in themselves and have the confidence to go back to public school settings. This is what achieves the high satisfaction rates. Ann also keeps her sessions small so that she can develop a personal relationship with each child.

Ann's marketing challenge is that these happy customers are not the purchasers of her service—their parents are. Yet she realizes the value of her personal relationship with each child in getting that child to come back. As a result, she sends personal letters to each child roughly six times during the school year just to keep in touch. Her letters are actually form letters summarizing what to expect in the next year, wishing them a happy holiday season, highlighting the past summer's events, and so on. Yet every letter has a personal handwritten note about something special to the recipient. Ann gets many responses from children and parents alike, thanking her for keeping in touch. Most important, she gets nearly 60 percent of her campers returning year after year.

Figure 5-2 shows one of Ann's letters and illustrates that simple, personal communications work.

Figure 5-2 *Sample "Personal" for Customer Group*

Dear Camper,

HAPPY THANKSGIVING.

Hi there. It is hard to believe that it is already time for Thanksgiving!

We are covered in snow here in the mountains, and it is snowing very hard as I write this. Once again, Flash and Sundown are at my feet, but this time it is because they are hiding from the weather! It is a stormy day outside, and I am very grateful to be in my office and not in a yurt today!

How is school going? I sure hope that you are working hard and having fun at the same time. Do you like your teachers? I hope so.

Tucker, Chris, and Tom are all out of school for a whole week at Thanksgiving, and we are headed to visit my Mom and Dad for the week. We are all very excited to be with our family for this holiday.

Have a wonderful Thanksgiving with your family.

I will write again soon, but in the mean time, know that you are never far from my heart or thoughts.

With Love,

Ann

Loyalty Programs

Beyond personal communications, there are other types of activities that help to influence customer loyalty. First and foremost is quality. Without quality in products and services, any loyalty-building program or marketing campaign in general will be a moot point.

Once you have identified your most valuable customers and what influences their purchasing decisions, you also can identify ways to reward them for their loyalty. Customers in a particular customer segment likely will have similar purchasing behaviors and product needs and attitudes. You can structure loyalty-based marketing efforts to appeal to various customer segments—most importantly your preferred customers.

Preferred-customer activities that build loyalty include

- Special communications such as premier catalogs for premier customers
- Customer appreciation events and user conferences
- Discounts on future purchases and complementary items
- Rewards for referrals and frequent purchasers
- Programs offering reward points that can be redeemed for goods or services

Loyalty programs are effective in accomplishing many important lifetime goals. And consumers like them. A Jupiter Communications consumer survey reported that 76 percent of online buyers belong to a loyalty program.

Benefits of loyalty programs include

- **Brand loyalty.** It becomes costly for customers to switch brands because they will lose preferred-customer status, which sometimes means losing valuable discounts, points for redemption on related purchases, and so on. Frequent Flyer programs command loyalty because of the opportunity cost associated with flying with an airline that does not contribute to your preferred mileage account. The same mentality applies to jewelry, lodging, dining, furniture, educational, and clothing purchases and more.
- **Enhanced brand satisfaction.** Customers feel appreciated when they receive special promotions or premiums and, as a result, establish a strong connection to their preferred brands. Special premiums include free upgrades on rental cars or seating upgrades on airlines.
- **Increased customer value or revenue.** Customers spend more for greater rewards.
- **Enhanced customer knowledge.** Companies are able to better identify and track the activities of their most valuable customers.

Some of the most successful programs have different levels of rewards for different levels of monetary value. These programs motivate current customers to remain loyal so that they can earn the rewards offered at the next level. Loyalty programs are discussed in greater detail in Chapter 8.

Getting Started—Lifetime Marketing Checklist

While customers may go through the same fundamental steps when making purchasing decisions, influencers are quite different. Customers make decisions according to their personal values, lifestyles, social status, and geodemographic and generational influences. Lifetime marketers learn what these influences are and cater their marketing accordingly.

Action Items

1. If your product category involves a high-risk/high-involvement decision, learn how to minimize purchasing risks by offering extended warranties, generous return policies, and other benefits that increase consumers' comfort levels.

2. If your product category involves a low-risk/low-involvement decision, create incentives that add value to your brand and increase the volume of goods purchased.

3. Educate customers about your category and brand so that they can make informed decisions. Teach them first about topics of value to them that are associated directly with their decision process. Teach them secondly about your brand. If you become their primary source of information, you likely will become their primary source of goods and/or services.

4. Give customers a reason to assign their loyalty to your brand after choosing your products in the first place. Do this through rewards for purchases, rewards for referrals, and personalized communication.

Worksheet: Are You Directing Customers' Decision Processes toward Your Brand or Waiting to See What Comes Your Way?

When answering the following questions, provide as much detail as you can regarding your current knowledge of marketing activities.

Do you know your customers' decision process?	
Is your product category associated with a high-risk/high-involvement decision or a low-risk/low-involvement decision?	
What problems are your core customers seeking to solve with your product category?	
List in order the greatest influences for purchases in your category. For example, price, convenience, quality, reputation, referrerals, return policies.	
What topics do consumers need to be educated about in order to make informed decisions?	
How do you currently educate consumers about key industry, product, or brand issues?	
How have you minimized the risk associated with purchasing your product?	
How can you further minimize consumers' perceived risk and add comfort to the decision to purchase your brand?	
When customers are in the decision evaluation process, how do you follow up to make the evaluation a positive one?	

What types of programs do you have to ensure that customers assign their loyalty to your brand rather than switch to a competitor for their next purchase?	
Do you provide multichannel options for your customers so that they can choose the most convenient method to do business with you?	
Do you know what activities your competitors have engaged in to direct the decision process in their favor? To secure postpurchase loyalty?	

Analysis

If you were able to answer most of these questions in detail, congratulations. Knowing in detail the decision influencers for your customers will enable you to quickly implement a lifetime marketing strategy.

If you struggled to answer these questions, get busy getting to know your customers today using the tools described in Chapter 4. The longer you delay knowing your customers and what influences them, the harder it will be for you to gain a competitive edge in your marketplace by securing the loyalty of your customers and attracting highly qualified prospects.

6 Identifying and Connecting with Your Best Customers

Learn How to Identify and Communicate with Your Most Valuable Customers for Individualized Marketing

Once you've identified the demographics, values, decision processes, and recurring trends and purchase patterns associated with your best customers, the next step is to create customer segments and assign customers accordingly. Your customer segments should be based on the behaviors and product uses that result in the greatest revenue stream and pose the highest lifetime value. The goal is to be able to assign all customers—and eventually your prospects—to specific segments that represent their transaction history and personal profile. By doing this, you will be able to create messages per segment rather than per individual and thus send "personal" messages to many customers at one time—far more feasible than sending one letter or e-mail at a time to hundreds or thousands of customers. Some companies have identified hundreds of customer segments so that they can communicate one to one and use their marketing resources wisely. A small business might have a dozen or less. It all depends on the industry in which you operate and the size and nature of your business.

There are many ways to segment customers. The first step is to define your segments in broad terms or by the type of business they represent, such as direct end users, resellers, commercial accounts, business accounts, or consumer accounts. Once you have determined your general categories, you then segment and segment again until you have identified all key purchase influencers that are worthy of direct attention.

Segmentation Methods

One of the simplest ways to identify your most valuable customers—those most likely to respond to lifetime marketing efforts—is through the proven analysis discussed in Chapter 4 that identifies customers according to *recency* of purchase, *frequency* of purchases, and *monetary* value—RFM analysis. Direct marketers have used this method for years. You probably have noticed that shortly after making an online or catalog purchase, your physical and online mailboxes are flooded with additional correspondence from the companies receiving your business. This is so because you have now been identified as a valuable customer likely to make another purchase in that business category within the near future. The selling company's goal is to keep its brand fresh in your mind and make sure that you are aware of all the many items it has to complement your most recent purchase. Tracking a customer's recency, frequency, and monetary value is one of the most efficient methods for capturing lifetime value.

Beyond the RFM analysis, customers should be categorized according to other key data, including

- Income
- Demographics
- Generation
- Category cycle (purchase readiness)
- Self orientation and personal values (for example, VALS status)
- Family orientation (for example, married, children at home, empty-nesters)
- Geographic/marketing region

- Education/occupation
- Satisfaction level
- Product usage
- Purchasing behavior

One of the biggest roadblocks in customer segmentation is lack of focus. You need to segment customers in a way that directly relates to your business's circumstances, needs, and realities, not according to a standard list of variables. Think about what truly separates some customers from others in terms of values and product/feature needs, spending patterns, and so on and how these issues relate to your brand and marketing capabilities. Then create segments that fit the way you will continue to do business.

Tips and Tactics

Do not segment just for the sake of practicing division. Segment because it makes sense for your business and the resources you have to apply to your marketing efforts. Be careful not to set yourself up for failure by creating too many categories and thus making your marketing program too complex to manage effectively.

Figure 6-1 is an example of how a lifetime marketer might organize customer data in a spreadsheet.

According to these data, Customer A would be tagged as the highest marketing priority for immediate revenue generation. Even though the purchase volume and household income are less than Customer B, Customer A's frequency of purchases is greater and thus represents a greater revenue stream (12 purchases at a $50 profit each = $600 versus 6 purchases at $60 each = $360 net income). Customer C represents a customer who is not likely to become a frequent or high-volume purchaser in the near future and thus would be a secondary marketing priority.

Figure 6-1 *Customer Data Spreadsheet*

	Customer A	**Customer B**	**Customer C**
Primary purchase	Custom code	Custom code	Custom code
Date of last purchase	12/02/01	6/02/01	11/01/01
Annual purchase frequency	12	6	8
Average purchase value—net	$50	$60	$40
Annual household income	$75,000	$90,000	$45,000
Self orientation	Maker	Fulfilled	Struggler
Family orientation	M2C	DNC	RET
Geographic region	Northeast	South	West
Category readiness	EA	INN	LAG
Category orientation	Custom code	Custom code	Custom code
Annual value	$600	$360	$320

Key: *M2C, married with two children; DNC, divorced, no children; RET, retired; EA, early adapter; INN, innovator; LAG, laggard.*

While Customer A represents the greatest revenue stream, Customer B represents a stronger potential for increased frequency of sales as this customer is currently purchasing only half the volume Customer A is purchasing. As a result, both Customer B and Customer A should be considered top marketing priorities; however, the message to each would be different.

Customer A

Customer A should be the focus of programs that

- Reward her for loyalty through discounts on her primary purchase or items purchased most frequently
- Promote complementary items or accessories
- Update her about sales, promotions, product news, and so on
- Encourage referrals

Communication frequency should be moderate. The customer loyalty appears to be strong at this point. The level of communications frequency should be enough to keep the brand fresh on her mind to prevent competitors from making any significant inroads.

Customer B

Customer B should receive marketing correspondence that

- Encourages repeat purchases
- Invites him to return to the point of sale (store, Web site, and so on)
- Offers an incentive for the next purchase, for example, a discount
- Inquires about customer satisfaction or change in needs
- Promotes new technology and products (customer is in the innovator category cycle, which indicates a desire to purchase new inventions quickly)

A level of frequency should be maintained that shows a brand's interest in serving the customer's needs. Caution should be given to overkill because that can be as annoying as telemarketers calling during your personal time and eventually whittles away your credibility and the readership of your messages.

Customer C

Customer C should continue to receive communications but on a less frequent level than Customers A and B. Less expensive mailers would be appropriate, for example, a scaled down product catalog or a flyer versus a comprehensive product listing that costs more to print and to mail.

Recency of purchase can be further segmented to identify customers who have lapsed within the past 6 months, those who lapsed within 1 year, and those current within the past 3 months. If your product purchase cycle is 1 month, for example, dog food, you will want to identify customers who have lapsed within as few as 3 months. Tracking customer recency and frequency data will help you to identify customers you are at risk of losing, as well as those whose potential is yet to be maximized, such as Customer B in the above example.

Each customer segment is assigned a priority value to help avoid spending valuable resources on low lifetime value customers, such as those

- Who have not purchased within the last two or three purchase cycles (for example, 6 months for a clothing purchase)

- Whose average purchase value is low
- In a maturing life cycle and thus not likely to purchase much longer

Dissecting the Segments

As true as the fact that no two people are alike is the reality that no two customer groups are alike. Within product groups, there are subgroups. Again, dog owners can be classified as those who see their dogs as children in fur coats, hunting animals, or sports companions. Each needs to be marketed to differently. Donors to a medical research organization linked directly to health care services might be patients, philanthropists, or manufacturers of medical devices and equipment. These could be segmented further into shoulder, knee, or hip patients; personal or professional philanthropists (for example, giving individuals versus foundations); and medical versus nonmedical corporate donors. The further you segment, the better you are able to identify specific decision influencers and thus appropriate personalized messages.

When you complete your customer group models, you will readily see why mass advertising alone will not help you build your business and will not enable to you to strengthen lifetime relationships with customers. With detailed customer segment profiles, you can now develop one "individual" message that appeals to many. One advertisement cannot speak to the emotions of every classification of customers, but a targeted personal postcard, specialized letter, or section of a newsletter can speak to multiple members in one group.

Customer segmentation is used to help organizations accomplish many important tasks, including

- Identifying the most profitable segments
- Identifying new products and/or product features most likely to succeed
- Determining pricing appropriateness
- Developing appropriate and relevant marketing programs

Customer segments vary greatly according to industry and product lines. A bank's customer segments might include

- Credit risk
- Current profitability

- Projected profitability
- Life stage—young with a high propensity to borrow versus retiring with a low propensity to borrow
- Attrition likelihood
- Channel preference (in-person versus online banking)
- Production activation (usage level for current products owned)

A jeweler's customer segments might include

- Wedding anniversary
- Birthday of spouse
- Birthstone
- Product descriptions
- Affluence
- Life stage
- Purchase frequency

Successful customer segmentation can produce extraordinary response rates to marketing campaigns. The Royal Bank of Canada has achieved response rates as high as 30 percent since implementing a customer segmentation strategy. Typical results for direct mail campaigns for the banking industry are only 3 percent.

When you define customer segments and develop marketing programs accordingly, you will gain valuable insights that will guide virtually every aspect of your business. You will understand which product benefits and features appeal to the greatest number of customers, which customer groups warrant the most resources for marketing and enhanced customer service, which features are most valuable and thus should be further developed and aggressively promoted, and which additional experiences you should offer your most valuable customers.

In essence, you will be able to market smarter because you can pinpoint which groups are mostly likely to purchase what, what messages will resonate, and which added-value services or promotions are likely to motivate trial or repeat behavior.

Managing the Data

To prepare workable customer segments, you must first establish a means for collecting, storing, managing, analyzing, sorting, and tracking data. The larger your business is, the more complex this process becomes. A local construction company may have only 25 customers over a 5-year period and thus is a candidate for an in-house program as simple as an Excel spreadsheet, whereas a larger company providing hundreds of customers with multiple products might need to invest in a large software program that does everything but turn the lights out at the end of the day. The goal of any tracking program you create should be to store multiple data points per customer, to update those data easily, to sort per individual fields, to share updated files easily with various groups and/or individuals in your company, and of course, to analyze the data to determine trends, patterns, problem areas, and strengths quickly and efficiently.

Whereas large businesses spend millions of dollars on customer resource management (CRM) systems and corresponding consulting, training, and implementation, smaller businesses can still record and monitor customer data affordably. Make sure that whatever system you use easily integrates with your existing network programs and allows you to easily perform the necessary functions. These include

- Being able to easily share customer data across your company so that customer interactions are consistent and appropriate based on the last transaction
- Being able to easily update a customer's file so that a new representative has access to the most immediate information, thus preserving the quality of your customer service
- Being able to easily sort data for key variables such as recency, frequency, monetary value, and purchase anniversaries
- Setting electronic reminders so that you are alerted to the prime time for customer communications, for example, purchase renewal dates

When reviewing potential database programs, keep your future in mind. If you are in a business with a high volume of customers and a likelihood to grow quickly, you might want to spend more money to get a database that will grow with your company so that you do not have to upgrade in the near future. If your business represents a small database of customers, for example, a property maintenance company focusing on a specific geographic region, a conservative purchase might be the smartest choice.

Tips and Tactics

Research database programs that are designed to help you track and monitor customers and their behaviors. Talk to software vendors about your specific needs, interview database managers of businesses in your category of similar size and scope, and read product reviews in current information technology and marketing journals to see what works.

The best way to determine the effectiveness of a database program—or any software program for that matter—is to ask end users rather than vendors how the program works. Vendors forget to tell you about long implementation schedules or systems integration issues, whereas end users will gladly share their experiences and frustrations. Selecting a system that will integrate easily with other enterprisewide programs is the smarter choice, even if it costs more. If you are not already doing so, you likely will want to link your customer database with your customer service, billing, and even training management programs.

Charles Schwab has a highly sophisticated CRM system for managing data about its customer segments, which represent about 7.1 million active accounts. It also hires a team of highly skilled information technology (IT) and marketing professionals to manage and analyze the data. A customer file is started at the initial contact or first transaction with a customer. Each time the customer calls, the call center agent can immediately access his or her file to learn about all past transactions and conversations. Marketing analysts review customer data and sort accounts according to gender, affluence, trading activity, channel preference, and transaction frequency. They also analyze the data to identify trends and make assumptions about the needs of specific segments. Marketing programs are then developed according to these "informed assumptions." For example, if the analysts find that multiple customers with similar demographics are requesting information about a specific product, the company will then execute a marketing campaign promoting that product and related products to that specific customer segment. As a result, Schwab's marketing campaigns are highly relevant and successful.

While it may not be appropriate for you to purchase highly sophisticated and expensive CRM software from a leading developer, you can still identify ways within your organization's existing resources to manage data. The key is being able to update the data quickly and sort them efficiently for different variables so that you can identify purchase influencers and trends and, of course, separate your revenue-generating customers from your laggards.

You also will want to sort customers according to their purchase anniversary and renewal schedule. If the purchase cycle for your product category is 1 year or more, you will want to create a file of customers whose purchase renewal date will occur within the current marketing year. You will want to communicate with them regarding their next potential purchase several months in advance, so being able to identify them easily is critical.

Creating a Customer Profile

Once you have collected enough customer information to identify trends, start making a list. List all the variables you can think of that influence purchase decisions and brand loyalty. Then prioritize this list. You will want to create segments for the primary behaviors and characteristics that influence purchasing and brand loyalty, such as those discussed in Chapter 4. Your A segments are those that represent traits or characteristics which result in high frequency of purchase, high-dollar-volume transactions, and a high likelihood of future profitability through up-selling, repeat selling, and cross-selling. When making your list, it helps to describe the rationale behind each trait. In this way, you can determine which categories are truly appropriate and most suitable for marketing communications efforts. Otherwise, you might create categories with little meaning and payoff.

Your customer segments should address both personal issues and transaction issues. You need to track influencing traits and purchase patterns in order to maximize the current and lifetime value of each customer. Figure 6-2 shows information categories for assessing individual customers as well as customer segments.

Figure 6-2 Segmentation Rationale Worksheet

Category	Rationale
Demographic	Communicate age- and income-related information
Values—principle, status	Appeal to emotions driving decisions
Generational	Appeal to emotions influenced by history or sociologic trends
Geographic	Market according to local interests, events, and attitudes, for example, seasonal clothing promotions for snow country versus beach country

Purchase renewal date	Identify renewal opportunities in 2003 versus 2004
Category orientation	Determine product lines for promotions according to orientation, such as family-oriented, single, adventurous, and so on
Product orientation	Identify attitudes toward product, such as practical purchases versus status, entertainment, image, and so on,
Annual purchase frequency	Determine amount of marketing to direct toward customer and when
Average transaction value	Determine value of customer and level of resources warranted
Market adaptation	Determine likelihood to purchase new products immediately or wait until proven or price reduced; determine whether or not to tease new product versus sales discounts
Purchase status	Identify lapsed purchasers, current purchasers, or past purchasers (lapsed referring to those having purchased in past cycle but not current cycle; past those not purchasing for two or more cycles)
Life cycle	Identify years remaining in purchase life cycle and thus years of potential revenue

Segmentation does not stop with drawing up categories and assigning customers; it is an ever-evolving practice. You must continue to learn about your customers so that you can assign new customers appropriately and reassign old customers as patterns, desires, or life cycles change; and you must create new categories as times change.

Since purchase decisions are multidimensional, each customer will fall into more than one category. You may want to send the same customer information about a new product for women in their fifties and information about a new line of status-oriented products. Prioritize your messages to avoid bombarding a single customer with multiple messages at the same time. If a purchase renewal date is approaching, make that your top priority and forgo sending messages about other aspects of the customer's behavior or relationship with your brand until another time. You need to get a feel for how much is too much in terms of communications frequency for your customers and then make sure that you do not cross the line. Overabundant marketing can seem like harassment to customers, and there are few other things that will kill a relationship quicker.

To keep current on your customer data, continue to ask customers to provide you with information via informal surveys and discussions. It is also a good idea to keep abreast of industry research generated by trade associations serving your business category and those of your customers. Again, state-of-the-industry reports and year-end analyses prepared by trade associations and publications can provide insight about trends and future projections. Industry information can help you to identify new customer segments and recognize which are most likely to grow in potential and which are likely to dwindle. You also can purchase reports from market research companies such as The Gartner Group, Forrester, The Aberdeen Group, and IDC Research. It also helps to read reports from financial analysts. Investment companies that produce in-depth reports on various industries include WR Hambrecht, Think Equity, Sun Trust Equitable, and US Banc Corporation/Piper Jaffray.

One of the best fallouts of segmentation exercises is that you will be able to see clearly which customers are profitable and which are not and assign your marketing resources and time accordingly. Figure 6-3 will help you to identify which customer segments are the most profitable and represent the greatest lifetime value for your business. Completing this figure for specific customer segments will help you to create a customer profile matrix that will help guide your marketing behavior.

Figure 6-3 *Customer Segmentation Analysis*

Variable	Description
Percentage of customer base	Percentage of current customers in specific segment
Size of opportunity	Indicates volume of prospects that represent a given segment, for example, percentage of overall market size, number of prospects in a specific database, market area, and so on
Average dollars per month or purchasing cycle	Represents average spent by the customer segment
Percentage of total revenue	Represents revenue contribution of segment and defines marketing resource priority
Extrinsic influencers	Physical aspects influencing purchase, for example, geography, price, convenience, and so on
Intrinsic influencers	Emotional aspects, for example, principle, status orientation, action orientation, and so on
Life phase	Seniors, baby boomers, adventurists, students, young professionals, and so on
Category orientation	Purchase for status, comfort, image, practicality, performance, and so on

Market/product adaptation	Likelihood to purchase new products immediately versus taking a "wait and see" approach; embrace or avoid trends; stick with proven products; and so on; indicates database for new product promotions
Accessibility	Ease of getting contact information, reaching individuals, expense of communications channel, and so on
Percentage of current purchasers	Lapsed, current, or past purchaser status for cluster
Information sources	Information sources that influence attitudes toward category and brand, for example, trade journals, associations, peers, magazines, and so on
Communications channels	e-Mail, hard mail, phone, magazines, news articles, radio, TV, and so on
Key message theme	Appeal most likely to resonate with this particular group
Assignment of resources	Worthy of high, medium, or low level of marketing budget and resources
Overall opportunity	Indicates likelihood of high lifetime value, marketing efforts to pay off quickly, and so on

Using the previous guides to create customer segment profiles and matrices will enable you to clearly identify the greatest opportunities for your business and determine the right messages and marketing activities for each customer segment. You also will be able to allocate your marketing resources more efficiently than ever. Figures 6-4 and 6-5 are examples of customer matrices for two different organizations.

Figure 6-4 *Sample Customer Matrix for Pet Supply Store Owner with Dog Owner Customers (Dogs Are Seen as Children in Fur Coats, as Hunting Animals, or as Sports Companions)*

	Children in Fur Coats	**Hunting Animals**	**Sports Companions**
Percentage of customer base	30	25	45
Percentage of market opportunity	60	25	35

(continues)

Figure 6-4 *continued*

Average dollars per month	$65	$25	$30
Percentage of total revenue	60	10	30
Extrinsic influencers	Comfort and appearance of dog; no price is too high or product to extravagant	Strong, healthy dog; price/value key	Happy, healthy dog; will pay for premium quality, not extravagance
Intrinsic influencers	Need to nurture and care for dog's every need	Desire for rugged strength, masculine qualities	Want comfort, security, sense of togetherness
Life phase	Seniors, single/childless adults, strivers	Adventurers, believers, baby boomers	Adventurers, generation Xers
Category orientation	Eager to provide dogs with latest comforts and pleasures	Seek after equipment-type products, training tools, and so on	Purchase sports toys for dogs, recreational leashes, backpacks, and so on
Market adaptation	Eager to try new fads; purchase cosmetics and clothing items	Stick with proven products, basic food, rawhide chews	Price conscious, but quality minded; like sporty type of equipment
Accessibility	Easy	Difficult	Moderate
Information sources	Pet journals, referrals	Other hunters, outdoor journals, sporting good stores	Pet store employees, promotions
Communications channels	Hard mail, in-store point of purchase	e-Mail	Hard mail
Key message themes	Your dog deserves the very best in comfort, pleasure, and apparel.	Healthy products result in stronger, more capable hunters.	Maintaining your dog's health and happiness means more playful years together.
Overall opportunity	High	Low to moderate	High
Resource priority	Top	Low to middle	Top

This matrix indicates that although people who see their dogs as children in fur coats are a smaller percentage of customers, their spending level is higher, and thus they should be a marketing priority over people who see their dogs as hunting animals or sports companions, who spend less and thus represent a lower lifetime value.

Figure 6-5 *Sample Customer Matrix for Nonprofit Health Care Foundation*

	Former Patients	Philanthropists	Corporations
Percentage that have given previously	40	25	35
Percentage of market opportunity	60	25	35
Average dollars	$500	$1000	$5000
Percentage of customer base	60	15	25
Percentage of total gift revenue	25	10	65
Extrinsic influencers	Outcome	Belief in mission	Product relationship
Intrinsic influencers	Satisfaction, excitement of restored ability	Desire to better world and people in it	Desire for visibility or access to outcomes
Life phase	Adventurers, strivers, fulfilleds	Actualizers, believers, traditionalists	Fulfilleds, strivers, believers
Category orientation	Users willing to pay for restored ability	Eager to be part of cutting-edge breakthroughs, excited about scientific advancement	Desire new outcomes that promote their products or improve product lines
Market adaptation	Highly committed if outcome was successful	Committed to popular, promising technology that benefits all	Skeptical to give without statistical evidence of claims
Accessibility	Easy	Difficult	Moderate
Information sources	Own outcome	Other givers, scientific, health journals	Trade journals

(continues)

Figure 6-5 *continued*

Communications channels	Direct mail	Direct mail, e-mail	e-Mail
Key message themes	Help ensure greater outcomes for yourself and others.	Millions of people each year gain restored ability due to research technology.	Research indicates that millions of people each year can benefit from such and such a product.
Overall opportunity	High	Moderate	High
Resource priority	Top	Middle	Top

Note: *Column headings represent the top three customers for donations to a nonprofit research foundation. After completing the grid, fund raisers can best determine where to target most of their fund-raising efforts.*

This matrix indicates that although philanthropists represent a higher donation than past patients, the percentage of customer base and total gift revenues is less. Past patients and corporations represent greater revenue streams and larger populations. Therefore, these two groups are higher priorities than philanthropists and thus warrant more marketing resources. Both groups are highly important in terms of lifetime value because one represents volume and the other represents greater revenue streams.

Once you have completed customer profile matrices, you are able to organize your marketing efforts. You should prepare schedules for marketing to the clusters with the highest value to you. Schedules will help you to identify timing for each cluster according to seasonality of message or past transaction history. For example, if you are marketing to past patients and have identified two prominent giving times—one during rehab or within 3 months of the operation and one 12 months after the operation—you would create a schedule for communicating appropriate messages according to those time frames and state of brand experience. Your schedule for marketing to satisfied knee surgery patients might look like Figure 6-6.

In order to effectively execute a customer segmentation strategy, you must have a strong database program that enables you to set up category files and matrices such as these and one that will allow you to easily sort and mine specific characteristics and traits. Being able to easily mine and export data is essential to creating results-generating lifetime marketing programs.

Figure 6-6 *Sample Schedule for Marketing to Postoperative Knee Surgery Patients*

	3 Months Postoperatively	4 Months Postoperatively	12 Months Postoperatively	Monthly
Message	Introduction to medical research activities	Thank you; push for continued donation	Summary of year's research activities and results	Newsletter discussing current research
Solicitation	Donation of $150 or more	Annual donation plan	Planned giving	Newsletter discussing current research

Large companies spend millions of dollars to treat customers like a small business can. And because of these personalization efforts, customers have grown to expect and demand personal treatment and interaction. If customers are getting individual attention from large Fortune 1000 companies, they will expect it even more from smaller companies.

According to IDC, a worldwide research firm, by 2004, worldwide revenue for data warehousing tools is expected to reach $17 billion, accelerating at a compound growth rate of 26 percent. Because of the personalization inroads that big businesses are making even at the cost of millions of dollars, it is even more critical that smaller-sized businesses learn to record and manage customer transaction and needs data. It is not just a good idea; it is imperative if you want to stay in business. Just find a way to make it work affordably and effectively.

Getting Started–Lifetime Marketing Checklist

Identifying consumer patterns and traits and sorting customers into corresponding categories will enable you to market smarter than ever before. Segmentation marketing, which allows you to deliver highly targeted and relevant messages to customers and address specific needs, will help you to achieve greater results and higher efficiencies than other forms of marketing.

Action Items

1. Find a database system that fits your budget and supports your existing computer systems.
2. List the customer variables that describe your customer base, starting with demographics and purchase patterns.
3. Identify the emotional influences for your customers through information surveys and discussions.
4. Select the variables with the most impact on sales and profitability.
5. Create customer files, and record each transaction.
6. Identify broad categories that represent customers, for example, dog owners and cat owners.
7. Segment each broad category into smaller subsegments, for example, dog owners who see dogs as children in fur coats.
8. Analyze your customer segments. Look for recurring patterns and traits among each customer segment.
9. Do your math. Calculate the annual and lifetime values that each customer segment represents for your business over the short and long terms.
10. Calculate the annual and lifetime value for each customer.
11. Develop marketing messages that apply to your most valuable customer segments.
12. Complete the customer profile matrix chart in this chapter to record valuable information about each customer segment.

Worksheet: Create a Profile Matrix for Your Most Profitable and Valuable Segments

Complete the following matrix for your most valuable customer segments.

	Segment A	Segment B	Segment C
Percentage that have purchased previously			
Percentage of market opportunity			
Average dollars			
Percentage of customer base			
Percentage of total revenue			
Extrinsic influencers			
Intrinsic influencers			
Life phase			
Category orientation			
Market adaptation			
Accessibility			
Information sources			
Communications channels			

	Segment A	Segment B	Segment C
Key message themes			
Overall opportunity			
Resource priority			

This worksheet can be accessed digitally at *www.mcmurtrygroup.com.*

Part 3

Harnessing the Power of Communications to Build Relationships

7 Getting Personal in a Big Way

Enhancing Brand Equity and Increasing Sales through Personalized Communications

Nothing got in the way of Anita Russell when it came to building personal relationships with customers for Coors Brewing Company, the third largest brewery in the United States. As the company's director of corporate communications for more than 20 years, she was committed to keeping people close to the brand, no matter what it took. At one point, it meant responding personally to nearly 15,000 letters a year from Coors' fans and those with complaints. Although it was a tedious task, not one letter went unanswered. Letters were composed for each consumer, thanking them for the hat made out of crocheted acrylic yarn and old Coors' beer cans, answering questions about calorie content and advertising campaigns, and explaining why all Coors' products were not available everywhere. Coors maintained a cultlike following with its customers for years in part because of these one-to-one relationships established and maintained by Coors' corporate communications, community relations, and sales functions.

The individual commitment to customer satisfaction and retention became a key value of the company. As the volume of mail grew, Anita worked to set up a consumer information center, advertising the newly established 800 number on cans and bottles to respond more efficiently to consumers' needs. Customer service professionals were trained to handle hundreds of questions, requests, complaints, and calls of praise for the company and its products. Special attention was paid to customers who voiced dissatisfaction, with Coors' representatives working to resolve all manner of issues. Sometimes members of the sales force would personally deliver replacement product to the doors of customers in order to satisfy them. Dissatisfied customers became satisfied ones and remained loyal consumers for Coors over the years.

No matter how large or small a brand is, getting personal with customers is critical to maintaining loyalty and competitiveness. With sophisticated customer resource management (CRM) technology, large companies are able to interact individually with customers in a way that used to be unique to small businesses. To a certain degree, this ability levels the playing field between large and small businesses when it comes to customer interaction and service. It used to be that the advantage of doing business with a small company was the personal attention and care that a small company could offer. Not any more. Big businesses have entered the game and are committed to interacting with each one of their thousands of customers as if they were the only one. Millions of dollars each year are spent on initiatives and CRM technology to help large enterprises do this very thing. As a result, customers have grown to expect personalized attention and service from all vendors with whom they do business—regardless of size. They want to know that you know their transaction history with your business, what types of products to promote to them, and what incentives interest them most and that if something goes wrong, there is a smart, caring, responsive person at the other end of the telephone. They want to know that you recognize their value and appreciate their business.

Quite often customers are often able to overlook a brand flaw but are not willing to overlook a breach in service. Customers demand high standards of customer service in exchange for their loyalty. When I hear friends complain about specific brands, it is rarely about the product and almost always about how they were treated rudely, kept on hold for an unacceptable amount of time, ignored when requesting information, or not allowed to return a product.

Getting Personal with Service

Harlan Bratcher, president of Armani Exchange, put it so profoundly: "Big businesses complicate things, and small businesses think too hard." In the early days of his career, Harlan was the director of personal shopping for Neiman Marcus.

Although Neiman Marcus has thousands of customers spending thousands of dollars each year at its many stores, each of Harlan's customers felt as if they were the store's most important. This was due to the high level of personal service he and his team offered, such as making house calls and assisting customers in ways that had nothing to do with Neiman Marcus's product line. He recalls listening to customers who just needed a friend and helping to plan a party. Neiman Marcus actually started a travel division as a result of the many requests for travel assistance that the company received from its "personal shopper" clientele.

The success of Neiman Marcus's Personal Shopping Division also was predicated on the philosophy of the company's founder, Stanley Marcus, of "giving customers what they want" and "the customer is always right." These two guiding principles ensured that sales representatives listened and offered customers what they needed, not what the store or clerk needed to make more money. Harlan's most satisfying sale was a $25 cotton sweater that he sold to Mr. Marcus for his wife's birthday. Clearly, Mr. Marcus could have afforded a much higher-priced item, and many sales clerks would have been tempted to exploit this. Instead, Harlan focused on what Mr. Marcus wanted and what his wife would use. As a result, he made a very small amount of money from the sale, but he earned the trust and respect of a very valuable customer and started a relationship that lasted for years. This is what lifetime marketing is all about: Focusing on what the customer's needs are and delivering on those needs even if it means a small monetary return at the time. Happy customers pay off for years to come.

At Armani Exchange, making customers comfortable is a key focus for Harlan. Sales representatives are trained to give customers what they want and refrain from giving them what they do not want (which is an intrusive, pushy sales approach). Harlan trains his sales representatives to greet, listen, and anticipate. In a sense, his employees are fashion concierges, listening to customers, getting to know them, and making recommendations on both known and anticipated needs. Employees maintain complete records of customers' transactions— only after having their permission to do so—and then follow up accordingly.

While Armani Exchange is a large company with nearly 50 stores in the United States and more than 1200 employees serving thousands of customers, it has found a way to personalize its brand and keep customers' loyalty for their lifetime. Customers who have a good experience with Armani Exchange are also more likely to shop the company's top line, Georgio Armani, as their life cycle matures and their tastes in clothing change. Good customer service transcends product lines and survives changes in customers' needs and interests.

When it comes to rewarding customers, the Armani Exchange philosophy is simple: Rather than offering discounts that could jeopardize the image of the brand, the company simply gives customers what they want from the very beginning—good products, good service, and relevant value. Online shoppers can earn a $50 gift certificate for every $500 spent. The convenience and personalization that comes from this, according to Harlan, is the best reward of all.

Tips and Tactics

Personalize your brand and reward your customers for their business in a way that directly enhances the brand image you want to achieve for your brand over the long term. If you do not want to be known as a mass discounter, do not offer discounts. Offer gifts or rewards points instead.

Nordstrom's is another good example of putting the customer first. Customers know that if they are unhappy with a purchase, even long after the sale date or after it has been used, they can return it with no questions asked. This policy takes the fear out of high-ticket purchases and creates a friendly atmosphere that often results in more sales. It gives people the comfort to buy something impulsively because they know they can always get their money back. Taking the fear out of the purchase process is key to closing the sale and to initiating a positive relationship.

Getting Personal with Rewards

A brand that has mastered the art of rewarding customers in a personal way is American Express. Through the company's Membership Rewards program, card members earn points toward free goods and services, and American Express earns incremental business.

In the early 1990s, American Express launched the Membership Rewards program to secure brand loyalty and lifetime value among its most lucrative customer segments. At first the program was designed to reward customers with points for travel outlets such as airlines and hotels. About 5 years into the program, savvy marketers realized that the reward structure was too limiting and took away members' personal choices and the opportunity to be rewarded with things that were relevant to their lifestyle, not the brand's. The company changed the program to allow members to redeem their points for a wide variety of goods and services, not just travel-related items. Members can now redeem their points for items at stores or specific products.

Since its beginning, American Express has been determined to have the best rewards program available in its category. The company does this by continually listening to its members to learn what is of value to them and what is not and then building its program accordingly. As a result, the Membership Rewards program has no expiration date or earnings cap. Members also can transfer their points directly to other programs such as Delta's SkyMiles frequent flyer program.

Membership Rewards has been a tremendous success. In a very short period of time and without any formal marketing, it accrued more than 4 million members. And these 4 million customers are among some of the brand's most loyal, using their cards frequently.

"When you give people something that is relevant and of true value to them, they absolutely give you their loyalty in return," said Susan Sobbott, the senior vice president overseeing the Membership Rewards program.

The spend rate among enrolled members is five times the average of all other American Express card members and is significantly above the industry average. The attrition rate is 75 percent lower than the average for credit-card customers in general. The success of this program is even more phenomenal when you consider that members actually pay to enroll in this program, so essentially they pay American Express to reward them. Why? Because the value the program offers them is greater than the investment.

Tips and Tactics

Reward your customers with something of relevant value, such as accessories to products purchased previously or information that will assist them with a specific goal, for example, getting a job promotion or reducing their monthly grocery bills.

What does all this mean? Customers like to be rewarded for their business and assign loyalty to the brands that do so. Rewards have to be meaningful, valuable, and, as illustrated by American Express's success, personal. Members can choose how they want to be rewarded rather than take whatever the company decides to offer. This personalization is a key contributor to the success of such programs.

According to Sobbott, "We are amazed ourselves how large the program is and how important it is to our business, not only in terms of volume of customers, but in terms of the volume of business they give us. We have higher than average customer behaviors because of the loyalty created by the program."

Not only are the rewards personal, so too are the communications. American Express segments customers according to the type of transactions made with the card. For example, a customer using her card largely for dining purchases will get notices about points being offered through new dining partners, and those using the card for high volumes of travel purchases will receive incentives to use the card for even more travel purchases. If the company wants to motivate a customer segment to try a new product category, it will offer points for using the card for related products. Members can go to the program's Web site to request news about specific product categories and corresponding partners.

Communications vehicles vary in order to ensure that members are reached in a way that is most convenient for them. Tools include

- The Membership Rewards Web site
- e-Mails containing point balance statements and mentioning new partner offerings
- Magalog, American Express's term for seasonal mailings that focus on a specific element of the program (For example, the Magalog released in November 2001 focused on the theme the "Spirit of the Season" and showcased holiday-related products offered by partner companies such as Sony and Saks Fifth Avenue. It also had articles on features and benefits of the program and a section showcasing products to which points could be applied.)

Communications are frequent enough to be of value to members yet not so frequent that they become annoying. Members receive monthly e-mails pertaining to their specific purchase patterns and needs, quarterly statements, and seasonal catalogs.

To keep customers loyal for a lifetime, you need to seek ways to reward them that are relevant to their needs and provide a real value. American Express has succeeded because of its commitment to do just that. Rewards need to be as personal as your communication. Give customers a choice as to how they want to be rewarded, and continue to give them incentives to earn more rewards with your business by offering new rewards on a regular basis.

Rewards programs are also strong tools for capturing customer data. When customers perceive that they will gain something of value, they are more likely to give you personal data for future marketing purposes.

Online retailers have found point programs to be highly successful. Some retailers have found that shoppers who are enrolled in points programs spend as much as 15 percent more than those who are not and that promotions offering points have outperformed other promotions significantly. Again, the key is rewarding customers for their business in a way that is personalized to their needs.

Getting Personal with Promotions

The whole point of lifetime marketing is to get to know your customers on as individual a basis as possible so that you can implement what I refer to as *personalized promotions*. Personalized promotions are just that—offering customers promotions based on their personal history with you. If a customer has most often shopped your sales, then send him promotions offering discounts. If a customer only purchases at holidays, offer her a holiday shopping guide. If a customer only purchases one product category repeatedly, offer him discounts for volume purchases and discounts for complementary products to entice the customer in broadening his shopping patterns.

Tips and Tactics

Referring to customers' past transactions, questions, or needs is an excellent way to personalize your brand and let customers know that you appreciate and recognize their business. Little things that make customers feel valued go a long way in marketing, just as they do in all of life's relationships.

Booksellers do an excellent job of personalized promotions. Barnes & Noble, Amazon.com, and others keep a record of the titles you have purchased with them and then send you communications about new titles on related themes. These messages, which typically come via e-mail, often offer a discount if you purchase one of the products they mention. Barnes & Noble has created numerous e-newsletters that discuss new releases and a number of other themes. Visitors to the company's Web site are encouraged to sign up for the newsletters that reflect their individual interests. By offering numerous newsletters that cater to just as many interests, Barnes & Noble is personalizing its correspondence according to customers' requests. Information sent to customers is specific to their needs and, with their permission, goes much further than generic communications that cover multiple themes and are sent out randomly to a company's database of customers.

Barnes & Noble takes personalization a step further through its Barnes & Noble University. Each month the company posts 50 new online courses on its Web site and offers them free of charge. The courses are based on books sold by Barnes & Noble and include personal interaction with the books' authors and other students. In this way, consumers can have a very personal experience with an expert in their field of choice and gain valuable information specific to their individual needs. And Barnes & Noble secures valuable learners to its brand and sells books related to the free courses offered. This is a good example of win-win marketing and personalization. All parties win. Customers gain valuable information specific to their interests, not what is pushed on them by a brand manager; authors get to promote their books and their expertise; and Barnes & Noble gains loyal customers and increased sales.

Amazon.com does a fabulous job of personalizing its home page to each customer. Whenever I sign on, the most prominent graphic on the home page is a direct salutation to me. The title of the home page is now "Jeanette's Store." In fact, the home page created just for me mentions my name four times, has a tab for Jeanette's Store, and uses the word *you* 11 times and *your* 23 times for 34 personal references. Underneath the title of "Jeanette's Store," the page mentions that Amazon has some special recommendations for me. It then lists a series of books and music products that relate directly to my past purchases. It also has a sidebar with the headline that says, "Jeanette, look what's new for you." It then has links to a message center that contains messages about new titles related to my past purchases and to my shopping cart. Amazon.com automatically creates a new Web page personalized to me each time I browse the site. After reviewing a few products, I can click on the tab "Page you made," and it will show me a personalized page listing the products I reviewed and recommend similar ones.

While your business may not be able to afford the type of infrastructure required to personalize Web sites such as these, you can still personalize your promotions. Instead of using a Web site to communicate directly about past purchases and related potential purchases, you can do it the old-fashioned way—via mail or telephone. If you keep good records of customer transactions and have a simple database management program, you can easily identify clusters of customers with similar purchasing histories, create a letter offering a promotion that is relevant to this segment, merge the letters, and mail them. If your message is relevant and your promotion is of direct value to your customers, you likely will get the same kinds of results as those generated by sophisticated e-commerce sites. Depending on the size of your business and the number of core customers, you even may be able to produce truly individual letters for each customer.

Tips and Tactics

Personalization can be as simple as taking your customers to lunch, sending them thank-you gifts that reflect their hobbies or personal interests, or writing thank-you notes to people who stopped by your booth at a trade show. Use personalization activities to initiate a relationship with a desired customer and to make existing relationships more meaningful.

Getting Personal with Communications

Customer information centers (CICs) are also a great way to personalize each experience with your brand for each customer. CICs are essentially robust, comprehensive customer service centers and are often integrated with a CRM system so that operators can pull up personal information on each customer and review their data immediately. As a result, CIC representatives are able to correspond with customers about past experiences and transactions and more effectively cross-sell and up-sell. Consumers can interact with CICs in any manner they choose—via telephone, e-mail, hard mail, or faxes. While the costs can be high for effective CICs, so too can be the rewards. Even the smallest of businesses can find ways to review existing customer data and respond and reward accordingly.

Personalization pays off at all levels. It does not need to be in the form of expensive Web sites or attached to extensive CRM systems or CICs to generate a return for businesses. It can be as simple as a hand-written note that is often the most successful form of personal marketing. John Vail, senior relationship executive for American Express, generates phenomenal results with handwritten notes. Prior to exhibiting at trade shows, John's team sends out a handwritten note to every attendee on the preshow mailing list inviting him or her to stop by the company's booth and get a free mystery prize. This number is often into the hundreds. For one particular show, John's team sent out 250 handwritten invitations and generated 38 direct responses for more than a 15 percent return. Once the invitees arrive at the trade show booth, the personalization continues. Each person is made to feel appreciated and respected. John's team does this by listening to the prospects rather than lecturing them on the company's products and corresponding benefits. By listening rather than selling at the initial point of contact, John's team has been able to get 50 percent of booth visitors to complete a survey and, most important, has generated qualified leads.

Vail has been highly successful as a relationship manager and sales representative by focusing on the customer as an individual or person first and as a sales lead second. Because he has taken the time to establish a personal relationship with each of his customers, he has been able to avert many crises and brand-switching threats.

Many brands have the difficulty of rarely having direct contact with the end purchasers of their products. Brands whose products are sold at independent retail outlets are at the mercy of sales clerks with little or no accountability to them. To make matters worst, many department sales clerks have few selling skills. In an attempt to circumvent this issue, Anne Klein II started a program called "At Your Service." Each item of clothing had a tag on it with a phone number to call for personal fashion advice. Both sales clerks and consumers were encouraged to call this number—sales clerk for advice on what other Anne Klein items to show the customer and consumers for personal fashion advice from a professional fashion designer. Shoppers were encouraged to provide contact and other personal data in exchange for a free video on upcoming Anne Klein fashions. With these data, Anne Klein was able to build a powerful database of new shoppers who now were attached to the brand in a personal way. This program gave shoppers confidence and the polished look they were seeking.

Lifetime marketing efforts cannot focus solely on the end purchaser. As illustrated by Anne Klein's At Your Service program, they also must focus on the sales channel. The same principles that apply to customers also apply to channel representatives. Securing their lifetime value and loyalty is critical to staying in business. Do not overlook this important step when creating your lifetime marketing plan.

Small businesses have many advantages over large businesses when it comes to personalization. Not only can they implement affordable personalized technologies such as cookies and display templating on their Web sites, they also can offer live interaction and highly personalized communications due to lower customer volumes and geographic immediacy. One of my clients is a construction company specializing in high-end mountain properties. The company was involved in building the commercial properties for a golf-resort community situated on top of a mesa in Colorado's Rocky Mountains and wanted to secure contracts to build residential properties as well. The anticipated value for each home was $3 to $5 million. Choosing a contractor is a highly involved decision, especially when it comes to purchases as expensive as this. Property owners and developers base a large portion of their decision on service and attention to detail. Therefore, the company's marketing efforts to this elite group of homeowners needed to be in line.

Rather than send out generic information and a soon-to-be-trashed brochure, we opted for a highly personalized campaign. We took photographs of the magnificent views from each lot that had been purchased and framed each photo in a custom-built wood frame that had the construction firm's name, Evans Chaffee Construction Group, engraved on it. We sent a framed photograph to each property owner, congratulating them on the beautiful views that were soon to be theirs and introducing them to the unique point of view the construction firm has when it comes to the overall building process. The campaign involved three housewarming gifts with personalized letters and an invitation to a personal tour of the Guest Clubhouse, a premier facility built by Evans Chaffee. Follow-up phone calls were made to all recipients to further initiate the relationship and schedule a personal tour or invite them to an open house. Not only was the company communicating with its target audience in a very personal way, it was giving them a gift that was highly appropriate and one that was sure to gain visibility on a daily basis. Because the database of names was small, only about 50, it was possible to make personal calls to get better acquainted with each prospect and therefore create a highly personalized campaign that would command attention and respect. And because the gifts reflected the values of the company's audience, the campaign was received very positively. In fact, the company received a thank-you note from one of the recipients—a result unprecedented in my career and I dare say that of most marketers.

Tips and Tactics

When it is necessary to contact prospects through mass media or form letters, your communications should emphasize and appeal to the personal values of your audience. The language used, the look and feel of your materials, and the promotion or gift offered need to be appropriate for your audiences' stage of life, lifestyle, and attitudes.

When using mass communications, such as newspaper and radio, you can still personalize your messages. You do this by identifying the personal issues associated with your category and then addressing them appropriately in your advertisements. One of my clients, SteamMaster, a cleaning and restoration business, had purchased a large block of print advertising in the local newspaper and needed help developing an ad campaign that would freshen the brand in the minds of customers. Most companies in this category focus on promoting their long lines of services provided and offering periodic price discounts. Instead, SteamMaster decided to personalize the campaign by addressing personal issues. People hesitate to have total strangers in their home and are typically a bit nervous at first about having their homes worked on by someone they do not know.

To address this issue, my team and I decided to personalize the brand by introducing the people providing the services. SteamMaster's primary competitive strength is that its technicians are highly trained and certified in their area of cleaning. Yet no one on the outside knows this. We positioned each technician as an expert in a specific area of cleaning and listed any certifications from professional associations they had earned. Our campaign included a 15-part series that showcased each technician and each service line that SteamMaster offers. This approach personalized the brand by focusing on the people who were the brand and put homeowners at ease by informing them that a highly trained technician would be coming to their home and caring for it properly.

The campaign was very successful in many ways. First, the personal nature of the communications got noticed in a highly cluttered newspaper setting and resulted in many positive comments about the campaign in general. It also gave an aura of familiarity to the technicians and the brand and created a new level of confidence among customers and prospects. This was one of the bottom-line goals because the company caters to owners of expensive, custom homes, many worth several millions of dollars, and thus needed to convey that its technicians and service upheld a higher standard than its competitors.

In addition to achieving direct results with customers and prospects, the campaign had a profound result on the employees. Because of the strong image created for each individual's expertise, employees had a stronger sense of their own personal value and were better able to identify with their roles in the company. As a result, the company was restructured into divisions according to the technicians' areas of expertise.

Personalizing Your Brand Image

Personalization goes beyond personal communications. It involves personalizing a brand in a way that draws people to it. Your brand image should reflect the personality of those with whom you are trying to establish a relationship. Companies targeting adventurous generation Xers create far different advertisements and graphic presentations than those trying to reach sophisticated actualizers. Everything about your brand's presentation should reflect the persona of your most valuable customer. Your business's persona is presented, for better or for worse, by the colors of your logo; your graphic identity down to the fonts you use in your marketing materials; the decor of your place of business; the dress, style, attitudes, and mannerisms of your employees; and so on. All these factors create a personality. If you have not done so already, take inventory of these and other image-building factors in your business to make sure that you are presenting the personality that will be the most inviting to your best customers and your best prospects.

Tips and Tactics

When creating an image for your brand, do not forget the shoulder segments or wanna-bes. These are the audiences that are either too young or too old to fit your demographic or generational profiles but want to experience the lifestyle of your core customer group. Building an image that appeals to core and wanna-be segments will broaden your appeal and market base.

Personalization has a direct impact on customer satisfaction. After Palm invested in a CRM solution, it was able to track customers' conversations better and record needs, inquiries, and requests so that all call center representatives could immediately pick up where another representative left off. Because of the enhanced ability to serve customers' needs immediately with less hassle and time involved, the company's call centers, which handle 4 million calls annually, were able to improve their personalization. Customer satisfaction subsequently increased by 12 percent.

No matter the size of your business, the nature of your industry, or the personality of your customers, you can personalize your brand through customer service, communications, and the overall aura you create for your brand. Identifying affordable ways to do this should be one of the top priorities of your lifetime marketing plan.

Getting Started—Lifetime Marketing Checklist

Personalization is the key to succeeding in business today. Customers expect to be addressed according to their relationship with you. As a result, mass mailings with impersonal approaches are generating dismal results, whereas personalized communications and promotions are achieving high returns.

Businesses can get personal with customers in many ways:

- Personalized service
- Personalized rewards
- Personalized promotions
- Personalized communications

For businesses with large numbers of customers, personalization takes place at the segment level. By sorting customers into segments, customers can receive information, promotions, and so on based on their history with you in a way that appears to be individually targeted toward them.

The more personal in nature the communication, the more likely it is to generate response and help strengthen the relationship between your brand and consumers.

Action Items

1. Integrate personalization at all contact points:

   - Marketing programs
   - Sales interactions
   - Customer service
   - Promotions

2. Train employees, resellers, and distributors to personalize their selling processes and communications when representing your brand.
3. Identify meaningful methods for rewarding customers according to their specific transactions and value to your business.
4. Be creative. Find ways to personalize your messages to individuals and customer segments that are memorable and compelling. Most of all, make sure that your messages are relevant and motivating for designated recipients.

5. Personalize your brand for employees because this will help to bolster your desired brand image and increase their satisfaction, which will have an impact on customer service.
6. Reference the emotional influencers of your core customers when executing mass communications in order to personalize your brand.
7. Find ways to reference customers' transactions or history with your brand in at least one communication activity per year.
8. When responding to personal complaints or requests, always call your customers by their first name.

Worksheet: How Personal Is Your Business?

	Yes	No
1. When interacting with customers, do you call them by name?		
2. Does your marketing material use first-person references such as *you* and *yours*?		
3. After closing a sale, do you follow up personally, for example, a handwritten note, thank-you gift, or phone call?		
4. Do you follow up with past customers with news about new products available?		
5. When working with a current or past customer, can you readily access information about his or her past experiences with your brand?		
6. Does your brand have a personality that your core customers and prospects can relate to?		
7. Do your signage, marketing messages, store appearance, product lines, employee appearance and attitude, and so on reflect an appropriate personality for your customers and prospects?		
8. Is your business consistent in presenting the desired personality for your business?		
9. Do you communicate with customers and prospects in a way that is more convenient for them than for you?		

	Yes	No
10. Do you frequently send correspondence to customers that is customer-oriented versus business-oriented, for example, thank-you notes, anniversary notes, congratulations, and so on.		

Score

Five or more questions, yes. You are on the right track for personalizing your business. Continue to refine your process, and find new ways to personally communicate with your audiences.

Five or more questions, no. Start focusing on your customers rather than on your sales quotas. Define the personality that is appropriate for your brand, and identify ways you can personally connect with your customers.

This worksheet can be accessed digitally at *www.mcmurtrygroup.com.*

8 Using the Power of the Web for Lifetime Marketing

How to Create Web Sites That Provide You with Valuable Data and Customers with Added Value

The most powerful lifetime marketing engine of our times is clearly the Web. There is no other methodology that allows you to truly personalize your marketing messages and brand presentations on a one-to-one basis. Lifetime marketers use the Web for much more than promoting their products or services. They use the Web to initiate new relationships, to strengthen existing relationships, to build brand equity, and to collect valuable customer data for future lifetime marketing efforts.

Web technology supports lifetime marketing principles like no other medium. A company can offer its customers an individual, relevant, and thus highly convenient experience each time they visit the company's Web site, which is key to bringing customers back and increasing lifetime value. Marketers benefit a great deal as well. Web tracking technology allows businesses to track virtually every move a customer makes on their site, determine the length of time customers spent reviewing a specific product or informational theme, what products they considered purchasing, what products they abandoned, and so on. Such technology also can identify whether or not an e-mail was opened. No other medium allows marketers to define the lowest possible denominator of open rates and do so precisely with actual and real data, not statistical inferences. Mass advertising cannot come close to identifying actual or individual response rates.

By capturing data each time a customer visits a site and fulfills a transaction online, businesses are able to compile detailed personal profiles on customers that go far beyond the limitations of demographic profiles.

Web tracking software can record every move a customer makes on a specific site and create individual customer profiles. Whenever a visitor logs onto a site, his or her personal profile can be called up automatically. It can then dictate to the Web engine which messages to present, even which graphics to display. Imagine if you had the task of creating a separate brochure or catalog for each of your hundreds or thousands of customers. Daunting. Yet that is exactly what Web sites are doing. The potential for personalized marketing has never been greater.

Tips and Tactics

Web tracking programs help you to identify which marketing programs are most successful at driving consumers to your site, what information interests your customers most, where they are coming from, and when they most often visit your site. A popular analysis program for small to medium-sized businesses ranges in cost from $1000 to $2500. Complex packages can run several thousands of dollars.

The Web provides marketers with an unparalleled ability to execute three of the most critical rules of lifetime marketing successfully: *personalization, relevance,* and *value.*

Personalization

With today's Web technology, every experience your customer has with your brand online can be a unique event based on his or her individual customer profile, transaction history, specific interests, purchasing patterns, and so on. Registered members of *www.armaniexchange.com*, have access to a personalized fashion finder. When they register on the site, they enter data on their personality, needs, and likes. The site then places their profile in a fashion category and then shows them clothing items that support their profile. Through this process, Armani Exchange is able to collect valuable information about the individuals interested in its brand and follow up with highly personalized, relevant e-mails and other communications. The company is also able to have an impact on its bottom line. According to Ann Colvin, vice president of e-commerce for Armani Exchange, the personal interaction provided on this site through the fashion finder, regular follow-up e-mails, and other tools has resulted in repeat visitors and increased revenue.

"Visitors return if they had fun the first time they visited and had a positive experience, and they purchase more," says Colvin. "Our goal is to give them value and a complete brand experience online."

Online sales data support this theory. In a 3-month time frame, almost 15 percent of purchasers made two or more purchases. The site's best customers purchase five to seven items per order, whereas the average for all purchasers is two items. And according to Colvin, members shop frequently and remain loyal customers of Armani Exchange.

Personalization can be taken to an even higher level. For some online retailers, no two customers experience the same Web site. As described in Chapter 7, each time an Amazon.com customer signs on to *www.amazon.com*, she sees a home page created specifically for her. The person's name appears throughout the page, a tab is titled after her (in my case it is "Jeanette's Store"), and links are created to take the customer to sections of the site directly related to her past transactions. Amazon.com lists products on the home page specific to past purchases and even goes so far as to have a message center for each customer. Of course, the messages are from Amazon promoting new products related to the customer's identified areas of interest. You can't get much more personal than this.

Babycenter.com provides its registered members with a highly personalized service, one of the best I have found on the Web. Parents or expectant parents register on the site and, by doing so, enter the name and age of each of their children. They can then opt in for various newsletters and e-mails pertaining to their needs. When submitting the registration form, a family profile is automatically created. Members can then designate how they want the site to be personalized for their next visit. It can be specific to the corresponding needs of a child's age or personalized for an expectant mother. Members also can designate which version of an online newsletter they want—the mom version or the dad version.

As a mother of a 2-year-old and 5-month-old twins, I can access two versions of Babycenter.com, each customized for the different ages and needs of my children. When I log on to Babycenter.com, I get a page that caters to the needs and issues of my twins. This home page leads with an article about how my 5-month olds are growing and how this could be changing my life (although I think I have a handle on this topic already). It has links to articles on shopping tips and monthly topics of interest. When child care was the theme of the month, articles covering varying aspects of child care were listed. In that same month, other hot topics pertaining to 5-month-old babies, such as feeding issues, were listed on my personalized home page. I also receive e-mails covering special themes and relevant topics.

For my 2-year-old, I log on to Parentcenter.com or access it through a link on Babycenter.com. The home page lists my child's name and then offers many articles of interest for parents of 2-year-olds. Both sites are highly relevant to my individual needs and offer me many reasons to stay at the site and return often. There are chat boards and dozens of articles on virtually any parenting or pregnancy topic. I also can store and share family photos on this site, create and send out digital birth announcements, develop a personalized pregnancy calendar, and engage in many other added-value activities. Each time I receive a monthly e-mail from Babycenter.com, the current age of my child is in the subject line, thus making it timely, accurate, and highly relevant. One month, the subject line will say, "Information for your 33-month-old" and the next month, "Information for your 34-month-old." All these activities are designed to build equity in the Babycenter.com brand so that I am less likely to switch to a competitor and more likely to come back to the site often.

While I get all these services, Babycenter.com gets valuable information about me and now knows exactly which types of promotions to send and which not to. Sending me information on products for an 8-year-old child would be pure advertising waste; however, sending me an e-mail advertising a new service or product to help me better cope with having three children under the age of 3 would get results. Babycenter.com is the epitome of a successful Web site that embodies all the critical rules of Web marketing: *personalization, relevance,* and *value.*

Relevance

Ken Burke, one of the leading minds in e-personalization and e-commerce and the founder of Multimedia Live (*www.mmlive.com*), maintains that the most critical goal businesses need to keep in mind when building Web sites for their brand is relevance. "Personalization is relevance," claims Burke. According to Burke, "Relevancy is the single most important element in a Web site, whether it be an informational or e-commerce site."

Without relevancy, you cannot personalize a site, and without personalization, your Web site is nothing more than a digital brochure and a waste of valuable resources. Relevant information, services, or promotions are those which directly relate to your customers' needs, expectations, values, and so on. These capture their interest immediately and keep their interest as they are highly meaningful to them and their current situation.

Marketers need to create sites that are relevant to their customers' needs, make it easy for them to accomplish the tasks and objectives at hand, and provide them with value according to their personal profiles. To do this successfully, you need to first identify your global customer segments and your corresponding subsegments. Your Web site strategy should then focus on the values, tasks, and needs of your most valuable customer segments. Successful sites typically cater to about three core segments and make it easy for these groups to find needed information and accomplish the personal objectives that drove them to the specific site.

Relevant information gives visitors reasons to stay longer at a site, browse deeper, and return for more information or services, all of which are essential to building relationships and generating sales and thus lifetime value. Loyalty programs, which will be discussed later in this chapter, are a key part of relevancy.

Value

The World Wide Web was developed initially as a research tool, and it is still being used in this way. Consumers use it to research purchases and compare products. Sites that provide them with valuable product information and help guide their decision processes are the sites they go to first and deem most valuable.

A 2001 study by J.D. Power and Associates shows that use of the Internet as a research tool is growing rapidly. During that year, approximately 43 percent of all used-vehicle buyers used the Internet to find information on potential purchases as part of the shopping process. This was a 27 percent increase over 2000. These consumers first visited an informational site versus a manufacturer's site when seeking information. Although 45 percent of used-vehicle shoppers researching the value of a specific automobile on the Internet visited a manufacturer's site, only 12 percent went there first, and only 8 percent of these found it to be the most useful site.

Providing customers with valuable, objective information on your site will give them a reason to come back to your site again and again. And of course, while they are there, they will be exposed to your brand's latest messages.

Value goes beyond information. Not only do consumers want valuable information, but they also want a valuable experience and value for their time spent at your site. A valuable experience can be defined in many ways. For some people, it is being able to find product information; for some, it is the convenience of online shopping; and for some, it is being able to manage personal finances and other accounts. Another aspect of value is efficiency. Consumers want to go to a site and get what they want without interruption, confusion, or difficulty. As much as you would like consumers to spend hours at a site you have spent many hours and dollars creating, most often their objective is to log on, accomplish their task or goal, and log off, freeing up their time for other activities, such as family, recreation, or work. Your site will be more valuable if you help your visitors achieve these goals. Value is defined by customers' expectations when they visit a site and their ability to fulfill direct and immediate needs.

Following is a summary of some of the steps, principles, and practices essential to creating a Web site that will help you capture lifetime value.

Step 1: Defining Objectives

To build a lifetime Web strategy, you must first determine what you want your Web site to be. Far too many companies build a Web site according to what management thinks it should be, not what customers need or expect it to be. And many companies do not set clear and quantifiable goals at all. When companies do not set clear and measurable goals, they often end up building a site that is a great display of technology and graphic design but offers little for initiating relationships. As a result, it fails to generate incremental sales and retain customers.

An organization's goal when creating a Web site should be to build relationships period. Businesses that define sales as their primary Web goal miss the point of the Web and tend to fall short of expectations. Web sites are relationship-building tools not selling machines. Multimedia Live has created highly successful e-commerce Web sites for large global brands by adhering to these principles. Online sales goals have been achieved by putting customers' needs and expectations for site experiences first.

Basic goals that all Web sites should address include

- Increasing conversion ratios
- Increasing average order size
- Increasing frequency of purchases
- Increasing customer loyalty

The more personal and customized your Web site is, the higher will be your chances of achieving these goals. Meeting the preceding goals will help you to achieve a positive return on your Web investment and to increase sales and profitability for your business overall. Meeting these goals is not done through aggressive sales techniques but rather through dedicated relationship building.

The most successful Web sites integrate innovative loyalty strategies and tactics. As defined by Ken Burke, who is a leading expert on loyalty strategies, loyalty tools are simply those which offer convenience, options, and added value. And in a volatile and fiercely competitive market place, having a strong Web presence that provides customers with purchasing options, information, and brand experiences can be the difference between businesses that fail and businesses that succeed. Creating loyalty should be a key objective of all Web sites.

The beauty of Web technology is that it allows you to embrace many critical aspects of lifetime marketing in one medium—and in one customer experience. For example, a Web site can

- Offer valuable information
- Collect customer data
- Track customer behavior and interests
- Provide immediate rewards
- Capture referrals
- Respond immediately to customers' inquiries
- Create personalized messages and promotions instantaneously

No other medium offers these valuable functions and benefits. To take advantage of the power of the Web, organizations must set clear objectives for their sites and then use existing technology accordingly. Each site should be built according to clearly defined guiding principles.

Critical objectives Web sites should strive to achieve include

- Collecting visitor data and e-mail permission. This should be your number one priority. Personalized marketing depends on creating personal profiles that enable you to communicate about specific transactions, needs, requests, and so on. You get personal data and permission by

- Requesting visitors to register on your site for specific information of value. Promotional information will not get you anywhere; information that helps visitors achieve set goals or tasks will.
- Contests for free product giveaways whereby visitors must enter their names and contact data to be eligible to win.
- Initiating and building relationships that can be developed over a lifetime.
- Providing customers with valuable information beyond the scope of your product line.
- Simplifying consumers' decision processes by providing guidance and information that supports their research, trial, and purchase processes.
- Making a site convenient and easy to navigate.
- Providing valuable information that will draw people back to the site.
- Providing interactive tools that engage people on the site to get them to stay longer, involve them in the brand, and motivate them to return.
- Achieving personal fulfillment by giving people the information or experience they desire in a fun, simple, and satisfying way.

Step 2: Planning

When John Tedstrom, managing director of business development for marketing company FFWD, builds a Web site, he creates distinct value propositions for different types of users based on user profiles. He applies what he calls the "five Cs" to organize thoughts about content and functionality of a site. The five Cs include

- Content
- Commerce
- Community
- Context
- Collaboration

Marketers need to provide something of value to key users in each of these areas. With interactive and other current Web technologies, these areas can be personalized for the customer segments you are targeting and ultimately individual customers.

Content

The content of your Web site addresses your product and must be organized according to the needs of your customers. How can you describe your product or service in a way that personally resonates with your target customer segments? Wojtek Tilbury, Web designer and creator of Somnyo.com, a Web consulting company, suggests getting multiple parties to contribute to your site's content, such as partners, industry leaders, and even employees, because this will broaden the perspectives you provide and give your site more depth. It also builds equity in your site among the different contributing groups.

Commerce

Ask yourself the following key questions:

- What online shopping options are you able to offer your customers?
- Does your commerce functionality address the priority tasks of your visitors?
- How can you make online shopping simple, secure, satisfying, and personal?
- How can you motivate repeat purchases and channel loyalty to your online programs versus in-store programs if this is a goal?

e-Points, programs that reward customers for repeat online purchases through points that can be redeemed for discounts on future purchases or free products, are often successful in increasing customer loyalty. Through its e-points program, Armani Exchange is increasing the lifetime value of its online customers by giving a $50 reward for every $500 in purchases. On average, customers spend an extra $100 in incremental purchases when using their $50 reward.

Community

Creating a sense of community among visitors to your Web site through interactive tools such as chat rooms, message boards, and other relevant and valuable interactions helps to create a lasting bond to your site and, ultimately, your brand. Community is achieved when visitors or members of your site gain a sense of belonging, as if a member of a select crowd. Armani Exchange creates a strong sense of community among its Web members through its *Zine* program, an online magazine. *Zine* profiles cities and events representative of the Armani personality and highlights appropriate fashions to help members create the total look for their total person. Essentially, *Zine* is about "buy this, do this, wear this here." And it works. Armani Exchange's site has grown rapidly throughout its existence without any formal marketing. Ann Colvin attributes part of its success to its "Tell a Friend" program that generates numerous qualified referrals and thus builds a greater sense of community for members.

iVillage.com, an informational/resource site for women, represents Internet communities at their best. Members can log onto chat rooms; find women their age to communicate with; participate in mom-to-mom e-mails; post messages on bulletin boards; read others members' reviews of products, comments, and suggestions on specific themes; post their own evaluations; access information from industry experts; shop; and so on. Women can even pose questions to "Mr. Answer Man" about their personal struggles and mystifications with the male sex. Sites such as this one have created strong communities that actually create barriers to other sites. Once you are entrenched in a strong community at iVillage.com and have established trust for the resources provided, you are not likely to want to go elsewhere for similar information.

Tips and Tactics

You can create a strong consumer community on your Web site by providing specific customer groups with valuable information and encouraging them to interact with each other via message boards and so on. Web seminars and similar programs help bring visitors together for a common purpose and thus further build a sense of community.

Context

What is the framework in which you are presenting your messages? Do the colors, graphics, fonts, and animation features appeal to the core groups you are targeting? Do they involve them in the site and encourage them to stay longer and come back frequently. If yours is a high-tech company, your messages need to be housed in an environment that showcases the latest capabilities of Internet technology. By not incorporating flash animation, vivid sound, streaming video, or other presentation features, you are creating the impression that you are not current with technology, and for a company providing computer technology of any type, this is not a desired image.

Collaboration

Can your site offer opportunities for visitors to collaborate with other consumers and customers, with brand representatives, and so on in activities related to the decision process? By offering collaborative experiences, you are building equity in your site because people have to return to your site to access relationships and resources that are valuable to them and unique to your site. You are also creating a strong community and forum for word-of-mouth marketing.

When considering personalization strategies for your site, think of how you can have an impact in each of the preceding areas.

Step 3: Developing a Strategy

When developing profiles of your most valuable customers, you need to define their expectations for your brand in terms of e-commerce and Web support. Do they expect product information, industry news, or decision-guiding tools such as a loan calculator? Do they expect to purchase products on your site?

No matter what type of business you have, you simply cannot remain competitive without a customer-oriented Web site. A site that shouts all your brand's accolades, evangelizes your leadership team, and boasts your products' superiority is simply ineffective and does nothing to initiate and build lifetime relationships. Such Web sites are simply digital brochures. Customers expect more than this—and they should.

Visitors to Web sites expect interaction, information, and immediacy, or what I refer to as the *three I's of Internet marketing.* They want to *interact* with a brand or others affiliated with that brand through e-mails, product demos, chat rooms, message boards, and the like. They go to Web sites to gather *information* about various products and corresponding features, warranties, and so on. And they expect *immediate* fulfillment. If they go to a brand's site expecting information, they expect it to be up to date, easy to find, and of value to them as they go through the purchasing decision process or seek product support.

The Three I's of Web Strategy

Interaction

Visitors want to be able to interact with your company's representatives directly and in real time. Many sites, such as *www.the-dma.org* for the Direct Marketing Association, are addressing this issue by including buttons to push to automatically dial up a live representative to get immediate answers. Customers do not want to wait days or weeks to get responses to their e-mails.

Information

In addition to getting information about your products and brand, visitors often want information about industry issues and trends, advice, and tips for how to achieve personal goals. This is especially true in the business-to-business community. If visitors can get job-critical information at your site that will enable them to make better and faster decisions, learn something new and useful, or look good to their bosses, chances are they will return and return again.

Immediacy

Shoppers do not want to wait, either by phone or via Internet. Direct merchant Norm Thompson discovered that its sales go up significantly when it can answer the phone with a live representative instead of a recorded message in a few seconds versus a few minutes. If you can respond to Internet requests immediately, you will better meet customers' expectations and increase your chances of capturing their lifetime value. Smart e-marketers get this. Many send immediate order confirmations via e-mail once an order has been placed to assure customers that their transaction was completed successfully and is being processed immediately.

Your brand's Web site must meet customers' expectations in order for your brand to achieve customer loyalty and hence lifetime value. Consumers' expectations have never been higher for the brands they patronize, and companies that do not meet these expectations in both product quality and support simply fail.

Once you understand the needs and expectations of your core customers, you must then resolve to build a site that is highly relevant to these customers. It does not take tens of thousands or dollars to create sites that adhere to these principles. My team has completed highly interactive and sophisticated sites for less than $20,000.

Informational versus e-Commerce Sites

There are two fundamental types of business-related Web sites:

- Informational/product support sites
- Commercial/e-commerce sites

Web sites that are informational do not offer e-commerce activities but rather information about a company, a brand, products available at bricks-and-mortar locations, consumer issues, and product support, for example, care and warranty information. e-Commerce sites offer all these services *and* the capability to purchase products online.

Clearly, the type of business you are in dictates your ability to engage in e-commerce. A sporting goods retailer can execute a strong e-commerce strategy, whereas a general contractor cannot. However, regardless of your industry, a Web site is a critical part of a successful lifetime marketing program. Your Web site is the gateway to your brand for customers and prospects and is a primary source consumers turn to when seeking information to assist them with decision processes involving your business. It is also one of your best resources for gathering consumer data and individual profiles for customers and prospects.

e-Commerce makes it easy to collect consumer data and gain permission to communicate with consumers in the future. If someone shops on your site, she expects to give you data and expects to hear from you regarding her transactions with your brand.

Informational/Product Support Sites

If an informational or product support Web site is most appropriate for your brand, you need to find tools that build loyalty outside of e-commerce. There are many ways you can do this.

First and foremost, you must understand what information is valuable to your customers and what information will directly address the decision process and have a positive impact on their behavior. You need to know with no uncertainty what your customers are expecting from your Web site and what they intend to accomplish during a site visit. All this information should be in your customer segment profiles.

When building a site strategy, it may be impossible to address the personal needs of each of your customer segments, especially if you have several subsegments. Again, you need to define three core segments and develop your site's messages, presentation, interaction, and functionality to meet the needs of these subsegments. Trying to address more than a small handful of subsegments will result in a meaningless, confusing site that is not likely to accomplish your relationship-building goals.

Second, you must incorporate activities and information that will keep your customers coming back to your site frequently. Again, the Web was developed initially as an information tool, yet in the age of burgeoning e-commerce, many businesses tend to forget this. Consumers have not forgotten it. Consumers use the Web to collect information, to research products for potential purchases, to exchange ideas, and to interact with brands and people. Successful Web sites that help to achieve lifetime value—or lifetime Web sites—offer valuable information and tools to customers in a way that encourages them to return to the sites.

Information provided to visitors can include

- General industry news, for example, research reports, news summaries, and so on
- Resources and links to third-party sites such as trade associations, think tanks, and magazines covering industry news
- White papers on new technologies, techniques, methodologies, market analyses, and so on.

Tools that add value and encourage repeat visits include

- Maps
- Weather stations
- Web cams
- Health calculators (such as ideal body weight)
- Project calculators (such as mortgage loan calculators)
  - The Direct Marketing Association's (DMA) Web site has a calculator that allows you to determine the proper sample size for a specified margin of error desired for a market research project.
  - Banks add significant value to their sites by offering loan calculators.

Alpine Bank, a regional business serving the mountain communities of Colorado, offers a variety of loan calculators to help visitors determine costs and savings associated with home mortgages, personal financing, and investment issues. Alpine makes it easy for customers to identify which tool best serves their immediate need by assigning frequently asked questions to each function. The breadth of questions ensures that the tool is relevant to a wide range of visitors.

When visitors click on the questions that apply to them, they access a calculator designed specifically for that need. Following are questions associated with Alpine Bank's home financing calculators:

- Should I refinance my home mortgage?
- What would my payments be for a fixed-rate loan?
- What would my payments be for an adjustable-rate loan?
- What would my payments be for a balloon loan?
- Should I rent or buy my home?
- Which loan is better, fixed rate or adjustable rate?
- What would I save if I make extra payments?
- How much house can I qualify for?
- How much house can I afford?
- Do I need an advanced mortgage calculator?

These tools make Alpine Bank's site worth going back to time and time again.

Providing valuable tools that consumers will use frequently is essential for two reasons: First, these tools provide value to the customer, which, in turn, builds brand equity and respect, and second, they get customers to come back to your site for subsequent uses, and while they are there, they get exposed to your brand's latest messages. This is why updating a home page with "new news" is a critical part of a successful Web strategy.

One of the most valuable ways that your Web site can enable you to initiate and build powerful relationships is by collecting key customer data. e-Commerce sites can collect these data easily through an online transaction. If your site is strictly informational, you need to be more creative. You need to give visitors a reason to give you their contact data and, most important, permission to market to them in the future. You can then build a highly qualified database for future marketing programs. The information you collect should help you to determine which customer segment they fall in and how you can personalize the site for future interaction.

To do this, you must ask qualified questions about your visitors, and this takes time. Consumers are most willing to do this if they get something in return, such as access to project calculators like those described previously. For information-based sites, information that directly applies to one's job or helps one to achieve a personal goal is often enough to compel consumers to provide you with personal data and permission. Information can be offered in the form of a white paper, research report, how-to guidelines, or customized news and information. Again, Babycenter.com's success is partially based on the wide range of customized information services offered to visitors when they register to become a member of the site. These services include a number of free e-mail newsletters and access to chat rooms and message boards with parents facing similar challenges, and e-commerce links. For e-commerce sites, customers may be compelled to take the time to register if they are offered a discount on their first online purchase, a free gift, or free shipping.

Tips and Tactics

Polling visitors to your site about relevant industry issues or trends is a creative way to get customers to register their contact data at the site. To participate in a poll, you can ask visitors for demographic and lifestyle data that qualify their responses and give you valuable information about your customers and prospects. By asking permission to contact participants with relevant future information, you also can add qualified names to your database.

e-Commerce Sites

Personalization of e-commerce sites is highly effective and perhaps one of the most valuable methods for creating online sales and lasting customer loyalty. Web-based personalization strategies help e-commerce companies achieve such critical goals as

- Increasing average order size
- Increasing order frequency

- Reducing abandoned-cart rates
- Improving customer loyalty and increasing retention
- Improving overall site experience

The technology behind personalization strategies can be expensive and result in sites costing hundreds of thousands of dollars. If your site does not generate revenue directly for your business, you may not want to invest in technologies that personalize your site on a one-to-one basis, such as greeting your customers by name, presenting summaries of past transactions, recommending products according to known interests, and so on. Instead, you likely will be better off personalizing your site in terms of presentation, messages, personality, and values that reflect your core customer segments. While it may not address individuals directly, your site can be a reflection of their personal values and interests.

Step 4: Integrating e-Commerce

Why sell online? Because customers expect it. Period. e-Commerce is growing at exponential rates. Retail brands that do not incorporate this option as part of a multichannel selling strategy will fail to be competitive. It is that simple.

A report published by Jupiter Media Matrix predicted that online retail sales in the United States would reach $104 billion by 2005 and $130 billion by 2006. In 2001, online retail sales reached $34 billion. eMarketer predicted e-commerce revenues to reach $156 billion by 2005. This report also projected that the online purchasing population would continue to grow at a healthy rate, reaching 130 million online shoppers in 2005. Consumers are turning to the Web to purchase from long-time trusted brands. Sites for bricks-and-mortar businesses are growing significantly, whereas pure dot-com sites have continued to dwindle. This statistic clearly points to the importance of multichannel selling. In 1999, nearly one-quarter of all U.S. households made a purchase over the Internet, according to a survey by The Conference Board.

The Internet is quickly taking over telephone sales. The Center for Customer-Driven Quality at Purdue University conducted a study that showed 56 percent of respondents shopping on the Internet and 40 percent shopping on the telephone. More than a third of the respondents to this survey claimed to use the Internet to research potential purchases. This same study showed that 97 percent of consumers still prefer making purchases at store locations versus Web sites.

However, this latter statistic is misleading. While customers still prefer in-store purchases where they can actually touch and physically see a product, they expect to have the option of where and how to conduct business with your brand. Even though many consumers use Web sites to research products prior to purchasing at a store, they still expect the option of being able to purchase online.

As Ken Burke so deftly stated, "A Web site without e-commerce is like going to Disney Land and not seeing Mickey Mouse. If customers feel let down, or have to take another trip to fulfill their needs and expectations, chances are they will assign their loyalty elsewhere."

Meeting customers' expectations by offering online shopping options can build loyalty and strengthen relationships with customers. If your brand does not offer consumers the convenience of online shopping or the option to choose how to transact business with you—online, through a catalog, by telephone, by mail order, and through in-store shopping—they may choose to take their business elsewhere. This is where multichannel selling strategies come into play.

According to Burke, who has built successful direct marketing strategies and e-commerce sites for global brands including Armani Exchange, the key to consumer loyalty is not only personalization as discussed previously but also multichannel convenience. His company has realized this for many of its customers by building loyalty-generating sites for direct marketing companies such as Norm Thompson, Swiss Colony, and Burpee. Beyond catalog and direct mail sales, these companies have expanded their brands significantly by offering customers the option of online sales. Burke has seen some brands increase revenues by up to 40 percent as a result of offering multichannel options.

Building loyalty is all about offering convenience and letting customers do business with you on their terms, not yours. Traditional businesses realize the value of this trend and have been entering the online world at a rapid pace. According to Jupiter Media Matrix analysts, offline brands are becoming the dominant force in e-commerce. Bricks-and-mortar retailers outnumbered Internet-only retailers in 2001, according to Jupiter. In March 2000, Internet-only retailers held 62 percent of the top retail sites. In March 2001, 56 percent of the top sites were held by bricks-and-mortar retailers, and this figure is expected to reach 63 percent by 2006.

Understanding the importance of Web site fulfillment is crucial. For example, in a study conducted by Binary Compass Enterprise, on-time delivery was a key predictor of customer loyalty, with 96 percent of shoppers who received their order on time saying that they were "likely" or "very likely" to shop at the site again. Delayed deliveries reduced the percentage of customers likely to patronize a site again to 60 percent.

Affinity marketing activities can also strengthen a Web site's ability to build equity and loyalty among its visitors and e-commerce customers. You can do this by

- Creating messages and graphics or personalized displays for your most active customer groups, for example, mothers of toddlers or environmental enthusiasts
- Listing purchases made within that group (for example, Amazon.com lists "other products purchased by other people that also bought this book, CD, and so on")
- Creating forums for communications between the members of these select customer groups

Tips and Tactics

Create confidence in purchase decisions by listing which items are your most popular, and increase your chances for upgrades and incremental purchases by letting customers know what similar customers are buying. By doing so, you are subtly addressing consumers' insecurities, up-selling, and taking the fear out of doing business with your brand.

Even the smallest of businesses can engage in e-commerce at some level. It can be as simple as taking orders via e-mail or integrating a simple order form into your Web site. You do not have to have all the latest bells and whistles to offer online purchasing options. However, you will have to pay for a security system that protects the privacy and account information of your customers.

After making the leap to e-commerce, regardless of how sophisticated it might be, you are then ready to personalize your brand in ways that no other medium will allow. Following are some technologies and functionalities that will help you to maximize the power of the Web to capture the lifetime value of your customers.

Step 5: Personalizing Online Shopping

Ken Burke is one of the most frequently sought after experts on e-commerce personalization, and he preaches his doctrines to marketers at direct marketing conferences nationwide. He starts by defining the four types of e-commerce personalization:

Basic personalization
- Personalization is limited to registration and account information.
- Web site recognizes user names.

Rules-based personalization
- Customer group models are built into the Web infrastructure, users are assigned to a specific segment, and then rules or messages, functions, and so on are applied to individual users based on corresponding values.
- Messages emphasize if-then scenarios and offer appropriate responses.

Collaborative filtering
- The Web site attempts to determine the appropriate customer group from a user's click stream and other data and then offers messages accordingly.
- Messages emphasize actions of others in segments, for example, "Customers like you have also liked . . . ," thus establishing an affinity for that customer.

Predictive modeling
- The Web site recognizes users, calls up data from past transactions, and attempts to determine the likelihood of a particular user taking a certain action and then responds accordingly.

Predictive modeling can have a significant impact on the effectiveness of an e-commerce site and thus a business's profitability. When applied correctly, it can

- Reduce abandoned-cart rates
- Provide different levels of content display based on behavior
- Solve customer service problems by providing help with specific behaviors or situations
- Increase the effectiveness of cross-selling efforts

- Personalize overall site messages and merchandising for specific behaviors and consumer patterns

Essentially every aspect of a Web experience can be personalized: content, graphics, promotions, recommendations, and even displays. A personalized Web site offers a different experience for each customer segment. For example, a regular customer with an annual value of $500 could log on and be directed to a Web site that is far different from that for a first-time visitor who needs first to be converted to the brand. In a direct mail campaign, you would approach these individuals differently—varying your messages, offers, and rewards or incentives. Web technology allows you to apply this same successful segmentation strategy much more efficiently and personally. The difference is that customers can direct and influence their experience in real time, and businesses can track every move such customers make on a Web site and build an individual customer profile accordingly so that the next visit is even more appropriate.

Every phase of a customer's life cycle can be personalized as well—from lead acquisition that is personalized by appealing to the values of a specific customer segment, to conversion that involves encouraging qualified prospects to become customers by appealing to their personal needs and influencers; and lastly, to retaining customers by offering them promotions, offers, and products that fit their individual personal profiles and transaction histories.

Tips and Tactics

Personalize your Web site for existing customers by having a "client only" section that enables them to access updated account logs, project notes, budgets, and payment schedules. This will bring customers to your site frequently so that you can expose them to your newest marketing messages.

Beringer Vineyards, a Multimedia Live customer, has executed a successful personalization strategy, and as a result, it is one of the leading online wineries. The company sells $20 to $300 bottles of wine and caters to the discriminating wine connoisseur. Their top line of wine is their Reserve label. Buyers of this label view wine as an experience, not a beverage, and are willing to spend hundreds of dollars on one bottle. They also view the wines they drink as a symbol of the status they have achieved in life. To keep this segment loyal to the brand, Beringer offers them a personalized experience each time they go to the Web site. Rather then entering the site in the same manner as first-time customers, Reserve customers are automatically recognized through cookies and are directed to a home page that displays only wines appropriate to their taste and attitudes.

Beringer thus directs Reserve customers to a separate template based on their past transactions, personal data, and specific experiences with the brand. This template has graphics and text that was designed specifically for them and their personal tastes. Ken Burke refers to this practice as "display templating," which is essentially remerchandising your site for each visitor. It is similar to a bricks-and-mortar store changing the displays for every customer who walks in the door so that they only see the items most relevant to them and those they are most likely to buy. Display templating, or individualized merchandising, is yet another great example of the exclusive power of the Web for lifetime marketing.

You should consider display templates, pages personalized for specific customer segments, for your most valuable customer segments. You can further personalize your Web site according to site usage patterns or click streams and to visitor behavior and customer data. A customer's data profile should include behavior with your brand online and offline. By aggregating data pertaining to customers' various experiences with your brand through multiple channels and data-specific to customers' values, influencers, and demographics, you can build appropriate templates and a successful overall Web site.

Step 6: Incorporating Loyalty-Building Strategies

Integrating loyalty tools into your Web site is critical to obtaining lifetime value. e-Loyalty tools range from the simple to the complex. In essence, they are little more than tools that provide convenience and added value. Following is a list of effective e-loyalty tools:

- **Product comparisons, brand comparisons.** Circuit City does an excellent job of this. When shopping for a handheld organizer, I was able to quickly compare the functionality, prices, and warranties of various brands carried by the store. This service greatly affected my decision-making process and has caused me to return to the site every time I need to research electronic or computer products. Comparisons also can be done for companies not involved in e-commerce. For example, a service provider can compare its customer satisfaction rates, prices, package offerings, and so on with those of competitors.

- **Decision wizards.** These tools ask a series of questions and then make product recommendations. This functionality helps consumers understand what they need. These are extremely valuable when consumers are making decisions about complicated and technical products that they do not fully understand. They help purchasers understand what functionalities they need and do not need based on anticipated product usage. Dell and Gateway both offer decision wizards to help customers make appropriate and relevant decisions for their needs and budgets.

- **Reminder services.** Brands that sell gift items such as jewelry, specialty clothing, books, and music remind purchasers of upcoming events for which they have previously purchased items. These might be Valentine's Day, wedding anniversaries, Mother's Day, and birthdays. You can actually register for reminders at some sites.

- **e-Hints.** Helzberg Diamonds takes reminder services a step higher. Instead of sending reminders to potential purchasers, the company has created a service whereby the potential gift recipient sends the reminder. This is done in the form of an e-hint. Customers go to *www.helzbergdiamonds.com* and find a gift they would want, for example, diamond earrings, an anniversary band, or a tennis bracelet. They then can pick a customized e-card from a series of templates offering a broad range of messages and graphics. They select the greeting and closing and send it. Quick, simple, relevant, and personal—and in my opinion, brilliant.

- **Gift registries.** Gift registry services are a great tactic for building brand equity. Consumers register for wedding or baby gifts at specific brand sites and thus are committed to using that brand's products. Gift registries are also a great way to get potential new customers because people affiliated with registered members come to the site to shop for the new bride- or mother-to-be. Crate and Barrel offers an online registry that assists members in selecting the right gifts and simplifies the purchasing process for gift givers, who can access registry information online or at any store location. Customers registering for gifts at the company's site access not only the services of *crateandbarrel.com* but also the services offered by the company's retail outlets. Members can update their accounts at either location—a good example of multichannel marketing. When registering, members get valuable information and guidance as well, such as gift-selection tips and product information. Registrants are also given up-to-date information about their accounts and products for the lifetime of their relationship. If a product they purchased is scheduled for discontinuation, Crate and Barrel notifies members and assists them with finding replacement items while they are still available.

- **e-Point and frequent-user programs.** e-Points, like frequent flyer programs, cement customers to a brand like few other things. Even consumers with high discretionary incomes relish points and getting something of personal value as a reward for brand loyalty. The trick is to offer something of personal value and to allow customers to choose their rewards, as discussed in earlier chapters.

Vail Resorts has implemented a very successful e-point program called the Peaks Program that works much like an airline Frequent Flyer program. In fact, it was developed under the direction of Vail Resorts' CEO, Adam Aron, who helped develop the frequent flyer program for United Airlines and reward programs for other major travel companies. The Peaks Program has hundreds of thousands of members who receive rewards for skiing at any of Vail Resorts properties, such as Vail, Beaver Creek, Keystone, and Breckenridge, all premier Colorado ski resorts. For every lift ticket purchased, members earn points that can be redeemed for additional lift tickets, meals at Vail Resorts' restaurants, ski lessons, or items at Vail Resorts' ski shops.

The Peaks Program has been tremendously successful because customers can choose how they want to be rewarded for their loyalty, and Vail Resorts gets valuable contact information and permission to market to customers about future and complementary services and events. In addition, the program has helped to increase patronage as well as overall revenue. By listening to customers and providing them more of the experiences they enjoy, the company's non-lift ticket revenues represented 71 percent of total resort revenues in 2000, up from 52 percent in 1996 and 44 percent in 1992. In addition, Vail Resorts' summer revenues have more than quintupled in the past 5 years.

Although the Peaks Program has been successful, Aron warns that it is harder to execute frequent-use programs for products or services that are not used frequently. He maintains that frequent-user programs can be helpful for a noncommodity product because they clearly have an impact on the decision process when it comes to brand, but they are not effective for increasing incremental sales. For building increased sales, these types of programs are more successful with commodity-type products or items that are used more frequently.

Regardless of the type of business you are in, frequent-user programs are helpful and should be developed as appropriate because they bond consumers to the brand. Frequent-user programs are powerful because of the information you are able to collect about customers for future marketing efforts and the cost efficiency they provide.

No matter how large or small a business is, loyalty programs should be a top priority. Collecting customers' names can be as inexpensive as asking customers to give you their business cards for a prize drawing. The idea is to collect customers' names, follow up with them, and reward them. The scale on which this is done fluctuates based on business category and size, yet the results are the same. Successful loyalty programs can be simple or complex, inexpensive or expensive. Regardless of your business, it is important that you develop and execute them on some level, and use the Web to collect data and community.

 Tips and Tactics

Collect customers' names and contact information through prize drawings, customer service profiles, warranty registrations, guest and user registries, and so on. Find clever methods for getting prospects to give you their information and marketing permission online.

"I can't imagine any successful marketing program today without a loyalty program," said Adam Aron, who has built a successful career, going from the marketing department to CEO's office, on his development and execution of loyalty programs that achieved lifetime value for critical customer groups.

There are direct and indirect programs or offerings that build loyalty. Some of the more indirect ways include the following:

- **Multichannel and order options.** Customers want options. They want to be able to shop when, where, and how they like, and they want the convenience of being able to transact business on their terms. The DMA conducted a study that showed that multichannel buyers represent four times the annual value to a vendor than a single-channel buyer for business-to-consumer companies. Offering simple conveniences such as allowing for multiple shipping addresses for multiple-item orders or being able to return online purchases to bricks-and-mortar locations goes a long way with customers. Eddie Bauer offers this service, which sends its customers the signal that their convenience is more important than the brand's. When I have not been offered the opportunity to return online purchases to physical store locations, I have found myself irritated with the brand at hand and less enthusiastic to purchase. Customers need the comfort of knowing that if an online purchase is not so exciting in its real versus graphic presentation, they can return it without incurring extra costs for shipping or the hassles of waiting in line at the post office.

- **Innovative conveniences.** The idea behind any successful Web site is to make your customer's life or job easier and thus become a valuable tool and resource. The more your site can do to assist customers or visitors with their individual goals, the higher your customer retention and loyalty will be. One of Multimedia Live's clients is an online library supply provider. The main visitors to the Web site are librarians; however, librarians are not the ultimate decision makers when it comes to purchases. They have to get approval from a chain of influencers, and this takes time. Therefore, the selling process can be long and cumbersome. Multimedia Live brilliantly integrated a process in the client's Web site that would automatically send an order estimate to every person involved in a given visitor's purchase process. Each influencer could bless the estimate simply by clicking on an approval button. The results? Shorter selling cycles, greater sales volume, and highly satisfied customers with deep-rooted loyalty to the site and the brand.

California Closets allows customers to view specific closet designs and create a file of styles they like. Customers can click on a photograph they like and easily e-mail it to an associate such as their interior designer. Each time they visit the site, they can view different styles and create new files of ideas for their own projects. This allows potential customers to store a file of ideas that can be accessed easily from their own hard drives and to quickly share ideas with others that may influence their decisions. This is a brilliant strategy because it works to secure two key customers to your brand: the end user and the influencer.

For either informational or e-commerce sites, the foundation of success is to

- Determine precisely what the customer's most compelling needs are
- Identify how your brand and Web site can simplify their job or life
- Build your site and functionality accordingly
- Provide desired and valuable information and resource materials
- Reward customers with added values and added conveniences, free products, or discounts

If you build your Web site to adhere to lifetime marketing principles and design it to motivate and capture repeat business from existing customers, you will significantly increase your potential for long-term profitability. According to a study of Internet shoppers by Binary Compass Enterprise, new customers of a retail site spent an average of $127 per purchase, whereas repeat customers spent an average of $251.

Step 7: Tracking Visitors and Identifying Trends

The beauty of the Web is that it tracks itself. Unlike any medium, it pinpoints customer behavior down to the individual level and the precise moment of interaction. It can reveal more about your customers than any other marketing tool. This alone justifies the effort and expense involved in creating a lifetime marketing Web site. Data collected via your Web site can help you to learn to think like your customers and understand their push points and disconnects and other relevant behaviors and influencers. A 1999 survey by The Conference Board showed that only 7 percent of businesses were using the Internet to capture information from visitors in order to customize visitors' experiences. Nearly 50 percent of the respondents claimed to have a Web site that delivered information to visitors, yet they did not have in place a system to capture information about visitors. Fortunately, the number of sites capturing visitor information has increased since then, and it continues to increase.

Web technology can reveal the following patterns about your customers and site visitors:

- Total time spent browsing
- Products browsed and time spent per product

- How many visitors came to site during specified time intervals
- Entry page—or how visitors came to site, for example, through a URL used exclusively for marketing purposes or through a search-engine referral
- Pages or information most accessed on your site
- Frequency of purchases
- Abandoned-cart rate
- Past purchases—products and categories
- Items viewed during specific visits
- Discounts and promotions redeemed
- e-Mail open rates
- Click-through rate from e-mails
- Loyalty tools used

Tracking these patterns will help you to make decisions about the development of your site and will provide ideas on how to enhance your site and business in the future.

Most Web servers create a log file that will provide you with answers to some of the preceding questions. Be sure to access this file frequently so that you can use this valuable information to further develop, monitor, and polish your Web strategy. Log analyzer software can give you detailed activity reports, including the following information:

- Number of visitors
- Number of total visits for a given time period
- Number of new versus returning visitors
- Number of requests that the server received (or *hits*)
- Number of page requests
- Most popular pages on your Web site (information of greatest interest to visitors)
- Top downloads (documents, applications, and so on)
- Top entry pages (the first page at which a visitor arrives)
- Top exit pages (the last page a visitor accesses)
- Most popular paths through your site (the order in which pages are accessed)
- Top geographic regions (based on location of the visitor's Internet service provider, not the actual location of the visitor)
- Most active organizations (based on the owner of the visitor's Internet service provider's domain name)

- Average length of visits to your site
- Number of client or server errors
- Amount of data transferred to visitor's computers (bandwidth)
- Top referring sites (these are sites that are linked to your site and send visitors to you)
- Top search engines (see which search engines are sending you traffic)
- Top search phrases and keywords (search terms that direct users to lists of related sites including yours)
- Top Web browsers your visitors are using to view your site
- Top operating systems

While this information helps you to identify global usage trends and activity levels for your site, it does not give you information at the individual level. To do this, you will need to incorporate *cookies* (small identification files that are placed on visitors' hard drives) so that your site recognizes them each time they return.

Knowing your customers' patterns will enable you to develop Web sites accordingly and execute highly relevant e-mail campaigns.

To measure the impact of a specific campaign, create a separate Web address directing consumers to your site. For example, if you want to see how many visitors came to your site from an ad promoting 50 percent off, you might use the URL *www.companyname.com/50off*. To see if radio ads are generating more leads than print ads, you might use the URL *www.companyname.com/print* in your print ads. Your log analysis software could then tell you which entry points brought in the most new visitors.

e-Mail Marketing

Since the early years of e-mail marketing, public relations professionals and marketers would send out "e-mail blasts," hoping that their randomly sent messages would get read by interested editors or consumers. I call this *e-mail roulette*—click the send button and wait to see what happens. Today, e-mail marketing has taken on far more effective dimensions. With the advent of permission marketing as spirited by Seth Godin, marketers can develop campaigns that are meaningful and deliver messages that are anticipated and even desired. e-Mail is much more than a blast; it is an integral part of a business-to-consumer relationship and is based on providing valuable and desired information.

While at one time the returns for sending e-mail blasts to prospects and customers were high, the returns are diminishing, even when opt-in lists are used. A survey conducted by Forrester Research indicated that e-mail no longer has the high response rates it once did. Forrester's data showed that consumers are buying fewer products and services that are advertised via e-mail. Additionally, of people who had been online users for less than 1 year, 18 percent made Internet purchases in 2000, and only 6 percent claimed to have done so in 2001. Even with diminishing returns, the volume of marketing-related e-mail in the United States is expected to triple to 424 billion messages by 2005.

There are various ways to use e-mail as a successful marketing medium, and these will be discussed shortly. To start, you must determine to whom you will be sending your e-mail messages. You can purchase opt-in lists, or you can use qualified in-house lists.

Opt-In Lists

Customers register with various Web marketing companies such as yesmail.com to receive e-mails about specific products, services, events, themes, or categories. e-Mail marketing companies then take these names and resell them as opt-in lists to marketing companies in the same way that list brokers sell names fitting demographic profiles to direct marketers. Even though e-mail marketing has higher response rates than direct mail, the effect is the same. You are sending your messages cold to consumers who have no relationship with your brand and have expressed no interest in hearing from you specifically. Because of the large volume of e-mails sent to opt-in mailing lists, the effectiveness is diminishing significantly.

Tips and Tactics

To be efficient, in-house e-mail lists need to be updated regularly to ensure that your communications are pertinent to customers' or prospects' current relationships with your brand. Inappropriate information, such as sending new-customer offers to existing customers, makes you look sloppy and can damage relationships.

Qualified In-House Lists

Just as successful lifetime marketing is founded on having robust customer databases and individual profiles, so too is successful e-mail marketing. e-Mail is most effective when used as a way to continuously communicate to customers specific information about their accounts, interests, and needs and to offer rewards and incentives. All your marketing efforts should work toward helping you build your in-house customer database. Your Web site can help you build a personalized customer database and a highly qualified prospect database by motivating visitors to register on your site in return for something of value, as discussed previously. Once you get their contact data and permission, you can then send e-mail campaigns to people who know who and what you are and are likely to be interested in what you have to say. Personalizing e-mails to people who have a true relationship with your brand is what lifetime e-marketing is all about. Just make sure that you update your customer data frequently. It is irritating to get new-customer incentives or introductory offers when you are already a paying customer. I have been a member of AOL for 8 years, and I frequently get CDs in the mail offering me 1000 introductory hours for free. This is insulting to me because I now know that my business has gone unrecognized and that because I am a loyal customer, I do not get the same deal as someone who has not given the company a dime. It also contradicts the personalization of the AOL member welcome screen, which uses my name many times, and the e-mails personally addressed to me, which give me the impression that the company knows who I am and the details of my relationship with them.

Marketing programs should drive customers and prospects to your site to learn more about your business or your category or to access other information of value to them. e-Mail campaigns should address issues specific to each customer. Again, this is done by drilling your messages down to the subsegment level, creating messages that appeal to each of these segments, and then sending these "personalized" communications accordingly.

You can build a database of leads for your e-mail campaigns from those who have visited your site and given you permission to contact them and from leads you generate at trade shows and other events. The key here is to make sure that you use qualified names and that you have permission.

As you collect addresses from those you want to contact for future marketing purposes, make sure that you clearly state your intentions to contact them with promotional messages and share your privacy policy with them. People want to know if their names and addresses are going to be shared with others or sold, and they want the option to opt out.

e-Mails need to be relevant to the individual receiver and need to be an extension of your Web strategy. They need to be developed in a way that helps to convert prospects or site browsers to customers, motivate customers to upgrade or purchase complementary products or services, and encourage customer loyalty and build brand equity by offering added value, rewards, and so on. All e-mails need to say something meaningful to the recipient, not to you or your marketing team. Do not send e-mails just because you can. Send messages that are relevant, meaningful, have an impact, and provide value in terms of either information or an offer.

Tips and Tactics

Increase customer loyalty by sending e-mails that communicate valuable information that says nothing about your brand or products. By sending news about your industry, consumer issues, trends, current research, or market or technological projections, you can create brand equity and gain consumer respect.

To be effective, e-mails should be sent out immediately after a purchase. If the first e-mail is not effective, a second e-mail should be sent that offers a discount on related purchases. By doing this, you are first making customers feel recognized and appreciated for their business and then rewarding them with something of value and direct relevance.

Personalizing e-Mail

Open rates are much higher when e-mail subject lines are personalized. Personalizing e-mail according to the recency-frequency-money (RFM) model is a highly effective approach. If you are a recent customer, you are likely to be interested in a vendor's message. If you are a frequent or high-dollar purchaser, the same applies. The open rate for RFM customers is higher if you personalize the subject line, again referring to their most recent transaction with you. You might consider going so far as to make the subject line specific to their very last transaction, for example, "How do you like your new DVD player?" This approach is simpler than it may appear. If you segment your customers according to purchase and date of last transaction, you can send the same e-mail to all purchasers of a specific product within a specific time period.

e-Mail Content

Beyond the text, some e-mailers incorporate colorful graphics in e-mail messages. I personally do not like this approach for two reasons. First, it appears far too commercial, and e-mail is best used as an informational medium, and second, it complicates readership. Some people's computers take a long time to open HTML e-mails, and thus you risk having people delete the message before ever reading it. Of course, there are some circumstances when graphic e-mails are appropriate and should be used. Just make sure your judgment is based upon customers' needs, not your own.

Personalizing the Link

When you direct people to your Web site via a URL in an e-mail, you need to make sure the entry point, or page they are directed to, is relevant to the message that got them there in the first place. When possible, develop a unique entry point that addresses the promotion or message in the driving e-mail.

Reference Your Privacy Policy

People want to know how you intend to use their names. Let people know what your privacy policy is by either listing it in the fine print of your e-mail text or including a link to a site where it can be found easily. Consumers want to know if you intend to sell or share their names with other organizations and for what reasons and how their personal data will be used within your own organization. By not divulging this information, you risk losing trust, respect, and ultimately, business.

General e-Mail Tips

Be Relevant

If you want someone to read your e-mail, give him or her something worth reading. It is that simple. Do not waste their time promoting products of no relevance to them, and do not insult their intelligence by sending hyped claims about how wonderful your business is and what you can do for them. Be direct, honest, concise, and meaningful. A good rule is to ask yourself how you would react if you received the same message from a vendor with whom you have transacted business. If the subject matter would be less than interesting or appealing to you, reconsider your plans.

Even with relevant e-mails, give recipients a chance to opt out of future messages. This shows you respect their privacy.

Figure 8-1 is an example of a highly relevant e-mail sent to me from Amazon.com based on a past purchase. Notice that it includes an easy way for me to opt out of future e-mails and offers me a reward for being a valued customer.

Figure 8-1 *Sample of Highly Relevant e-Mail Message*

Dear Amazon.com customer,

We've noticed that many of our customers who have purchased albums by Sarah Brightman also enjoy the music of Charlotte Church. For this reason, you might like to know that Charlotte Church's new album "Enchantment" is now available. You can order your copy at a savings of 26 percent by following the link below.

http://www.amazon.com/exec/obidos/ASIN/B00005OWEJ/ref=mk_pb_aai

Of course, we couldn't expect time to freeze its relentless path and forever preserve the Welsh sensation Charlotte Church in a chrysalis of precocious youth. And yet, at 15 and now taking bolder steps into expanding her repertory on "Enchantment," the soprano remains a marvel of a prodigy. Here, she scours a wider range of sources than on her previous albums. Church moves with breathtaking ease from classic Broadway (*West Side Story, Show Boat, South Pacific*) to traditional Celtic, film ballads, . . .

To learn more about "Enchantment," please visit the following page at Amazon.com:

http://www.amazon.com/exec/obidos/ASIN/B000050WEJ/ref=mk_pb_aai

Sincerely,

Thomas May
Editor
Amazon.com

PS: We hope you enjoyed receiving this message. However, if you'd rather not receive future e-mails of this sort from Amazon.com, please use the link below or click the Your Account button in the top right corner of any page. Under the Your Account Settings heading, click the "Update Your Communication Preferences" link.

http://www.amazon.com/your-account/

Develop Your Own List

As discussed earlier, developing your own list is not only more effective in generating responses, but it is also less expensive over the long term. Wojtek Tilbury offers the following suggestions for building in-house lists and getting permission to use them:

- Start an e-mail newsletter and encourage visitors to your site to join. Provide a subscription or sign-up form in several key places throughout your site.
- Require visitors to register at your site to download valuable resources or industry news.
- Whenever visitors download a file or access a new resource, encourage them to sign up for your e-newsletter.
- Make sure that you also collect e-mail addresses while interacting with prospects and customers offline.

- Provide a private area on your Web site for your employees to add and remove e-mail addresses from your e-mail list so that you can keep your list accurate and up to date.
- As you add contacts to your contact management system (CMS), add their e-mail addresses and indicate whether or not you have their permission and for which types of promotional messages. You can then mine the data and import them into your e-mail list.
- Based on the registration process for your site, avoid the use of "must fill" fields that require data entry before the user can complete the registration process. Not only is this irritating, but it also defies the concept of permission marketing, which centers on consumers having control and deciding whether or not to give you their data.
- After a visitor has completed the registration or sign-up form, always send a confirmation autoresponder e-mail. After the user submits his or her e-mail address, the server should immediately trigger back an autoresponder e-mail that confirms the user's registration. These e-mails not only should confirm a successful opt-in process but also should give details as to how to opt out.

Get Permission

Spam is still inappropriate, and just because someone has done business with you does not mean that they have given you permission to bombard their e-mail boxes. At one point, Motorola customers who received a series of unsolicited e-mails from an independent distributor sent numerous angry complaints to Motorola's customer service department and even to the CEO. Although they were customers, they felt violated by being sent offers without their permission. While customers typically do not react in the same way to hard-mail campaigns, many deem their e-mail boxes as highly personal and private. They do not want them jammed up with meaningless e-mails, and they certainly do not want to be subject to crass advertising on their personal computer. Consumer reactions to spam or "perceived spam," which can happen if messages are sent that may not appear to be within the realm of given permission, have become such a potential public relations nightmare that many companies require a double opt in. Consumers opt in when they register on a Web site and then confirm that opt in by replying to a confirmation e-mail.

Tips and Tactics

Always offer recipients of your e-mail campaigns a chance to easily opt out, even if they are your most valuable customers. It is not just an expected courtesy; in many cases, it is the law.

Spam typically has generated only a 1 to 2 percent response rate, only slightly higher than banner ads, whereas permission e-mail has generated as high as 15 to 40 percent response rates.

Beyond the risk of being labeled a spammer, there are other fallouts of sending nonpermissioned e-mails:

- **It's the law.** Many states require businesses to have permission or a previous business relationship in order to send an e-mail ad. Congress is currently considering an antispam law.
- **Customer service nightmare.** Mailing unsolicited e-mail most often will result in a flood of reply mail from angry recipients, as illustrated by the Motorola example. Floods of reply mail to spam campaigns have crashed companies' Web sites and internal mail systems, let alone resulting in much negative publicity.
- **Loss of Internet service provider.** Nearly all Internet service providers (ISPs) terminate service to customers they believe send nonpermission commercial e-mails. In addition, an Internet watchdog group called the Mail Abuse Prevention Service (MAPS) will blacklist any company it believes conducts non-permission-based e-mail marketing. Nearly 2000 ISPs use the MAPS Blacklist, which can cause up to 40 percent of a marketer's outbound e-mail to go undelivered. This mail does not "bounce" back. Rather, the participating ISPs simply choose to filter and not deliver the returning e-mails to their subscribers.

Make an Offer

e-Mails that get the greatest responses are typically those which offer recipients tangible value. If you personalize e-mail messages for specific customer segments, you will be able to make relevant offers that will get attention and higher response rates than most other forms of marketing. You should make it easy for recipients to respond to the offer by giving them a link to your Web site where the offer can be realized or simply allowing them to reply to your e-mail to activate the promotion.

Master the Subject Line

In any type of advertising—print, outdoor, or Web sites—headlines are the most critical component. What you say in a headline dictates whether or not the rest of your message gets read. In e-mail, the subject line is the headline and should be crafted carefully to motivate or instill curiosity or interest. It also needs to be highly relevant, such as "Per your recent order with ABC store." Your e-mail text is also critical. Again, make it interesting, simple, and catchy. Never use misleading subject lines to try to trick people into opening and reading your message. There is never any justification for deceitful marketing, e-mail or otherwise.

Keep It Brief

Whenever I get long e-mails, even from valid sources, I save them until I have the time to leisurely read them—which more often than not is never. As a result, I rarely read e-mails that are more than a paragraph long. Time is the most valuable asset we have. Do not waste it—yours or your customers. Get to the point quickly.

Always Include an Easy Unsubscribe Option

Make it easy for recipients to unsubscribe, and then honor those requests. You can offer a URL to go to or simply request a reply message. Make sure that you update your database often so that you do not end up sending an e-mail to someone who has opted out. Every state law, every proposed federal law, and the DMA all mandate that marketers include an unsubscribe option on every outbound message. Penalties for not providing an unsubscribe option range from civil to criminal, with fines up to $500 for each nonconforming message.

Send Messages in Both Plain Text and Rich HTML

If you do decide to send a graphic e-mail and your mass e-mailer supports multipart MIME e-mail messages, compose and send your messages in both plain text and HTML. In this way, if the recipient's e-mail application supports HTML messages, then he or she can easily view fonts, colors, images, and links. If not, then the recipient's e-mail application will ignore the HTML version of the message and only show a plain-text version, which avoids the irritation of getting an e-mail that is time-consuming to open.

Integrate Metrics

Test your subject lines, your copy, your offers, your messages, and your customer segments' responsiveness by setting up separate reply addresses and URL links for each campaign. Measuring is simple and inexpensive on the Web, so take advantage of the opportunity to learn what messages and offers attract the most response and from which customer segments.

As discussed previously, you will want to invest in a tracking software program to help you measure who opens your e-mail messages, when they open them, and how they respond, as well as the open rate for specific messages. This will help you to test the open rate of each message, subject line, and customer segment, a highly critical variable for e-mail success. Keep in mind that the most critical success is determined by conversion rates, not raw visitors. If you are successful at driving people to your site via clever e-mail and other marketing activities but cannot convert them to customers, you need to rethink your Web and overall marketing strategies.

Getting Started—Lifetime Marketing Checklist

First and foremost, always have a Web strategy. Set clear and measurable objectives for your site, and make sure that they are realistic and doable given your budget and other restrictions.

Action Items

1. Design your Web site to cater to your most valuable three or four segments.
2. Develop messages, graphic presentations, tools, and so on that appeal to these groups.
3. Include content that is relevant, meaningful, and objective. Do not just include content that shouts about your brand. Supply content that gives visitors a reason to come back often.
4. Update content often, at least on your home page, so that visitors gain something new on subsequent visits.
5. Identify ways for building a sense of community among your visitors. Create interactive and collaborative opportunities for visitors with the site, other customers and visitors, and with your team.
6. Find ways that your business can immediately respond to requests made to your Web site, e-commerce or informational.
7. Develop loyalty programs that are relevant to your top customer segments or, if possible, individuals.
8. Provide customers with multichannel purchasing options by offering some form of e-commerce.
9. Track visitors and individual behavior so that you can respond appropriately and guide future marketing efforts.
10. Develop e-mail campaigns based on relevance, loyalty, and permission.
11. Create and communicate a privacy policy.
12. Personalize, personalize, personalize.

For updated information and tips on Web strategies, tools, tracking methods, and so on, visit *www.mcmurtrygroup.com.*

Worksheet: Defining Your Web Strategy

Answering the following questions will help you to determine your current strengths and weaknesses as you develop your lifetime marketing Web strategy. A digital version of this worksheet can be found at *www.mcmurtrygroup.com*.

What is the primary objective you are hoping to accomplish with your Web site?	
What are the secondary objectives you want to accomplish?	
What value can you offer customers and visitors to motivate them to register at your site and give you permission to market to them?	
What content or information can you offer visitors that is of direct value to them besides content about your business or products and services?	
How can you foster a collaborative community on your Web site that pulls together visitors, employees, and customers?	
Can you realistically add e-commerce functions to your site?	
If e-commerce is not appropriate for your site, how can you otherwise support the purchase process?	
How can you better develop customer interaction on your site?	

How can you respond more immediately to visitors' requests and needs?	
What types of tools or utilities can you offer to make your site more valuable and draw people back to your site?	
What types of activities are likely to motivate loyalty among your Web visitors or customers?	
How can your site make your visitors' jobs or lives more convenient?	
Are you currently tracking general visitor and individual behavior?	
Do you conduct e-mail campaigns among your registrants?	
If so, how are you measuring the success of your efforts?	
What is your investment threshold? Or what is the level of money you can spend making your site more sophisticated without diminishing your point of return?	

What's Missing in Marketing's Four Ps?

Adding the C, or Customer Perspective, to the Four Ps of Marketing—Product, Place, Price, and Promotion

Before you can create a comprehensive lifetime marketing campaign, you must first review the basic tenets of marketing—product, place, price, and promotion, or the four Ps. While marketing programs clearly are built on these four areas, the most important aspect of a successful marketing plan is missing—the *customer*.

Lifetime marketers build marketing plans that address the Ps and the C of marketing. The C component, the customer, is the most critical part of a marketing plan. If marketers do not understand the customer inside and out, they cannot properly develop the P components to satisfy customers in a way that will allow them to capture lifetime value.

For a marketing plan to be successful in achieving lifetime value, it must incorporate the customer aspects into each of the four Ps. This concept seems so obvious, yet it is amazing how often it is missed. Until now, we have discussed the C of marketing in great detail. Now we will discuss how to apply this information to the Ps.

Product

While your business may have dozens, hundreds, or even thousands of customers, today's customers want to feel like they are your only one. They expect to be treated as your most valuable customer through back-bending customer service, and they expect you to personalize your product to meet their individual needs, as outrageous as they may be. Customers can get away with these expectations because companies can deliver and have delivered. With all the customer resource management (CRM) and e-commerce technology available today, personalized brand experiences are becoming more common.

Too often businesses build products that meet their needs but are not relevant to customers. High-tech companies are a good example. Many companies spend hundreds of thousands of dollars, even millions, developing systems and functionalities dreamed up by forward-thinking computer programmers who are trying to outsmart engineers working for their competitors. While many times the functionality and corresponding "bells and whistles" provide real value to end users, often they do not, and companies end up creating systems nobody wants or perceives a need for.

The e-learning industry suffered from this problem in the late 1990s. Many companies spent millions of dollars developing the next new function or comprehensive system that would revolutionize and digitize every aspect of corporate training. The problem was that companies were not ready to drop their instructor-led training and put all their money and resources into online training. They simply did not perceive a need for the remarkable capabilities developers were producing—at least not for the price required.

In the days when e-learning was considered to be the "next killer app," as described by Cisco Chairman John Chambers, many companies scrambled to hire as many program developers as possible to outpace the competition in developing innovative functionalities. In just a few years, these same companies were significantly downsizing, had been acquired by larger companies, or were out of business altogether. SABA, one of the market leaders that had pursued an aggressive development strategy, had a stock value of $2.29 in August 2002, just 2 years after reaching a high value of $38.81 in August 2000.

A company by the name of Learnframe pursued a similar strategy and also failed. With the millions of dollars the company's CEO had raised from private investors over a 10-year period, a team of programmers and developers worked away at building a fantasy learning management system. It would have all the capabilities and features even remotely possible, and the development team would stop at no cost to create it. Learnframe went about hiring as many computer programmers as possible, even when it did not need them, because it was certain that someday the company would, and it would be best to get them on the payroll and locked in. As a result, the cost of the program kept growing at an enormous rate. And so did the complexity of the project. Every time a competitor announced a new feature, Learnframe would add that functionality to its dream system.

Originally, the project had a 1-year development schedule. Years later, the project still was not complete, leaving Learnframe with little to sell. As a result, the company lost revenue, investors, employees, and its role as a viable contender in its industry. Eventually, the company consisted of a handful of owners and investors trying to revive a dead business.

Tips and Tactics

Let your customers define your product development strategy. Regularly survey customers and qualified prospects to discover what their current needs are, future anticipations, and likes and dislikes about current technology. Use your findings to develop future products and define your business's position strategy.

What went wrong? SABA, which had been praised by analysts and developers as the king of the industry, had a stock value a fraction of its past worth and was in a pattern of downsizing instead of growth, and Learnframe, with its talented programmers, could not sell its products and in just a couple of short years had gone from a company of nearly 200 employees to virtually nothing.

Management and other issues aside, both these companies built products that made them proud yet were not based on real and valid issues, needs, purchasing patterns, and learning trends of customers. Both companies spent millions of investors' dollars and valuable personnel hours on a dream rather than on researched and validated customer needs. Customers did not care about the bells and whistles and all the other fancy features they were trying to build faster and better than anyone else. Customers simply wanted a basic delivery and management tool that was easy to implement and integrate with existing enterprisewide systems and that actually worked. They wanted basic features and basic prices with stellar service.

SABA and Learnframe were creating exorbitant systems at exorbitant prices. As a result, the basic products on the market with a proven track record sold, and others lost their shirts and a golden opportunity to establish dominance in a growing market. The lesson here is to take the time to find out what your customers want, which features and functions are likely to get used and which are not, and then build your products accordingly. Your first priority should be to learn and listen. The second priority is to find realistic ways to fill real and valid needs better than anyone else.

An associate of mine dreamed of having his own business. To this end, he refined a business idea and developed a thorough white paper on the product category covering in-depth the technology that would be used, the potential market volume, the potential revenue and thus profits, and all the logistics of building the business. He forgot completely about the most valuable factor of all—the customer. Nowhere in his business plan did he talk about who was most likely to purchase the product, who would influence his potential purchasers, and what their needs were regarding the category and how they were likely to use the product. He had researched the moneymaking opportunities but had failed to define a target audience and then research the audience to discover their needs and general interest in the product and corresponding category. Not surprisingly, he failed before he was even able to hit the road.

Tips and Tactics

Before beginning on any business or new product plan, get as much information on your customers as possible. Review secondary research from associations, news organizations, and periodicals. Survey customers about needs and purchasing issues. Analyze competing brands' products and customers. All these activities will help you to develop a sound plan for product development.

No matter how good a business idea is, it cannot succeed without first focusing on the customer. New products and technology should not be developed without knowing with absolute certainty your potential customers' attitudes toward and interests in the given product and propensity to purchase.

Personalizing your products or product line can be relatively simple. It just takes the time to listen to your customers individually and then find a way to personalize either the product itself or the experience with your brand. You can do this by polling your customers to find out what their recommendations are, as well as their needs, issues, concerns, and so on. Then you must listen to them.

If your business is in retail, you likely will not be able to customize products from third-party manufacturers, but you can personalize customers' experience with your business. Sears recently rolled out its Tool Territory program, which consists of a master craftsman on hand to advise shoppers, a counter to use when testing power tools, and tool testing stations that enable customers to experience tools before purchasing them and where shoppers can pound away, scrape away, and tighten screws to their heart's delight. Music stores have listening stations so that customers can listen to CDs before committing to purchase them. Computer stores can personalize their customers' experiences by offering personal tech experts. Clothing stores can personalize their brands by providing image consultants to help customers find the colors and fashions that look best on them. To help personalize a fashion retail experience, customers with an annual value of $1000 or more could receive a free color and fashion analysis by a personal image expert once a year. They also could schedule an appointment to shop with the image expert each time they come to the store. Think of the volume this could generate in up-selling alone. Regardless of the business you are in, there is likely a way that you can personalize the shopping experience.

You also can build in varying levels of experience for the different values customers represent to your business. Customers of a computer retail business with a specific annual value could qualify for free consultations with a computer expert to help them understand the benefits and cost-benefit ratios of specific products, technologies, and so on. This service would be especially helpful for small business customers wanting to keep ahead of the competition by working smarter and faster but not knowing enough about business technology to know where to best invest limited funds.

Personalization of products is no longer a competitive distinction for many industries—it is an *expectation*. The computer industry is a good example of this. Dell Computers quickly took over the personal computer market by offering customers exactly what they wanted in a computer rather than a prebuilt system based on what an engineer thought consumers should have. Automobile companies are also offering customized cars. Both industries realize that when consumers are investing in an expensive product they will have to live with for years in order to get their money's worth, it needs to be exactly what they want, not what someone else is telling them to want. People do not want to pay for bells and whistles that mean nothing to them; they are willing to pay for what they will use—nothing less, nothing more. Yet you continue to see companies build products for their portfolios, not their customers' lifestyles and needs.

The way you personalize a product needs to be relevant to consumers and their purchase process. At one point, a leading blue jeans manufacturer launched an attempt to offer custom jeans. Unfortunately, this product was not met with the success anticipated, possibly because people were not dissatisfied with how their current jeans fit to the degree that they were willing to spend the time getting sized for customized jeans, pay the price, and then wait for them to get done. Jeans are a practical purchase, but the process to get them customized was not. The product and the personalization process need to be in line with each other.

Another way to personalize a product is to let customers choose how to be rewarded for their business. Again, American Express and Vail Resorts do a great job of this by allowing members to choose how to redeem the points they earned through qualifying purchases. Both programs have been very successful in generating repeat business and customer loyalty.

Your company's value proposition should reflect not what you want your business to be, but what solid customer research tells you your customers want your business to be for them. How you position your products in the marketplace needs to be a direct reflection of your customers' needs and wants. Your positioning strategy must address these issues in a way that resonates with customers' emotions and thus further draws them to your brand.

As summed up by Al Ries and Jack Trout in their book *Positioning: The Battle for Your Mind,* positioning is what you do to the mind of the customers, not the product.

Defining a market position for your brand is critical to developing a successful marketing strategy and for helping your brand stand out in a cluttered marketplace. Putting stakes in the ground to show what your business is committed to or has superior expertise in helps to define your competitive strengths in the minds of your target consumers. Many customers prefer to work with businesses that have specialized in their area of need because it builds confidence that they will receive the most advanced skills or products. Choosing a product or service brand is sometimes like choosing a health care provider. When you want the most advanced skills, you choose a specialist, such as an orthopedic surgeon versus a general practitioner. Positioning strategies help to build this type of confidence.

Place

Consumers have more shopping options than ever before. First, we shopped at stores; then through catalogs; then through shopping networks such as Amway, Avon, and Mary Kay; then via TV; and finally via the Internet. As customers, we have grown accustomed to having multiple purchasing channels to select from, and we are demanding it more and more.

Even with the demise of thousands of pure-play dot-coms in the 1990s, Internet shopping continues to grow at dizzying rates. For 2001, analyst firms submitted e-commerce revenue estimates that ranged from $37.1 billion to $117 billion. eMarketer, which provides research reports on the e-commerce industry, projected that e-commerce revenues will reach $156 million by 2005, four times their estimate for the year 2000. eMarketer's 2001 report on e-commerce also showed that the population of online buyers is growing rapidly, with 79.3 million shoppers in 2001 alone. This is huge when you consider that in 2000, there were only 116.5 million U.S. Internet users. The firm also projected that there would be 130 million Americans who have shopped online by 2005, up from 64.1 million in 2000.

With statistics like these, many may wonder why so many dot-coms went out of business. Simple. Consumers want the convenience offered by online shopping, but they also want the service and comfort of shopping with the retailers they have frequented and trusted for years.

Many of the failed dot-coms were new names with unproven product quality, service, and delivery on promises. The successful e-commerce sites are those of companies that also offer consumers "bricks and clicks"—bricks so that customers can physically review the products they saw online and clicks so that they can have the convenience of shopping anytime from the comfort of home rather than the chaos of crowded shopping malls. Traditional merchants have increased their brands and revenues significantly by offering customers both shopping choices under the same umbrella of customer service and satisfaction guarantees. The success that traditional retailers are having online is so large that pure-play dot-coms are seeking ways to associate their brands with bricks-and-mortar retailers in order to offer customers the advantages associated with bricks and clicks. Amazon.com has been pursuing this strategy recently with national retailers.

Developing an online store to supplement a physical store is a highly expensive and intensive business commitment. It is not for every business, and it is not the only way to personalize a brand. There are numerous other ways to personalize your place of business for customers. Retailers are doing this by offering experiences, not just shelves stocked high with products. For example, REI has added climbing walls and other recreational items to many of its stores, giving customers a chance to experience a taste of the adventures REI sells and interact with personnel and products directly. REI also offers travel services and guided excursions to unusual places, thus offering customers the means to fulfill personal dreams of adventure.

Bookstores, such as Barnes & Noble, have added coffee bars to create a relaxed, warm, and inviting place of business that makes people want to stay longer and potentially buy more products. Keeping people in your store is as critical to physical sales as keeping people at your site is to online sales.

Regardless of what type of business you are in, you can create an environment that will help to enhance your customers' overall shopping experience. Your total environment is the aesthetics of your physical structure and the emotional well-being or feelings you generate among your customers through staff interaction, service, and the like.

Typically, I dread taking my car to get serviced and having to wait in a smelly, dirty, uncomfortable lobby that more often than not looks like it has not been cleaned for weeks or months. I was forced to stop at a Big O Tire store in Evergreen, Colorado, when my windshield wipers failed to work in a snowstorm. I was stressed and anxious because the drive had been tedious, having to stop every few minutes to clean my windshield along the road with facial tissues and struggling to keep on the road because I could not see it. I also was late for a very important business meeting but could not go on because my visibility was just about zero.

To my surprise, the Evergreen Big O Tire store was clean and had a lobby with free donuts, drinks, and a customer courtesy telephone. The sales staff made sure that I was comfortable, offered me a phone book and food, and then got a crew working immediately on my car. I was not there to buy tires, the company's main source of revenue. I was there for a very minor service. Yet the sales staff treated me like I was the only customer that day. The clerk knew I was late for a meeting, so he gently nudged his team to work faster to find out why my windshield wipers did not work. A few minutes later, he emerged to tell me that I had frozen water lines and that they were thawing them out as quickly as possible. A few moments after this, he handed me my car keys, walked me out to my car, which had a newly cleaned windshield, and wished me a safe drive to my meeting. He refused to charge me a dime. I had such a good experience at that store that I looked forward to going back and found myself planning an oil change around my next trip down I-70.

The manager of the Evergreen, Colorado, Big O Tire Store knew the power of creating an atmosphere where people feel comfortable and appreciated. This atmosphere was founded on having an inviting lobby, free food and phone service for customer convenience, and an unexpected level of customer service.

Tips and Tactics

Integrate customer service into every aspect of your marketing plan. Train employees to think like their customers so that they can anticipate their needs and fill them faster, or before being asked. Motivate employees to apply the golden rule to customer interactions by linking their performance to their paychecks.

Customer service is a large part of any business's place or distribution strategy. For mail-order, online, and catalog companies, it is the only interaction with a brand. There is no other aspect of a place strategy that can compensate for a negative experience. A customer may go back to a bookstore because of its convenient location, coffee service, reading rooms, and large selection even if he or she had a bad customer service experience on occasion. However, if a customer has a bad experience with a brand that can be replaced easily by competitors offering the same level of convenience and types of products, such as shopping on another Web site or using a different catalog, the likelihood of retaining that business is significantly lower.

A study of 300 adults conducted by Mobius Management Systems showed that due to poor customer service:

- 46 percent of respondents had dropped a credit card provider
- 43 percent had dropped a bank

- 32 percent had discontinued an Internet service provider
- 30 percent had dropped a phone company
- 22 percent had dropped a pager or cellular phone vendor

When it comes to defining customer service, 54 percent of these same respondents said that if they are on hold for more than 5 minutes, they consider customer service poor. Nearly this same percentage claimed that the most frustrating part of customer service is trying to get through automated phone systems.

You need to define customers' expectations in order to meet and exceed customer service expectations. Find out what the pushing points are for your customers, and then deliver.

Jupiter Media conducted a consumer survey to determine the effect of responsiveness on customer satisfaction. They found that 57 percent of respondents said that the speed in which an online retailer responded to an e-mail inquiry would affect their decision to purchase from that vendor. Even more revealing, 53 percent of respondents claimed that they would be less likely to buy from the online retailer's bricks-and-mortar locations if they were not happy with the customer service from the online store. Again, customer service is the most critical aspect of a place strategy. People shopping from their homes experience only two aspects of your brand—product and customer service. In today's marketplace, the distinctions between competing products in several consumer categories are getting dimmer and dimmer. Thus the most important aspect is customer service.

Sometimes the simple things are the biggest influencers in making your brand a personal and rewarding experience for customers. Stores can be personalized not only with conveniences for customers but also with elements that appeal directly to the personality, emotions, and lifestyles of your most valuable customers. If your store sells adventure, do what REI does and add some adventure to the shopping experience. If you sell music, offer personalized listening demonstrations. If you sell high-tech products, offer customers the chance to play with the latest products rather than just read about the technology in a point-of-purchase display. Your goal is to create an atmosphere that appeals to the mind set of your best customers and puts them in the right frame of mind to want to linger longer in your store and return for more of a positive and unique experience. Your place of business should work toward creating an overall experience with your brand—product sampling, customer service, comfort, convenience, and value. Doing this does not have to be expensive. Find ways to personalize the shopping experience for your customers that are in line with your resources, environment, and customers' expectations.

Another aspect of a successful place strategy is to identify what you can do to make the distribution of your product more convenient for your most valuable customers. If you market to elderly people or others who have a difficult time getting out of the house to shop, for example, mothers of young kids or the physically disabled, offer delivery services to make shopping easier for them. Distribution strategies should consider the customers' needs and convenience first and the needs of the business second.

Tips and Tactics

Be creative with distribution strategies. Offer drive-up service for busy customers, take mail orders, or make house calls. Do whatever it takes to ensure that your customers can continue shopping your brand even when their life stage or circumstances change.

Brand presentation and customer service are critical for defining what your business is to consumers and for creating an environment to which people want to return. Like a Web site, stores must be designed to motivate repeat visits. Offer a valuable experience that supports your product line, and then offer the best possible customer service.

Price

How you set your prices says a great deal about your product and business and your customers. Businesses that want to attract strivers or consumers seeking status and approval from others will tend to have higher-priced merchandise. Brands marketing to teens typically will set higher prices because teens feel a sense of achievement and association with status-oriented groups when they purchase high-priced items. Businesses wanting to penetrate a marketplace by selling as many goods or services as possible to mainstream or middle-of-the-road consumers will list lower prices. Whatever your pricing strategy is, the most important consideration is your customers' expectations and thresholds toward price.

Lifetime businesses know their most valuable customers and prospects inside and out and thus know how price affects their purchase decisions. Businesses need to know the influence price has on first-time purchases, repeat purchases, and up-selling and cross-selling efforts. If you are successful at getting a new customer based on value pricing, chances are that you will retain this customer and generate lifetime revenues by continuing to offer value pricing.

Tips and Tactics

Develop a pricing strategy that directly reflects your positioning strategy. Carefully monitor competitors' prices to ensure that you are in line with the market and the image you want to achieve. Ask your customers for their input.

A successful pricing strategy is not only one that considers global marketing issues such as supply and demand, competitive pricing, and consumer thresholds, but it also considers the impact that price has on its most valuable customer segments. Each of your customer segments may react differently to price. Strugglers likely will shop for the best price and look for discounts and sales. Achievers likely will value convenience and time over price and thus will be willing to pay more.

Pricing is a significant aspect of personalized promotions. Rather than offering price discounts across the board to all customer groups, you will be more successful by offering price-oriented promotions designed on a customer-segment basis. Your customer profiles need to contain information on the pricing needs and expectations of each customer group so that you can develop appropriate communications and promotions.

Another successful pricing strategy is *customized* pricing. This occurs when businesses let consumers shop from a price orientation and thus set their own price. Some companies go so far as to let customers set their own price within reason. Priceline.com is an excellent example of this, allowing customers to define up front what they are willing to pay for travel expenses. Gateway Computers allows customers to set a price value at the onset of their online shopping experience. The Web site asks visitors for their price range and then shows products that fit within that defined range, thus maximizing the value of their time and simplifying their overall shopping experience. By allowing customers to customize prices, you are again personalizing your brand for them and increasing satisfaction with the overall shopping experience, which is key to acquiring and retaining customers and capturing their lifetime value.

Promotion

The whole purpose of developing customer profiles is so that you can develop and execute *personalized promotions*. While it may not be practical to send personal thank-you notes and congratulations cards to all your customers, you can communicate with them in personal ways by sending them correspondence that is in line with their personal values and product orientation.

When creating customer segments, you need to create segments that reflect the purchasing patterns, not just the personal patterns, of your customers. For example, one of the ways your customers should be categorized is according to the type of promotion most likely to get their attention and business. You can then develop promotions that cater specifically to the values of each segment. You may want to offer segment A an extended warranty plan for a discount and segment B a 10 percent discount, segment C free shipping, segment D a free gift with purchase, and so on. By doing this, you are personalizing an offer that addresses real and valid needs and desires.

Communicating with customers is like communicating with friends. The more you talk about your self, the less they listen. Communicate what you can do for them, how you can make their life easier, and why they should listen to you. In essence, communicate your qualifications for being their brand of choice.

Your personalization efforts always should communicate to your customers in the first person. With all the technology available for doing this, there is really never a reason not to. e-Mail and hard-mail messages should include a direct salutation and, when appropriate, reference the latest transaction with your business. You can still develop one piece of communication for each segment; just make sure that you have the ability to merge personal information throughout. As simple as it is, referencing people by their first names, in person or via digital or print communications vehicles, goes a long way. My bank has a glass bowl containing dollar bills at each teller station. On the jar is a note telling customers that if the teller did not say their first name at least once during their transaction, they should take a dollar out of the jar. While this may seem like a contrived effort, the message is that this company wants you to feel like a valued and recognized person, not just a number or revenue source.

Promotion is far more complex than sending personal communications and offering personal promotions. In order for your personalized communications efforts to have the needed credibility to motivate behavior, you must have brand recognition and credibility. This is where the use of mass communications comes in. Although mass communications are not going to achieve lifetime value for any brand, they can strengthen lifetime marketing efforts. However, mass communications must be looked at as a complement to personal communications, not as the primary means for promoting a brand and generating sales. Chapter 10 shares some tips for how to efficiently use traditional forms of promotion and mass media to support your lifetime marketing efforts.

Getting Started—Lifetime Marketing Checklist

Why "Customerize" the Four Ps?

Applying the customers' perspective to the four Ps of marketing will

- Enable you to develop highly relevant products for your most valuable customers
- Save you money in research and development because your activities will be guided by known needs rather than assumptions or developers' dreams
- Allow you to personalize the shopping environment and experience in ways that makes customers want to come back for more
- Enable you to identify the distribution and shopping options that make it easy and convenient for your valued customers to do business with your brand
- Communicate in a highly personal and effective way

Action Items

1. Identify the features and benefits that mean the most to your consumers.
2. Identify features and functionalities that have little appeal to customers or their usage history. Find ways to eliminate these in order to make your product more in line with customers' expectations and budgets.
3. Determine price influences and thresholds among your best customer segments.
4. Identify ways you can offer pricing options, packages, and so on to meet various needs and widen your customer base.
5. Analyze your place of business. Does it appeal to or reflect the values, principles, or image of your most valued consumers?
6. Identify ways that your place of business can offer personal experiences with your product or service.
7. Identify knowledge, information, or support that you can offer customers and shoppers that adds credibility to your selling efforts and motivates them to come back when needing further knowledge.
8. Identify the communications channels most used by your customers so that you can reach them most efficiently.
9. Identify key messages that resonate loudly with your key customer segments.

Worksheet: How Customer-Oriented Is Your Business?

The following questions will help you to understand just how personal your business really is.

	Yes, No, or I Don't Know
1. Are your products designed according to your needs or customers' needs as identified through research activities?	
2. Do you know which features and functions of your product have the most meaning to customers or have the most impact toward helping them reach their goals?	
3. Does your pricing strategy reflect customer purchasing trends and requests? Does it provide optimal flexibility?	
4. Can you personalize your products according to specific customer needs, for example, custom-built computers?	
5. How do you collect feedback from customers about your products and service?	
6. Have you defined a market position for your brand and product? If so, is this position based on customers' needs and attitudes or those of management?	
7. Do you offer customers distribution options, such as in-store versus online, mail-order, or phone shopping?	

	Yes, No, or I Don't Know
8. Does your place of business appeal to the values and attitudes of your most valued consumers?	
9. Does your place of business offer experiences, knowledge, and support that make it worth going back to?	
10. Do your employees offer memorable customer service that gives customers a sense of belonging to your brand family?	
11. Do your promotions relate to customer behavior patterns and expressed needs or changes in demand?	

Score

Five or more questions, yes. Keep up the good work. You're on your way to capturing customers' lifetime value.

Five or more questions, no. It is time to start building your business for your customers, not yourself or your business associates. Start paying more attention to customers' needs and patterns.

Five or more questions, I don't know. You need to decide what you want your business to be when it grows up. It is also time to start taking your business and its marketing needs seriously.

Part 4

Building Your Lifetime Marketing Plan

10

Applying Lifetime Marketing Techniques to Traditional Communications Vehicles

How to Make Mass Communications Media Support Personalized Marketing

I f you ever received a love note or valentine from an anonymous admirer, you likely remember feeling flattered, even excited for a brief moment, and then quickly forgetting about the mysterious attention and refocusing your energies on the admirers you knew. This same principle applies to lifetime marketing. You can send the most compelling personalized communications and valuable incentives for promotions, but if no one is familiar with your brand and what it can do for them personally, your efforts and money will likely go unappreciated and be meaningless, and thus be ineffective. As I mentioned earlier, mass communications can be used effectively to build credibility for your brand so that when your personal communications reach their intended audience, your message is credible, understood, and acted on.

When using mass media to promote your business, make it a part of an overall marketing program, and maintain that perspective. Companies that rely solely on mass media to promote their businesses risk going out of business in today's highly competitive marketplace. Consumers now have more choices than ever for just about every product and service imaginable. And they expect personal attention and service. This does not just apply to how they are treated once they purchase from you; it also applies to how they learn about your products, how they interact with your representatives, how they receive information about your brand, and how you manage their personal relationship with you. A company may be able to boast the most clever ad campaigns and most awards on their trophy shelves, but that is not why anyone is in business. Long-term profitability is the only measure that counts, and the only way to achieve this is through personalized lifetime marketing efforts. Use mass media to help you generate new leads for lifetime relationships and add credibility to your personalized communications.

When developed to support lifetime marketing activities, mass advertising can be an effective means to

- Generate exposure for your brand and key messages so that lifetime marketing efforts have more credibility
- Learn what works and what does not, for example, which messages and vehicles get the most response
- Expose your brand name to qualified prospects
- Keep your name alive and on the forefront of consumers' minds
- Drive consumers to your Web site or business to initiate a relationship

Mass advertising can be a strong tool for getting people to your place of business or Web site, where you can initiate relationships and collect contact and needs data for lifetime marketing efforts. To do this, advertisements need to be planned and placed carefully.

If you decide to use mass advertising to support lifetime marketing activities, do your homework to find out which communications channels are used most readily by your core customers. By surveying your customers, you can determine if they are most likely to be reached via newspaper, radio, specialty publications, or TV. Then pinpoint which outlets or brands of media are most appropriate. The same thing applies to purchasing media to reach prospects. Purchase the media vehicles that reach your best customers, and you also will be reaching your best prospects. If your target customer travels a lot, radio might be the most effective approach. If they value intellectualism, knowledge, and self-development, talk radio is likely the best fit. To reach customers with more leisure time on their hands, for example, retired persons, newspapers and magazines may be the best communications vehicle. You want to choose publications that correspond with your customers' values and interests.

When working with media representatives, always ask them to develop a metric for your ads so that you can determine the actual return on your investment. If they cannot do this, then you should not give them your business.

Following are some guidelines for integrating mass media into your lifetime marketing activities in a way that builds credibility and appropriate exposure for your brand.

Mass Advertising Guidelines

1. Develop Compelling Messages for Your Best Customers

Although mass advertising reaches an audience that is much broader than your target customer segments, you should treat your ad as if it were being sent only to your most qualified prospects. The message you deliver to your customers and prospects should be developed as if it were being delivered to one individual at a time. Write your text to appeal to your most valued customers and hence prospects. In this way, you are likely to get the attention of those most likely to respond. Always direct consumers to your Web site so that you can deliver more specific information and, more important, collect valuable customer data for individual marketing purposes.

Write your ad to reflect the values and purchase processes of your most valued customer segments. Your message should be brief yet compelling. Many ads give way too much information to be inviting to any consumer. Ads need to communicate the core value to the customer, include a promise and benefit, and then provoke a call to action. One of the most critical investments you should make when doing mass advertising is in a good copywriter. Too many small businesses rely on the media outlet to produce their ads. Do not give into this temptation just because it is a free service. Newspapers and radio stations, especially in small markets, typically do not have the quality of copywriters and designers that you can find through ad agencies, marketing consultants, or freelance professionals. In-house ads tend to look alike, read alike, and for radio or TV, sound alike. You want your ad to stand out from the clutter, and the most qualified professionals to do this are not employed by the same company as your ad rep. In fact, quite often the ad rep will create your ads himself or herself. Typically, this is not a good thing. You need to hire someone capable of presenting your brand and your messages in a fresh and interesting light. Pay the money to do it right, or don't do it at all. Poor advertising will hurt your brand image and fail to support your goals.

One of the main purposes of your ad should be to get people to visit your Web site or place of business so that you can initiate a relationship. Most often, new prospects will visit a Web site before contacting a business in person or via phone because this is an anonymous, pressure-free introduction to a new brand or business. Your ads always should invite consumers to visit your Web site. You might want to tie a free offer or promotional give-away to registering at your Web site. For example, your ad could mention that the first 100 people to register at your Web site before a specified date will receive a free gift. This tactic not only will help you to generate new leads for lifetime marketing, but it also will help you to track the effectiveness of your ads and media outlets.

Tips and Tactics

Develop advertisements as if they were personalized to your most valuable customers. In this way, you will appeal to the most qualified prospects, those with whom you want to initiate a lifetime relationship. Always encourage prospects to visit your Web site, where you can collect their data for lifetime marketing.

2. Ensure That Your Graphic Presentation Supports Your Desired Market Position

Appealing to the core values of your best customer groups goes beyond the written word. This also applies to the graphic presentation or tone of your advertisement. Keep in mind that communication is far more than the written or spoken word. It encompasses the packaging and style with which your message is presented. Even your color and font choices say a lot about your brand. This is also very important when developing your Web site. Too many times Web sites do not reflect the brand properly.

A client of mine is a developer of very sophisticated enterprisewide software. The company's products are truly the most advanced in the marketplace. However, the company's Web site at one time was perhaps the most technologically unsophisticated in its marketplace. It contained no animation and no interactive tools or functions. It was simply a flat digital brochure. Yet the company was trying to position itself as a leader in computer technology. Its Web site defeated this purpose and sent a very different message. As a result of its low-tech presentation, visitors did not leave this site with a strong impression of the company's technological capabilities, and in its particular industry, state-of-the-art technology is critical. On changing the Web site, the company was able to create a much more relevant experience for visitors and present its capabilities accurately both verbally and graphically.

Tips and Tactics

Create ads that reflect the emotions and decision influencers of your most valued customer segments and the values and expertise of your business.

Again, as you develop graphics for your ads and Web site, keep in mind the values, lifestyle, interests, and needs of your prime customer segments. This will ensure that you get the attention of those most likely to respond and will allow you to reach the shoulder segments or wanna-be audiences effectively as well.

3. Measure Your Efforts

Advertising programs should be learning programs. If you use mass media, you need to set up mechanisms to determine their impact on reaching and motivating your most valued customers and prospects to respond as desired. Direct marketing via print or e-mail can be measured down to the individual response. Mass advertising is not so easy to measure. You should test the vehicle in which you are placing your ads, the message, the creative execution, and the promotional offer. You can do this via various means, including those listed below.

Unique Response Mechanisms

- **Unique URLs for each ad or medium.** Many brands use a different URL for each ad campaign and medium for directing consumers to their Web sites. In this way, they can tell who came from the TV ad or the print ad and which message was the most motivating. Dell Computer measures its TV ads by directing viewers to *dell.com/tv* and measures its catalog by directing readers to *dellforme.com*. Web tracking programs can easily identify entry points for each visitor to a site, how long they stayed at that site, and where they went from there. Such programs also can tell marketers if their e-mails were opened so that they can test the open rate for various subject-line statements, opt-in lists, and so on.
- **Separate toll-free phone numbers.** Many companies use separate toll-free numbers in each media outlet in order to see which outlet or message generated the most direct response.
- **Unique offers.** By offering different incentives in identical advertisements reaching the same populations, you can determine which types of offers actually motivate trial best. For example, do consumers respond better to free shipping offers, free gift with purchase offers, discounts, or two for one offers? Knowing this will help you to identity the types of offers that are most likely to help you generate new customers.
- **Business reply cards.** If sending out a reply card for consumers to return for more information, a free gift, or unique discount, code the card according to the message delivered, promotion offered, and customer segment represented by the recipient. The codes should be simple footnotes recognizable only to you, such as 12/2002–B–CS:12 to represent a December campaign, message B, customer segment 12.
- **Coupons.** Like business reply cards, a coupon distributed via direct mail, hard mail, or e-mail should be coded so that the impact of the offer and message can be measured.
- **Phone surveys.** Asking callers how they heard of you is not the most reliable metric, but it can be helpful.
- **Varying media frequency.** You also can test media frequency by using different frequencies in similar markets or different frequencies at

different times in the same media market. You will need to incorporate precise measuring devices such as those listed above to help you measure the impact of varying levels of frequency.

Tips and Tactics

Measure multiple aspects of your ads to help you gain a full understanding of what works and what does not. For example, you can measure

- The media outlet's impact on reaching customers
- The message's ability to generate inquiries
- The recall of the ad

Measurement of advertising efforts does not have to be reserved for big-business budgets. Small businesses or companies with limited budgets can conduct their own measurement activities such as those listed above. However, keep in mind that creating and executing your own tests may not yield scientifically valid results because they likely will not adhere to the statistical rules and guidelines employed by professional market research firms. However, they will give you a basic understanding of what works and what does not if they are conducted over a reasonable period of time.

Figure 10-1 is a sample test matrix that illustrates how you might go about determining which outlets and messages generate the greatest response. This is for illustration purposes only. Each test you conduct will need to be developed according to specific learning goals and market influences. Results from such a test will not take into account other market and promotional influences. When drawing assumptions from any test result, you will need to consider other factors in your marketplace, such as economic climate, seasonal influences, supply and demand, and so on.

Being able to track entry points to your business via separate phone numbers, URLs, business reply cards, and so on is critical to evaluating any type of advertising test. Do not rely on receptionists to ask callers where they heard of your business. This is highly unreliable because inquiries are not consistent, and neither are consumers' responses.

Figure 10-1 *Test Matrix to Determine Which Outlets and Messages Generate the Greatest Response*

Test	Newspaper	Radio	Magazine
Learn which vehicle generates the greatest response	Message A	Message A	Message A
	Promotion A	Promotion A	Promotion A
	URL A	URL A	URL A
	Message A	**Message B**	**Message C**
Identify which message generates the greatest response	Period 1— all outlets	Period 2— all outlets	Period 3— all outlets

If you do use mass media as part of your overall marketing program, make it work, and make it accountable. By testing different variables in the beginning, you will soon be able to maximize your investment and use mass media to fully support your more valuable marketing activities—lifetime marketing. If you do not know what works and what does not, you cannot eliminate waste from your budget and use your valuable resources in a manner that will most effectively build lifetime sales for your business.

Public Relations

The most credible form of mass communications is publicity, or brand mentions and features in the nonpaid media—the news. I often recommend that clients put their mass communications budgets toward public relations (PR) activities and leave advertising to the companies that have money to burn. By working with the media, you can generate more credibility than you could ever buy. However, there are some disadvantages, which is why many companies do both advertising and PR activities. These include

- **Lack of control.** The news media can choose whether or not to use your story idea or interview your company spokespersons and can determine which, if any, of your key message points to include in a story, providing you get mentioned. The media controls the words, headlines, length, and so on. You do not get a chance to preview the story before it gets published, so you are totally at the mercy of a third party.

- **Time.** Getting your story printed takes a great deal more time than buying media space and producing an ad. It often can take months to develop credibility with an editor and convince him or her to use your story angle and company as a resource or focal point in a news story. If it is imperative that you get your message out right away and generate visibility for your brand, you will need to supplement your publicity efforts with another form of communication. Advertisements that look like news articles or news programs on TV, "advertorials" and "infomercials," are marketers' attempts to capture the credibility of the news medium on their own terms and within their circle of control.

- **Potential backfire.** The job of the news media is to report both sides of a story. If there is a potential down side to your story or negative consumer issues involving your product category, your publicity efforts could backfire. Even though an editor might seem favorable to you and your brand, he or she could use your company as an example of what is wrong with your industry or shed some other potentially damaging perspective. Always keep industry issues in mind when promoting your stories to the media.

There are several ways to personalize your public relations efforts and give them a lifetime marketing spin. These include

- **Developing press release messages that address specific customer segments.** You can develop story outlines accordingly to specific customer segments' needs and current issues. Because the only cost of PR visibility is the cost of your time or your agency if you go that route, you can prepare many more story suggestions and message themes than with paid advertising. Just make sure that your story themes are relevant to your most valuable customer segments and newsworthy to the media. Reporters and editors want news or information that provides value to their readers by enlightening them about an important issue, sheds new light on an old topic, teaches them how to do something critical (for example, how to develop a winning Web page), or saves money on information technology (IT) purchases. How-to lists are often popular with the media.

- **Incorporating case studies into your stories.** By telling customers about another customer's personal experience with your brand and the results generated, you are enlightening prospects about the type of experience they too can have with your brand. While the story may not reflect their specific situation, it likely will strike a personal chord if it is developed correctly. Whenever possible, include before and after data in your case studies to show how a customer or a customer's business was directly affected by your product or service. Statistics add credibility immediately and show quantitative results that are critical to many consumers as they progress through the decision process.

Always include in your publicity material the name of an individual for the media or even consumers to call. This contact should be someone who can relate to the customer—the media representative—on a personal level both effectively and quickly. Prompt follow-up to any inquiries is key to starting a personal relationship off on the right foot.

PR is a very powerful medium for establishing and strengthening a brand's position. It can position your company as a valuable resource, innovator, and market leader if it is done correctly. There are many ways to do this.

- **Educational stories.** First, educational press releases are highly valuable to the media and consumers alike. For the media, it is their job to educate, and these tools, if written objectively, help them do their job faster. For the consumer, they provide valuable information that can help them make complex choices or decisions. Educational press releases typically cover how-to themes such as how to shop for high-tech equipment, what to look for when choosing a general contractor to build your home, what criteria should you insist on from your child's summer camp, and so on. The idea is to share valuable information that supports the decision process for your most valuable customers and to position your company as the leading source for industry information for media and consumer inquiries.

- **Friction.** According to the PR director for a leading national newspaper, "Reporters like friction. They need friction to find dramatic stories." He suggests that for businesses to get attention and story commitments from editors, they must identify the issues causing friction in the current environment and then try to tie into those trends and patterns. He advises, "Try to illuminate issues behind the trends editors are reporting on and build a story that is unique. Relevancy is key here." Again, develop stories on the friction that most strongly tugs at the heartstrings or consciences of the customers most likely to react, and choose story themes that will position your brand in a manner that is most appealing to your most appealing customers.

- **Create original and "new" news.** The media wants to write about stories that reflect the public pulse on issues relevant to their publications. By conducting a brief survey among key constituents of select trade publications, you can provide editors with valuable new information that makes them look smart and positions your company as the market leader. For example, American Express's Travelers Cheque Division wanted statistical support for its claim that the best gift is often one that is chosen by the recipient. Around Valentine's Day one year, the division polled numerous people to find out what was the strangest Valentine's Day gift they ever received. They wrote a press release around the results and suggested that people give American Express Gift Cheques instead of edible ties and the like. The story was clever, newsy, and got the brand's key messages across in a way that was meaningful to the media and consumers.

Conducting original surveys that produce scientifically valid results is typically an expensive endeavor reserved for large businesses. However, small businesses can conduct informal surveys on lesser scales. The key is to make sure that you do not make any population inferences or imply that the survey was bigger or more sophisticated than it really was. Be sure to communicate clearly how the information was gathered, who provided the information, and that your results do not indicate population trends.

When creating a survey for news-related purposes, keep in mind

- **Brevity.** Keep your survey brief and targeted. Ask only questions that need to be asked and that provide you with relevant information.
- **Accuracy.** Make sure that your questions are carefully worded so that the answers you get truly reflect the questions you are asking. This is where a market research specialist is valuable. You may want to create a list of questions that you believe are relevant to the marketplace in general and hire a market research specialist to review them to make sure that the data you will receive are as accurate and unbiased as possible.
- **Relevancy.** Ask questions that reflect the claim you want to make. Sometimes it is actually a good idea to work backwards by first formulating

the headline you hope to be able to communicate to the media and then build the questions that will get the data to back it up. This exercise will keep you focused and help you to draft meaningful questions.

- **Privacy policy.** Make sure that respondents know how you will use their information and whether or not their names and identities will be shared with other parties. This applies to all types of surveys, not just those prepared for PR purposes.

For help in generating a survey and determining its statistical significance, go to *www.mra-net.org*. You will find project calculators to help you determine the appropriate sample size, confidence intervals, and potential response and completion rates.

Tips and Tactics

Create press releases that are newsworthy and provide valuable information to a viable consumer segment. Press releases can contain information on industry trends, how-to tips, product reviews, and so on.

When preparing any type of information to send to the media, make sure that it is newsworthy. Sending promotional or nonnewsworthy stories will cause you to lose credibility so that when you do have something of value to say, nobody notices. Newsworthy themes include

- New product launches or introductions
- How-to suggestions and tips about new products or technology
- Industry and business trends
- Personnel news
- Awards, recognitions
- Acquisitions, mergers
- New technological developments
- Presentations made by personnel
- Community service projects, charitable donations, and so on

The media is always in search of good how-to stories that enlighten readers about how to do something better or differently or apply a new solution to an old problem. Figure 10-2 is a press release that sets forth a new idea or perspective for an established industry. This press release was highly effective in generating news coverage on both a national and a local level and positioning the company's founder as a credible leader in his field.

Figure 10-2 *A Press Release That Sets Forth a New Perspective for an Established Industry*

FOR IMMEDIATE RELEASE

Pioneer of Learning Technologies Urges Trainers to Change Perspective
Founder of Generation21 Presents Benefits of Individualized Learning Tools

Golden, CO—May 22, 2002 "Training is not an event, it is a continual process," Dale Zwart, founder and CTO of Generation21 Learning Systems told an audience of trainers and IT professionals at the company's third annual Knowledge Management conference in Englewood, CO, last week.

According to Zwart, successful training programs are those that enable employees to access job-critical information when they need it most—on the job. By being able to retrieve instructional information, procedural documents, research reports, organizational memos, etc. instantaneously, and from remote locations, employees can learn continually and thus complete tasks without interruption, preserving work schedules and meeting customer expectations. Yet most organizations continue to spend the majority of their budgets on formalized training programs that require time away from the job to complete, and result in low retention rates and overall inefficiencies.

- A recent study by Corporate Exchange University shows that 70% of online learners never complete their courses.
- A recent poll conducted by Generation21 among registrants to *www.gen21.com* indicated that learners turn to peers for information before accessing formal training programs.

These figures point to the need for a change in focus regarding training programs says Zwart, who encourages trainers to integrate both formal and informal training programs and find ways to make organizational knowledge more readily available. By providing learners with Instant Knowledge™, or immediate access to nuggets of information, they can increase the return on their training investments, and more positively impact organizational goals. He also urges trainers to consider the following perspectives in order to build highly effective learning programs:

(continues)

Figure 10-2 *continued*

- Information is a product that you need to manage.
- Trainers must meet learners' needs.
- Leverage organizational knowledge.

For a full copy of Zwart's presentation or more information about individualized learning or Generation21, please send an e-mail to *info@gen21.com*.

About Generation21 Learning Systems

TKM is the only comprehensive software system proven to deliver exceptional organizational performance by collecting, managing, and distributing all types of information to employees and customers—when and where they need it. Its uniqueness lies in its single-source demand-based knowledge database, which stores all the vital information staff members need to do their jobs well, and uses Universal Knowledge Object™ technology to ensure that this information is always current, consistent, and readily available. In addition, the TKM system provides customization for each learner, and maintains all content in a database for immediate on-the-job reference—a key element of the Instant Knowledge™ performance support feature. Access the Generation21 Web site at *www.gen21.com*. Generation21 is a subsidiary of Renaissance Learning Inc. (Nasdaq: RLRN), a leading provider of educational software and training.

This press release contains forward-looking statements made pursuant to the safe harbor provision of the Private Securities Litigation Reform Act of 1995, including statements regarding the introduction of new products and services. Any such forward-looking statements may involve risk and uncertainties that could cause actual results to differ materially from any future results encompassed within the forward-looking statements. Factors that could cause or contribute to such differences include those matters disclosed in the Renaissance Learning Inc.'s (formerly doing business as Advantage Learning Systems Inc.) Securities and Exchange Commission filings.

Press releases can be simple and still be highly effective. Note the press release shown in Figure 10-3 could be used by any brand of pet supply store to promote fun, relationship-initiating activities. Again, your imagination is the limit. The more fun or valuable the event, the more likely it is to get published.

Getting your story published takes more than just sending out a press release. For feature-type stories, you will want to follow up with specific editors via phone or e-mail to pitch a more detailed story to them. Your job is to

Figure 10-3 *A Press Release That Could Be Used by a Pet Store*

FOR IMMEDIATE RELEASE

Lights, Camera, STAY!

Town USA, January 1—Finally, your Felix, Max, or Henrietta will get their long overdue chance at fame.

ABC Pets is hosting its first-annual Pet Photo Contest that could make your pet the talk (or bark) of the town. Just bring in a favorite photo of your most beloved pet by February 1, 2002, and let fate determine the rest.

"Our pets are such an important part of our lives," said John Doe, owner of ABC Pets. "It's about time we get to show them off publicly and put their best paw, wing, or fin forward. We're very excited to give the pets of Town USA a chance to shine."

Photos will be judged according to creativity, originality, and expression. Categories include candid, posed, and creative (costume, stunts, etc.). All photos should be at least 5 inches × 7 inches and accompanied by a brief essay describing the pet, its personality, and the circumstances surrounding the photo. Winning photos will be displayed for one month at ABC Pets and will be submitted to the local newspapers for further exposure.

Entry forms can be picked up at ABC Pets at 111 Main Street from 9 a.m.–5 p.m. For more information, please call Jane Doe at 555.5625.

About ABC Pets

ABC Pets is a full-service pet supply store offering comprehensive product and service lines for dogs, cats, reptiles, and fish.

Tips and Tactics

Establish good working relationships with editors covering your industry. Position yourself as a source of credible, newsworthy information, not someone seeking free publicity.

personalize the story to their specific needs and illustrate the value to their specific audience. Offering editors an exclusive story when appropriate is a good way to build strong rapport with the media outlets you value most. Many publications will request an exclusive. Just make sure that you offer exclusives to the outlet that reaches the greatest number of your most valuable customers.

Beyond having a good story to tell, the secret to getting your story published is to build personal relationships with the editors in much the same way that you do with consumers. Do your homework. Get to know editors' specific needs, review their editorial calendars (often posted on Web sites), and get to know what their deadlines are. Many PR executives host breakfasts or lunch briefings with selected editors on a regular basis to share news and to strengthen personal relationships.

Direct Marketing

The fact that marketing agencies get excited about a 1 to 3 percent response rate from a direct mail campaign pretty much sums up this medium. Direct mail used to be one of the most widely used ways to communicate with customers for up-selling, cross-selling, and repeat-selling purposes. However, its effectiveness has declined sharply as e-mail and other more interactive methods of communication have taken hold.

According to Mark Jacobson, a direct marketing consultant specializing in fund raising for nonprofit organizations, the payoffs from traditional direct mail programs have changed drastically over the past 20 years. In the 1980s, the standard for a response rate was between 1 and 3 percent, and the cost might be 23 cents a piece, which included postage. Customers were satisfied with these figures. Now most organizations struggle to reach a 1 percent response rate on a cold mailing or one sent to names on a rented list rather than an in-house list of qualified leads or customers. At one time, the Direct Marketing Association (DMA) stated that the average direct mail campaign cost about $98,000 to reach 100,000 customers.

Typical costs for mailings average 60 to 75 cents per piece mailed, not including the postage, which typically is around 18 cents per piece. Thus, if you mailed out 10,000 pieces at a cost of 70 cents each plus 18 cents each in postage, you spent $8800. Let's say that you achieved the typical return of 1 percent (actually less in real life) and that your average return was $50 in donations or net profit, depending which side of the tax law you work on. This means that you gained $5000 after spending $8800 for a loss of $3800. This is not going to keep you in business for very long.

To compensate for the dismal returns achieved, direct mail companies changed the method of measuring effectiveness. Campaigns used to be measured by the cost per dollar earned. Some organizations have switched to measuring effectiveness by the cost per new donor or customer acquired. This is largely due to the fact that companies likely will lose money to initiate a new relationship but will make money over the long term by capturing the lifetime value of those new customers. Jacobson claims that more than 90 percent of nonprofit organizations lose money in the first transaction with a new customer achieved through direct mail. This number is even higher for most campaigns launched by commercial companies.

So why conduct direct mail campaigns? And how do you make them effective? Direct marketing—e-mail and direct mail via targeted databases—when done correctly, is much more effective over the long term than any form of mass advertising. By executing personalized mail campaigns versus mass direct mail campaigns, you can achieve quite high returns. The Royal Bank of Canada saw its response rate to direct marketing efforts rise above the industry average of 3 percent to as high as 30 percent after basing its campaigns on a customer-segmentation strategy.

Benefits of personalized direct marketing include

- **Increased retention rate.** Personalized direct marketing can make people feel emotionally attached to a brand and valued thus giving them a sense of personal equity and belonging.
- **Enhanced referral rates.** Highly satisfied customers with brand attachment are most likely to refer other customers. When customers are given rewards and incentives through personalized direct marketing, referrals tend to go up.
- **Higher sales volume.** Loyal customers are the best prospects for up-selling and cross-selling. When communicating with these groups, response rates are higher.
- **Lower direct costs.** Database marketing can reduce business costs by changing channels of distribution or allowing companies to better generate sales directly with end users. Insurance companies, credit card companies, and cellular phone companies are examples of types of businesses that have reduced direct costs through the proactive use of

customer databases. A software company might earn 90 percent of sales revenue when selling direct and only 50 percent when selling through retailers.

- **Lower marketing costs.** By marketing to targeted and qualified database groups, businesses minimize advertising waste and typically experience higher response rates, thus lowering the cost per lead. Because of the low-cost to execute many direct marketing campaigns, especially e-mail campaigns, you can afford to test various messages and promotions to fine-tune your marketing efforts and thus execute highly efficient programs over the long term.

Direct marketing is most effective when targeting customers within a database rather than an entire database en masse. The principles of mass advertising apply to in-house databases as well. If you send the same message to everyone in your database, your response rate will be lower than if you send targeted and relevant messages to specific customer segments. Again, the recency, frequency, and monetary (RFM) analysis is a successful approach to direct marketing.

Figure 10-4 shows the differences in results when marketing to a full database, sample database, or customers with the highest RFM scores.

Figure 10-4 *Full Database versus Partial Database Marketing Results*

	Sample Mailing	Full-Database Mailing	RFM Mailing
Response rate	1.58	1.34	2.54
Responses	474	13,434	7,394
Net revenue	$16,590	$470,120	$258,790
Pieces mailed	30,000	1,000,000	290,763
Total costs	$16,500	$550,000	$159,902
Profit	$90	($79,880)	$98,888

Note: *Sample data only.*

Like any lifetime marketing program, direct mail is most effective when sent to customers, not prospects, and when based on a customer's most recent history with your organization. It can be a very successful medium if it is highly personalized. The best form, of course, is a hand-written note in a hand-addressed envelope. Clearly, this is not practical for a business wanting to reach hundreds of people in one campaign. This is where the value of having subsegments comes in—allowing you to create specific messages and letters for each customer subsegment and thus personalize your message to many at the same time. Again, a letter to dog owners who perceive dogs as children in fur coats needs to be different from a letter going to dog owners who see dogs as hunting animals or sports companions.

One of the biggest reasons businesses fail to benefit from direct mail campaigns, says Jacobson, is that they do not track and record customers' past transactions properly. Marketers first need to learn why people chose to do business with their brand in the first place. They also need to understand why their customers purchased in one year and not the next. Direct mail communications, whether e-mail or hard mail, need to directly address these reasons and build on them. For example, if one of your customer segments is highly price conscious and a discount promotion first brought them to your place of business, then you need to continue to communicate special discounts and sales to this segment. If another purchases from your business only at Christmas time, you need to make sure that they are at the top of your holiday messages list.

Marketers also need to test the effectiveness of various messages and letters. Testing direct mail simply involves sending out various messages to specific customer groups, coding those messages, and then recording the return. You can create different response mechanisms for each message you test. For example, if you want to compare the effectiveness of two different promotions, you could send a message on a price discount to 50 percent of your database for customer segment A and a message on a free gift with purchase to the other half. Those receiving the price-discount message would be directed to a different URL or phone number than those receiving the free-gift message. By tracking the new leads generated to these mechanisms, you can get a fairly good idea which promotion is going to result in the most incremental business.

Testing various message themes is also critical to successful marketing. Some customers are likely to respond to highly emotional messages, and others are not. Some companies actually test the "emotional threshold" of their target consumers by running ads with varying levels of fear among clusters of customers with similar profiles. In most cases, companies have found that there is an emotional threshold for advertising messages, and when you cross that line, customers tend to disconnect from your ad and your message and thus your product.

There are several advertising variables worth testing through direct mail campaigns, including

- Price discounts versus free gifts.
- e-Mail versus hard mail.
- Response mechanisms—toll-free phone numbers versus Web sites versus business-response cards.
- Emotional appeals—these need to be based on the values of the targeted customer group. The level and presentation of the appeal is what you are testing.
- Topics of interest related to your product or service.

A critical success factor for direct communications in any format, print or Internet-based, is to keep it relevant. If your message is not highly relevant to consumers' needs and their relationship with your brand, you will lose credibility, waste your marketing resources, and risk losing customers.

Following are some relevant communications themes for direct marketing that work well either via print or e-mail:

- **Thank-you notes.** Thanking customers for their business goes a long way and typically costs little. Sending thank-you notes, hand-written or mass-produced, keeps your name alive in front of a valued customer and helps consumers bond with a brand. Thank-you notes should be just that, not another sales message. A subtle way to encourage sales via thank-you notes is to offer a discount as a thank-you gift on the next purchase within a specified time period.
- **Lapsed-customer communication.** Identifying once-valuable customers who have lapsed is an important part of any lifetime marketing program. These customers once were attached to your brand and, for some reason, have lost their connection. Correspond with them to find out why. If they have left for life-cycle reasons, for example, they have reached the end of their need for your product or service, take them off your list. If they have lapsed due to brand switching, loss of interest, or convenience issues, offer them a reason to try your brand again. Discounts, free gifts, or new convenience-based services often will help to rekindle an old flame.
- **Imminent offers.** A highly relevant form of lifetime marketing is to refer to a customer's past purchases with you and offer the customer acces-

sories or upgrades. If this is done immediately after the purchase, the success rate is higher because the consumer still has the product or service on his or her mind and is likely thinking about related products or activities. Offer customers discounts or other incentives related to their most recent purchase.

- **Gift-giving reminders.** This is an effective form of advertising for most retailers, especially jewelers, clothing boutiques, floral shops, and so on.
- **Newsletters.** Only do a newsletter if it is highly appropriate for your audience. There are far too many newsletters in this world and far too many that go unread. If you do a newsletter, save the trees, and make it digital. Generation21 Learning Systems produces a highly effective newsletter and e-mails it to nearly 10,000 customers each quarter. Many analyst firms produce regular e-newsletters that are widely read throughout their industry. When a newsletter delivers relevant and desirable information, the response rate is typically strong because it keeps people up to date about a product they have an expressed interest in, and it offers industry trends, not just product news.

Steadman Hawkins Sports Medicine Foundation produces every quarter a lengthy newsletter in print form that looks much like a small medical journal due to the number of pages and type-intensive articles. Yet it is highly effective and has generated many donations and media stories in and of itself simply because it provides highly relevant information for the audience, and the audience is passionate about what the foundation does. Their articles are written for both medical and lay constituencies, making it valuable to all its key customer segments. The foundation sends it out in hard form largely in part because its audiences have higher usage rates with hard copy versus digital copy. Many of the recipients are retired persons and doctors who do not spend hours in front of a computer.

Newsletters should reflect the core values of your customer segments and subsegments. You can create a newsletter for each segment or rotate features and articles that appeal to your various segments in a general newsletter. Always share valuable information that your readers can use; do not just shout about how wonderful your business is. Remember, it is called a *news*letter because it is designed to share news, not promotional messages. Always provide information that simplifies the decision process for your customer segments and positions your business as the expert who can provide them with valuable information.

Reward customers for reading your newsletters. Newsletters that reward customers for reading them by offering discounts or news of valuable benefits or savings can be highly successful. American Express's Membership Reward newsletters are highly read because of all the cost-saving announcements they contain.

The key to successful newsletters is to

- Make sure that your customer segments seek the type of information you plan to distribute.
- Produce the newsletter to reflect the audience's reading habits, for example, have time or desire to read full articles due to job-critical content or scan headlines only.
- Make sure that you distribute newsletters in a format this is most appropriate for your readers' lifestyles.

Tips and Tactics

If you produce a newsletter, write it to address the customer segments you are targeting, deliver it in a format that best reflects their lifestyles—digital versus print—and provide incentives for reading it such as information about price discounts, special offers, and so on.

- **Announcements.** Give your customers the courtesy of hearing new news from you first and the media second. Whenever you distribute a press release, send out a copy to your internal and external databases either simultaneously or ahead of time. This also helps ensure that your news gets read. You cannot control the usage rates of a press release, so if you have news you want customers to hear, send them copies of your press releases. Also send them letters or notes updating them about new products or acquisitions—anything that shows that you are a growing and progressive business, one that is worthy of their business and loyalty.
- **Satisfaction surveys.** Even though they may not take the time to respond to a survey, customers appreciate knowing that you want to hear from

them and value their input. Sending a brief survey is also another nonpushy way to get your name in front of them and get them thinking about your brand and offerings.

Overall, direct marketing, when executed according to lifetime marketing principles, pays off over the long term. Organizations need to view direct marketing as a learning tool and one that pays off for the long term rather than as a method for generating short-term gains or quickly moving unwanted inventory. Those that do and do it right will experience positive returns, typically far greater than with any other form of marketing.

Getting Started—Lifetime Marketing Checklist

Before conducting mass media campaigns, review the following checklists. A digital copy of these checklists can be found at www.mcmurtrygroup.com.

Advertising and Public Relations Checklist

1. Develop your ads to appeal to your most valuable customers. Write to an individual who reflects the values, influencers, and needs of your best customers.
2. Always build in metrics so that you can determine which media, vehicles, messages, and promotions are most effective for which customer segments.
3. Make PR activities a top priority.
4. Build personal relationships with editors and producers. They need you as much as you need them. Treat them like a most valued customer group—listen to their needs, send them only relevant and valuable information, and follow up with story ideas that fit their needs, schedules, and deadlines.
5. Identify news themes that are meaningful to the public and the media. Develop these stories and distribute them appropriately.
6. Prepare how-to and other types of educational stories frequently and distribute them to the media and consumers.

Direct Mail Checklist

1. Prepare separate campaigns for each customer segment, thus making your message highly personal and relevant.
2. Prioritize your mailings. Spend your resources developing and distributing messages and offers to the groups most likely to respond and to spend the most money over their lifetime.
3. Use direct marketing activities to learn about your customers and weed out the profitable from the unprofitable. Remember, direct marketing is a long-term initiative.
4. Present communications in a series. Do not expect your first mailing to pay off right away. Research shows that three exposures to a message increase the likeliness of a response.

5. Keep your messages clear, concise, and to the point. Make sure that everything you say is meaningful and useful to readers and applies directly to their needs, not your own.

6. Always keep in mind the educational level and product familiarity level of your audience and write appropriately.

7. Always test your messages, promotions, and lists. Otherwise, you will be wasting a critical opportunity to learn about your customers and how to build effective marketing campaigns. You also will learn how to use your resources to their highest efficiency.

8. Code your campaigns so that you can determine which segments best responded to which messages and promotions. You can code business reply cards or use different phone numbers and URLs in ads with different messages or placed in different outlets to see which variables produce the greatest results.

Promotions Checklist

1. Define the primary goals you hope to accomplish through mass advertising.

2. Focus on the customer segments that are the most likely to respond to advertising.

3. Identify which advertising media are most likely to reach your selected customer segment through customer surveys and appropriate research.

4. Determine which brands of media—for example, which newspapers, radio stations, magazines, and so on—are most used by your customer segments.

5. Establish your learning goals early on in the planning process. For example, what do you hope to learn from your advertising—the best messages, outlets, or emotional appeals for specific segments?

6. Implement a method for measuring the responses to your ads? For example, unique URLs, phone numbers, reply cards, and so on.

7. Identify any educational themes associated with your product or service that you can develop into newsworthy story angles for local, regional, and national media outlets.

8. Determine how selected educational themes support your brand's key messages and develop your communications materials in ways that subtly highlight your brand's strengths.

9. Identify the most important messages to test among your customer and prospect bases, those that will enable you to develop highly relevant and effective future campaigns.

10. Test various promotions, such as free shipping, discounts, free gift with purchases, and so on, to help you learn what will generate the most attention and get the greatest response among your best customer segments.

For samples of the following types of lifetime marketing materials, please go to *www.mcmurtrygroup.com*:

- Thank-you letters
- Introductory letters
- Product announcements
- Sample press releases
- Sample newsletter articles
- Sample customer update letters

11 Writing and Executing a Customer-Oriented Marketing Plan

Using Customer Information to Create a Workable, Measurable, and Successful Marketing Plan

Once you have truly gotten to know and understand your customers inside and out and have identified those most valuable to you, you are prepared to write a customer-oriented marketing plan. The purpose of writing a plan is to define your strategies, priorities, commitments, and activities in a way that serves as a guide for all your marketing efforts.

Without a plan in place, it is too easy to end up with "rocking chair" marketing activities—those which keep you busy but do not get you anywhere. A marketing plan commits you and your company to a specific direction and guides your allocation of resources. My suggestion is that if a new idea for advertising or another form of marketing comes up and it does not support your marketing plan, then your budget should not support it.

This chapter sets forth a template for creating a customer-oriented plan and guides you through the overall process from analyzing your current marketplace to defining your strengths and weaknesses and key messages. A blank template for your development purposes is included at the end of this chapter and is available at my Web site, *www.mcmurtrygroup.com*.

Your marketing plan should address the following areas:

- Situation analysis
- Strengths
- Weaknesses
- Opportunities
- Threats
- Competitive analysis
- Marketing goals
- Objectives
- Target markets
- Positioning
- Key messages
- Actions
- Measurement

Situation Analysis

Your first step is to define and provide an overview of the circumstances currently facing your business, such as the market environment, economic influences, and strength of existing customer relationships. You might be in an industry that has lost the trust of the general public due to a recent scandal or health issue, or your product category may be facing pricing challenges or technological limitations, or there might be a lot of new entrants in your marketplace claiming to do what you do cheaper and faster. All these issues affect the environment in which you operate and market your business. You need to spell out the issues influencing your market as thoroughly as possible in order to have a strong understanding of how they may affect your business and your ability to operate successfully.

By identifying your circumstances, you can better recognize your challenges and define what is realistic to accomplish given the environment in which you are operating. You do not want to take on anything that might be too lofty or too ideal at the given time for your resources.

Your situation analysis also should address the nature of your customer relationships and current changes in your customers' attitudes toward your category, pricing, product features, and other key issues. For example, if your company is new, you might have shallow relationships with your current customers that need to be deepened in order to prevent competitors from taking them away. Circumstances that affect the way you do business or your ability to sell your product and/or services and have an impact on your sales efforts and overall potential also should be included in the "Situation Analysis" section (Figure 11-1).

Figure 11-1 *Sample Questions to Answer Concerning Your Situation*

Situation Overview Analysis

1. What are the current market circumstances that have the most compelling impact on your business?
2. Are there any prevailing consumer attitudes toward your business category that may affect your ability to operate as usual?
3. What stage of the market cycle is your industry experiencing? For example, is your market growing, mature, or declining?
4. What market trends have the potential to affect your company's ability to succeed?
5. Are there any economic, political, or environmental issues affecting your market?
6. What factors most influence consumers' decision processes for purchasing in your category, for example, price, convenience, status, and so on?
7. What is the overall market climate in terms of consumer demand, purchasing trends, industry sales volume, predicted growth, and so on?
8. How will pending technological and new product developments affect your market environment?
9. Describe the selling environment. Is it a tightly closed community, such as on "old boys' network," or an open field with lots of opportunities?
10. Describe the growth trend for your company. How does it compare with others in your industry?
11. What internal factors may affect your ability to meet business objectives and growth goals, for example, lack of resources and budget, management support, technology, and so on?
12. What is the level of brand recognition you currently have among your most valuable consumer segments?

Strengths, Weaknesses, Opportunities, Threats

Analysis of your strengths, weaknesses, opportunities, and threats (SWOT) is a fundamental part of any marketing plan. Yet, for these issues to guide you toward successful lifetime marketing, they need to be considered from the customers' perspectives rather than just yours. You need to rely on your experience and understanding of your business and marketplace and the feedback and perspectives of your customers and outside associates.

Strengths

When assessing your company's strengths, try to do so through your most valuable customers' eyes. Your marketing plan needs to be developed to help you generate steady revenues and capture the lifetime value of your most valuable customers and prospects. Therefore, you need to write it from their perspective. In this section, outline all the things you are doing right. This includes activities involving customer service, product development and quality, distribution, pricing, and so on. Include internal activities as well. You need to create a strong company culture and selling environment in order for your marketing efforts to be maximized.

Survey a random sample of your customers so that you can accurately answer the questions listed in Figure 11-2 about your brand's strengths.

Reviewing these and other pertinent issues from the perspective of your most valued customers will help you to readily identify the strengths that attract people to your brand and keep them coming back. By capitalizing on these strengths, growing them, and building new strengths that may be defined in the future, you are preparing yourself to become a lifetime business.

Weaknesses

It goes without saying that assessing the weaknesses of your business is the most difficult part of building a marketing plan. Yet it truly is the most important. No amount of customer profiling, personalization, or innovative lifetime marketing activities can compensate for poor quality, sloppy customer service, inconvenience, or a shallow product line. Trying to assess your weaknesses from an internal prospective is like trying to look at the back of your head without the use of a mirror. You simply cannot do it. You can only see all your weaknesses clearly from the outside.

Figure 11-2 *Sample Questions to Ask Yourself and Your Customers Concerning Your Strengths*

Strengths Analysis

Questions to ask yourself:

1. What strengths do you associate with your product, for example, quality, price, functionality, features, and so on?
2. What strengths do you associate with your service, for example, lenient return policy, responsive sales personnel, prompt reply to inquiries and service issues, and so on?
3. What strengths do you associate with your transaction process, for example, multiple selling channels, same-day delivery, multiple payment plans/options, and so on?
4. What strengths do you associate with your brand's impact on consumers' decision processes? For example, do you engage in activities that educate consumers and reinforce purchase decisions?
5. What strengths do you associate with customer retention? For example, is your customer retention above or below the industry average? What are you doing right to retain customers' loyalty?
6. What strengths do you associate with your company's employee culture, and how do these affect your customers' experience with your brand?
7. What strengths do you associate with your company's selling environment? For example, is your place of business customer friendly, does it project confidence and quality attention to detail and customers' needs, and so on?
8. What do employees praise about your company?
9. What strengths do you associate with your current marketing programs?
10. What do customers most praise about your business, products, or service?
11. What do you believe is your company's overall reputation in the marketplace?
12. Have you received any industry awards for your products or business programs?

Questions to ask customers:

1. What is the single most important attribute our brand offers you?
2. What features do you most strongly associate with our brand—convenience, price, status, service, and so on?
3. What benefits do you most associate with our product—quality, function, features, durability, and so on?
4. What are our strengths associated with product quality?
5. What are our strengths associated with customer service and product support?
6. What are our brand's strengths when compared with competing brands you have experienced?
7. Why did you choose our brand in the first place?
8. What motivates you to continue to do business with us, for example, incentives or programs we offer to reward your loyalty?
9. What are our strengths associated with customer communications and marketing?
10. What are our brand's greatest strengths from your experience in doing business with us?

The best way to determine what is wrong with your brand or what could jeopardize a customer's lifetime loyalty is to ask the customer directly. Send your customers a satisfaction survey, and give them an incentive to complete it. This could be a discount off their next purchase or a free gift—just make sure that it is something of direct value to them, as discussed in previous chapters. Your customer satisfaction survey should address all aspects of your brand and also should let your customers express themselves. Do not just give them questions that require yes or no answers.

Make sure that your survey covers customer service as well as your product quality and features and overall shopping experience. When products appear to be equal, the primary differentiator between competing products is often service. This is one of the most important areas for you to explore.

Customer complaints are another good way to determine your weaknesses. Smart businesses do not just respond to complaints; they encourage them. Market research shows that companies retain 90 percent of their customers who received resolutions to complaints. Discovering what you are doing wrong and then making it right helps you to retain existing customers and avoid offending new ones. Resolving complaints simply makes the customer feel valued and appreciated. For the purpose of building a customer-oriented marketing plan, receiving complaints is valuable because they reveal critical issues regarding your product, service, and competitive environments that you otherwise might not have discovered. You can learn what is wrong with your product or your service and find out about the little things you had not thought of yet that mean a lot to customers.

There are several ways to encourage customers to share their complaints rather than keep quiet and assign their loyalty elsewhere. These include

- Sending out periodic customer satisfaction surveys
- Listing complaint hotline numbers on receipts, on point-of-sale materials, and on business cards
- Distributing comment cards at the point of sale
- Sending e-comment cards or brief surveys to customers regarding specific transactions
- Asking them in person via telephone or at the time of sale

Other weaknesses that are not directly related to customers' experiences with your product also need to be addressed in your lifetime marketing plan. These issues deal with your selling environment, distribution, market position, brand awareness and visibility, and competitive environment.

As you identify weaknesses, try to identify solutions as well. For example, if credibility is a weakness, your plan needs to include activities that illustrate the knowledge and expertise of your business and position your team members as leaders in your field. Your goals and activities should directly address strengthening your weak points and overcoming your challenges.

Figure 11-3 lists some questions you should ask yourself and your customers to help you to determine your weaknesses.

Figure 11-3 *Sample Questions to Ask Yourself and Your Customers Concerning Your Weaknesses*

Weaknesses Analysis

Questions to ask yourself:

1. What weaknesses do you associate with your product, for example, quality, price, functionality, features, and so on?
2. What weaknesses do you associate with your service, for example, not enough personnel and other resources to respond quickly?
3. What weaknesses do you associate with your brand's impact on consumers' decision processes?
4. What weaknesses do you associate with customer retention?
5. What weaknesses do you associate with customer acquisition or lead conversion?
6. What weaknesses do you associate with your company culture? How could these be affecting your selling environment?
7. What weaknesses do you associate with your marketing efforts?
8. What do employees say are your company's greatest weaknesses?
9. How do your weaknesses compare with those of your competitors?
10. What obstacles are in the way of your eliminating your weaknesses?

Questions to ask customers:

1. Have you had any problems with our product's performance and other quality issues? With customer service and sales support?
2. Do you have any concerns about our responsiveness to inquiries or customer service issues?
3. Do you find our promotions, rewards, and so on relevant and beneficial?
4. Are our communications timely, relevant, and of personal value to you?
5. Do you have any feedback regarding our policies on returns, exchanges, and so on?
6. How does our brand compare with competing brands you have experienced?
7. On a scale of 1 to 5 with 5 being high, how satisfied are you with our brand?
8. In what, if any, areas do you believe our company can improve?

Opportunities

Opportunities come in many forms—new users, new product uses, new markets, economic boosts, market developments, changes in the competitive climate, and so on. To recognize opportunities, you need to stay abreast of both your market conditions and customer needs and attitudes. If you understand your customers and your marketing circumstances, you will be able to more easily identify new avenues and strategies for revenue growth.

Years ago, Arm & Hammer significantly boosted its sales of baking soda by marketing a new use for its product—as an air freshener for refrigerators. Someone on the company's team recognized a consumer problem the company was prepared to solve and thus created a new use for an existing product. This single move generated significant amounts of incremental revenue without high overhead costs in research and development, testing, and product and packaging design. It simply involved a new marketing and positioning campaign.

Economic factors also must be factored into your opportunities. If your market is experiencing a slowdown due to a lagging economy, be creative. Can you adapt your product to make it more applicable or affordable to a new audience such as students versus established professionals? Can you expand your services to include a lower-cost option to maintain your cash flow during difficult or changing times? After the September 11, 2001, terrorist attacks on New York and Washington, the U.S. economy took a very hard hit. Resort towns and other travel destinations geared up for one of their worst years in recent history. Rather than sit back and wait for sales to slump and layoffs to become inevitable, smart marketers started looking for new opportunities. Some resort hotels offered huge discounts that served as a low-cost introduction to an audience that otherwise might not have considered their locations. Other companies started looking at new markets. Builders who traditionally focused on large commercial or residential properties started pursuing remodeling contracts that would help to expand their services far beyond a temporary economic downturn. Venture capitalists started looking at new ways to keep the investment market alive.

Customers quite often reveal opportunities through requests or special needs. A retailer of children's toys in a small resort town near my home was frequently asked by customers to help them get durable outdoor clothing for hiking and rugged outdoor activities for their children. These requests identified a new revenue-stream opportunity for the retailer. When conducting customer satisfaction surveys, ask leading questions regarding needs and desires that will help you

Figure 11-4 *Sample Questions to Ask Yourself Concerning New Opportunities for Your Brand*

Opportunity Analysis

1. What potential new uses exist for your product?

2. Which customer segments are most likely to benefit from any identified potential new uses? What is the core value of these new uses?

3. Can your product or service be adapted easily to appeal to specific needs of new audiences, for example, teens or seniors?

4. How can you adapt your product, service, or transaction process to address changes in consumer technology or market trends in general?

5. How can you adapt your product, distribution, or pricing to accommodate new or anticipated changes in consumer demands, attitudes, and use patterns?

6. What new technological developments could improve your products or business processes?

7. What partnerships or alliances can be formed within your direct or vertical industries that can boost your brand's exposure?

8. Are any competitors leaving the marketplace, thus creating prospects looking for a new vendor?

9. What new ideas, product uses, or technological developments do customers need to be educated about?

10. Is your market growing or declining? How can you adapt your business to address change?

to identify opportunities in line with customers' current and anticipated needs and your business goals. Figure 11-4 lists some sample questions you may want to ask yourself.

Threats

Like opportunities, threats or challenges come in several different forms, some with imminent implications and others more long term. Smith-Corona presents a good example of what happens to a company that ignores threats from functional alternatives. In the 1980s, computer developers were coming out with small, easy-to-use, and affordable computers designed for personal use in businesses and at home. Smith-Corona chose to ignore the growing trend and kept its focus on being the best typewriter company in the world. In just a few short years, typewriters became obsolete, and Smith-Corona became a name associated only with antiques and collectibles. Another leading producer of typewriters responded to the threat and pursued new product developments to keep up with changing technologies and customer needs. As a result, Royal Consumer Business Products (now owned by Olivetti Office USA, another past producer of typewriters) is still around, producing personal digital assistants (PDAs), calculators, organizers, time-management systems for payroll processes, and several other business tools.

Just like technology, customers change too. If you are marketing a product exclusively for teenagers, how will your business be affected when the current group of 12- to 20-year-olds matures? Will the next generation have the same interests? Will the population be larger or smaller? Lifetime companies continuously think ahead to ensure that their profit streams continue far beyond the current fiscal year, even beyond the consuming generation.

Like change, lack of visibility and brand recognition also can threaten the longevity and profitability of your business. Consumers, especially when making highly involved decisions, tend to choose established brands with proven track records, even if it means paying more. Consumers seek comfort in the decisions they make. The want to be comfortable knowing that they made a good decision, that they are getting value for their investment, and that they will be taken care of if anything goes wrong. A brand with high visibility tends to have more credibility with consumers making involved or risky decisions. Brands that do not have high levels of visibility are most often at a significant disadvantage when competing for new business.

If you are a newcomer to a marketplace, you have the additional threat or challenge of breaking into sometimes a closed, tight market community. The construction trade is a good example of this. Many decisions are based on long-lasting relationships with contractors and suppliers such as plumbers and electricians, many of which are strengthened at "boys' nights" at the local pool hall. If you are new and do not have as many deep-rooted relationships as your competitors do, you face the threat of being left out of bid processes and future jobs. Initiating relationships with established influencers thus needs to be a top priority.

When assessing your external threats, keep in mind that these are likely the same threats that your competitors are facing and gearing up to meet. Pay attention to their strategic moves while you plan your own.

Businesses face internal threats as well as external threats. Internal threats include

- A poor company culture that breeds more politics than products or new ideas
- Unhappy, disgruntled employees
- Employees who feel no ownership or loyalty to your company

- Departments or divisions unable to pay for themselves or turn a profit and thus causing undue expenses
- Inefficient operations that affect profitability and pricing capabilities
- Lack of research and development
- Lack of employee training, which can cause your business to fall behind in product development, sales, service, and efficiency
- Lack of proper tools and technology to allow your employees to perform at their peak
- Poor customer service
- Lack of follow-through on customer complaints, requests, and expressed concerns

Virtually anything that can disrupt the ability of your business to perform at its peak and exceed customer expectations is an internal threat to your ability to capture lifetime value and long-term profitability.

Figure 11-5 lists questions you should ask yourself about threats to your business.

Figure 11-5 *Sample Questions to Ask Yourself Concerning Threats to Your Business*

Threats Analysis

1. What is the corporate culture that is filtering down to customers? Is it friendly, attentive, or negative in ways that could be making customers uncomfortable?

2. How established are you in your marketplace compared with key competitors?

3. Could your business be run more efficiently, for example, operations, research, sales, fulfillment, administration, and so on?

4. Do you engage in research and development activities that will keep you one step ahead of the competition?

5. Are your employees trained to perform in line with current standards or customer expectations?

6. Do you have the technological infrastructure, tools, and human capital to execute sound management programs such as customer resource management (CRM).

7. Is your market shrinking or growing in terms of sales volume?

8. Is the number of competitors growing or shrinking?

9. How strong is the barrier to entry in your marketplace? How are you protecting your business against this threat?

10. Do you have the resources and capital to adapt your operations to coincide with changes in demand and consumer needs?

Competitive Analysis

If you want to attract and keep the consumers with the highest propensity to purchase frequently and spend the most money per transaction, you need to thoroughly analyze your competition to make sure that what you offer is better and more appropriate to your customers' personal needs. Your competitive analysis should list your most dominant direct competitors—other brands that offer the same product or service that you do—and the functional alternatives—different products or services that fulfill the same basic need or function. For example, margarine is a functional alternative to butter, and a paper-based personal planning notebook is a functional alternative to a PDA such as Handspring or Palm. While Day-Timers and Handsprings are not direct competitors, they are functional competitors because they achieve the same end, just through a different means. Smart marketers address both.

To compete with a functional alternative, you have to educate potential users about the benefits of your category. To compete with a direct competitor, for example, Handspring versus Palm, you must educate potential purchasers about the advantages of your brand. Educational marketing is a long-term proposition, whereas brand marketing can have quicker returns because the potential audience likely already knows the category benefits and is comparing brands as part of the purchase process.

The purpose of conducting a competitive analysis is to identify influences that may be pulling potential users and even customers away from your brand to another brand or functional alternative. You also want to know what incentives your competitors provide to motivate customers to remain loyal to them throughout their purchasing lifetimes. Figure 11-6 lists some questions to include in your competitive analysis.

For answers to these questions, you likely will need to do an anonymous survey among your competitors' customers and some mystery shopping. Some of your customers, partners, and resellers who deal with your competitors may be able to shed some light on these issues as well.

Marketing Goals

As stated throughout this book, the main purpose of any lifetime marketing plan is to capture the lifetime value of your most valuable customers and prospects and thus level the playing field for your company and big business competitors.

Figure 11-6   *Sample Questions to Ask Yourself Concerning Your Brand's Competitiveness*

Competitive Analysis

1. Who are your most direct competitors—those with similar customers, resources, circumstances, and goals?

2. What are your competing functional alternatives?

3. What is your competition doing right (strengths compared with your strengths) in the following areas:

   - Price
   - Product line
   - Product feature and development
   - Customer service
   - Marketing and promotions
   - Discounts and incentives

4. What is your competition doing wrong (weaknesses compared with your weaknesses) in the following areas:

   - Price
   - Product line
   - Product features and development
   - Customer service
   - Marketing and promotions
   - Discounts and incentives

5. How do competitors add value to their products or service?

6. What types of programs do competitors offer that build brand equity?

7. How are your competitors' brands perceived by customers in terms of price, product quality, customer service, and value?

8. What new products or services have your competitors introduced in the past year?

9. How do your competitors' business resources compare with yours?

10. What marketing claims do your competitors make, and how successful are they in fulfilling them?

You need to set goals that focus directly on this outcome. Goals need to be measurable and realistic and attached to specific time frames. Otherwise, they are often nebulous and unobtainable. I try to develop marketing plans that set forth 6- and 12-month goals initially.

While you need to have long-term goals in place, you will achieve more in a shorter period of time if you focus on short-term goals first. Businesses need to achieve victories and celebrate successes along the way to long-term goal fulfillment. It is also easier to manage if you can set goals for each quarter and thus realistic action plans over a short time period. Keep in mind that your staff's, and even your own, attention span diminishes if the goals are too far out of sight. Too many times marketing plans set forth "pie in the sky" goals that are unrealistic given the resources of the business and market conditions. When this happens, marketers and management get frustrated, and marketing plans end up in file cabinets rather than on desktops.

Appropriate and measurable goals include

- Gain at least one new customer in a given time period.
- Increase customer retention by 15 percent during fiscal year.
- Increase annual value per customer by 10 percent via cross-selling and up-selling efforts.

Vague goals that cannot be measured easily include

- Become the best dry cleaning service in a 30-mile radius. How will you know when you have reached the status of "best" among your customers and prospects? How do you measure "best"? How does "best" affect your bottom line?
- Achieve market dominance. While this is every brand's dream, how realistic is this given your current market status? If you are a newcomer, can you really achieve dominance in a specific time frame? Do you need market dominance to achieve profitability goals? Do you actually have the capital, human resources, and other assets that will allow you to achieve this in 3 to 5 years? A more realistic goal might be to carve out a niche among a specific segment and dominate that niche.

Absolutely all your marketing activities should directly address your goals and objectives. Anything that is not directly related is a waste of money and resources. To stay efficient and successful, your activities must stay focused. It is easy to spend a lot of money by reacting to all the special offers your local print and broadcast outlets may bring to you, but if it does not fit your goals and appeal directly to your targeted customers, you are wasting valuable time and resources, no matter how good of a deal it might be.

Getting ownership of goals is critical. If your business is small, open up the goal-setting process to managers of various departments. Representatives from your customer service, sales, finance, product development, fulfillment, and operations should all be invited to a goal-setting meeting. Of course, you and your marketing manager will need to sort through suggestions and define priorities, but overall, you will gain more support from various team leaders and departments if you involve them in the beginning. When various groups within an organization have ownership of specific marketing tasks that relate to a specific goal, the company tends to work better and have a higher chance of success. If your goal is to increase incremental business from existing customers, your customer service team will need to be committed to achieving this goal through better implementation of up-selling and cross-selling efforts while interacting with customers. Without their buy-in and ownership of that specific task, your chances of success are greatly diminished.

Objectives

Your plan needs to address numerous objectives that will enable you to achieve your marketing goal. Objectives are actionable minigoals or necessary steps for achieving your universal goals. Actions need to be attached to each objective. If your goal is to acquire new customers, your objectives might look like this:

- Generate visibility for your brand and exposure for your key messages through public relations activities.
- Create forums for initiating new relationships through special events for prospects, partners, and industry leaders.
- Develop incentives that will help convert leads to customers.
- Assist target audiences with the purchase decision process through educational marketing.
- Pursue new markets, for example, seniors or students.

Target Markets

Again, your marketing plan needs to be written to appeal directly to your most valued customer groups, those which represent the greatest lifetime value potential. In this section you need to define these groups and any new markets worth pursuing. Your lifetime marketing plan should profile your top three to four core customer groups.

Back to the pet supply storeowner analogy. If you owned a pet supply store, your core customer groups again might be as follows:

- Dog owners
- Cat owners
- Tropical fish owners

You then need to address the groups that influence your core audiences. Often marketing plans address the end users and direct purchasers but fail to include the influencers. Influencers can be those who control the purse strings, such as parents, and those who request money to be spent, such as teenagers. Influencers often include entry-level managers, politicians, religious leaders, peers, teachers, business colleagues and superiors, industry leaders, and the media. By building relationships with the people who influence your core target audience's decision processes not only will you gain a valuable new referral source, but you likely could gain new clients as well.

Influencers for purchasers of pet supplies might include

- Veterinarians
- Other dog, cat, and fish owners
- Editors of *Dog Fancy* and *Cat Fancy*

A developer of corporate training software might target the following groups and influencers:

Primary customers:
- Training managers
- Information technology managers

Influencers:
- Human resources professionals
- Quality managers
- Regulatory affairs officers
- Chief information officers and chief operating officers

Next, list any environmental, emotional, or social influences. For example, a company marketing clothing to young girls must address their need to be popular, their desire to look like a certain role model or teen idol, and their insecurities about not fitting in with the crowd. They also have to consider social and environmental factors such as parents' rules about what young girls can and cannot wear, school dress codes, and so on.

After identifying your core customer groups and key influencers, you need to extrapolate key information from your customer segment profiles that will guide your message development, strategic actions, and communications channel selection. Profiles should include their values, lifestyle, product orientation, and so on.

Customer Profiles

You need to keep current customer profiles individually and collectively. Following is an example of some of the variables a software firm might include in its profile for corporate training managers.

General traits:
- Female skew, 65 percent/35 percent
- College educated
- Human resources (HR) skills and orientation
- Report to HR department
- Feel increased pressure to train more people in less time and for less money
- Need to expedite training process and results
- Accountable for impact of training on performance and budgets
- Responsible for elective and mandatory training
- Purchase responsibilities include training courses and technology
- Tend to be strivers—young professionals seeking career advancement
- Tend to have limited function of technological issues but understand features and benefits

Influencers:
- Vice president of direct department
- Information technology (IT) officers
- Department heads and line managers
- Regulatory affairs officers
- Budget
- Simplicity of product use, installation, and integration
- Proven outcomes—case studies
- Industry and media reports
- Counterparts at other companies

Marketing priorities should be given to customers, customer groups, and influencers with the greatest potential return. If you have not done an analysis to determine the weight each of your customer groups has in lifetime value potential, do so now. To calculate the lifetime value of your core customer groups, you need to extrapolate averages from the data files in each segment and then factor in the corresponding values using Figure 11-7. Doing this will define your priorities and enable you to efficiently allocate your marketing resources.

Figure 11-7   *Determining Annual Profit and Lifetime Value per Customer Group*

Average sale value per individual	$100
Minus cost of goods sold	$50
Revenue	$50
Administrative costs: credit charges, percentage discounted for risk management	$10
Promotional costs: discounts, coupons, advertising per unit sold	$10
Net profit per transaction	$30
Average purchase frequency per year	5
Annual value per individual	$150
Average length of life cycle (in years)	15
Lifetime value per individual (annual value x life cycle)	$2250
Segment population	300
Segment lifetime value potential	$675,000

This calculation for segment lifetime value only holds true if all persons in your segment have the same number of years remaining in their life cycle. For example, the customer segment in the figure represents customers with an average of 15 purchasing years remaining. If your segment has varying life cycles, for example, women with red hair who represent an age span of 15 years, you will need to adapt your calculation to show a variance in life-cycle years remaining.

Positioning

Before embarking on specific marketing actions, you must first define the market position you are trying to achieve or the niche you want to fill. This space is not a tangible space but a perception. Positioning, again, is what you do to the minds of the consumers with regard to your brand's image. Thus your market position should be defined in terms that are relevant and meaningful to core customer groups and in terms that best present your brand's strengths and expertise. A positioning statement defines your business, your competencies, your commitments and priorities, and your core audience and motivates consumers to engage with your business.

Once you determine the market position that you seek to establish for your brand, you then need to develop a positioning statement to help you communicate that position to your customer groups. The purpose of a positioning statement is to briefly define your brand to consumers and establish a specific brand image. Positioning statements should be incorporated into all aspects of your brand from product development to promotion and distribution. In marketing, it needs to be easily identified in your key messages and overall graphic identity and used in all marketing pieces. It should guide the development of marketing materials such as brochures and a Web site. Both written and graphic communications should embody the personality and professional traits associated with your desired market position and hence positioning statement.

The most important part of selecting a positioning statement and brand persona is to select one that truly reflects the core competencies of your business in a way that is easily recognized and respected by target groups. Your positioning statement should sum up what you do, what you stand for, and what you aspire to be. For consumer brands, positioning statements often are synonymous with slogans. The key is to come up with a statement that conveys the value or benefit you offer—emotional or tangible.

Successful positioning statements for brands in various industries include

- Gateway: You've got a friend in the business.
- Kodak: Share moments. Share life.
- GE: We bring good things to life.
- Nissan: We are driven.
- The Learning Camp: Building confidence one child at a time.
- Porsche: There is no substitute.
- Coca Cola: The real thing.
- IAMS Dog Food: Good for life.
- Saba: The leader in human capital development and management solutions.
- VISA: We're everywhere you want to be.
- Foley's Department Stores: The right choice.
- Sears: Where else (changed from Where America shops).
- Wal-Mart: Always less. Always low prices.
- Evans Chaffee Construction Group: Defining excellence in mountain construction.
- Allstate: You're in good hands.
- Dell Computer: The world's leading computer system company.

These statements sum up in memorable terms what a brand is all about—what a brand is and strives to continue to be. Successful statements immediately tell customers what's in it for them. Positioning statements need to reflect customers' needs and desires, not management's egos or pride.

Key Messages

Key messages should address the issues of importance to customers and prospects, help to build the desired brand image, and reinforce the selected positioning theme. Your messages should be based on the values and needs of your core customer segments. They should be presented in a way that is appropriate and compelling, and they should be delivered in a manner suitable to your core groups' lifestyle and information-gathering processes.

Your brand's key messages should tout your strengths and distinguish your brand from those of your competitors. For example, if you have fewer product returns or repairs than a competing brand, this should be part of your key message strategy. Maytag has built its entire branding strategy on the key message that the company performs fewer repairs than other home appliances vendors. Thus, for years, consumers have seen the bored, idle Maytag repairman on TV. If your product developers or company leaders are visionaries in their field, pioneering new technologies and concepts, this should be a key message.

Key message strategies should be built on your customer profiles, appeal to your customers' decision processes, and be true and credible. There is never a reason to communicate a hyped or misleading claim. It will always come back to you in a negative way and jeopardize your brand's credibility among all audiences—consumers, influencers, and the news media. Once your credibility is damaged, it is very difficult to repair.

Actions

Coming up with clever and fun actions to help you fulfill your goal is the most fun part of marketing. When I worked for Ketchum Communications, a large public relations agency, we would often pull a team together to brainstorm clever and innovative ideas for achieving a client's goals. Our hours of idea generation were fun and fulfilling and resulted in many successful campaigns for clients. The challenge is to keep your ideas appropriate for the audience, relevant, doable, realistic, affordable, and measurable.

If you cannot measure an action's value against a defined goal, don't do it. Keeping your actions simple also will make it easier for you to execute them. Simple does not mean compromising quality; it just means simple. If you compromise the quality of a marketing event or collateral piece, you are essentially compromising your brand's image because you are positioning it as one that puts costs or profits before quality. No one wants to purchase a product of inferior quality. Execution is key to your image.

Potential action items include

- e-Mails or letters announcing updates or promotional messages to customers
- Personalized promotions
- Production of collateral sales kits or brochures
- Customer service programs
- Product modifications
- Product line expansions
- Web site development or enhancement
- Customer or partner appreciation events
- Public relations activities, such as media relations and publicity efforts
- Trade show exhibits
- Educational seminars

The list of potential branding and marketing activities is limited only by your own capabilities and imagination.

To keep focused and efficient, make sure that all the action items you develop are attached directly to your goals and challenges. Under each goal and challenge, you should list the actions that are needed and doable to support the goal or overcome the threat.

If your objective is to increase brand recognition in your marketplace, your actions might be to

- Conduct a consumer study to determine current level of recognition
- Develop newsworthy press releases and disseminate them to appropriate media

- Solicit presentations at association or service club meetings that attract qualified prospects
- Create a program that motivates and rewards current customers for referring friends and relatives
- Sponsor an event that caters specifically to qualified prospects and valued customers

Measurement

After identifying the actions you will take to achieve your goals and objectives, you then need to incorporate metrics. Everything you do should be measurable; otherwise, it is difficult to assess which activities are having the most impact and boosting your bottom line. You can measure activities by

- Number of leads generated
- New customers acquired
- An increased percentage of repeat sales
- Customer retention
- Dollar value per transaction
- News articles generated
- Feedback from customers, partners, and resellers
- Number of visits to your Web site
- Number of visitors choosing to register at your Web site

Again, my motto is, "If you can't measure it, don't do it."

Once you have outlined appropriate actions and measurements, the next step is to develop a project schedule and calendar. Doing so will help to ensure that you stay focused on executing appropriate projects and do so in a timely and pertinent manner. Project schedules should include project descriptions, due dates, task outlines, and ownership assignments. Figure 11-8 presents an example.

Creating a customer-oriented marketing plan is one of the most exciting and rewarding things you will do for your business. If you base this on actual customer and market data, it will be one of your most profitable endeavors over the long term of your business. Enjoy!

Figure 11-8 *Sample Project Schedule and Task List*

Project Description	Tasks	Owner	Due Date
Customer satisfaction survey to assess strengths and weaknesses of customer service	Update customer e-mail list	Employee A	March 1
	Develop survey tool	Team B	March 5
	Approve tool	Team VP	March 8
	Create response mechanism	Team C	March 5
	Create database for responses	Team C	March 10
	Distribute survey	Employee A	March 21
	Input data to customer profiles	Team B	March 22+
	Follow up with respondents	Team A	April 1
Initiate public relations efforts (newsworthy press releases to industry and local editors)	Develop media list for local outlets	Employee A	April 1
	Obtain editorial calendars	Employee B	April 8
	Identify news angles	Team A	April 15
	Write first potential press release	Employee C	April 22
	Distribute press release	Employee C	April 29
	Pitch editors	Employee B	May 1
	Set up tracking device	Employee A	April 22
	Monitor publicity		May 1+

Getting Started–Lifetime Marketing Checklist

Following is an outline to help you write your own lifetime marketing plan based on the principles set forth in this book. A digital copy of this worksheet can be found at *www.mcmurtrygroup.com*.

Writing Your Lifetime Marketing Plan

Situation overview	
Your strengths	1. 2. 3.
Your weaknesses	1. 2. 3.
Market and brand opportunities	
Market and brand threats	
Competitive analysis	List primary competitors and their imminent threats to your success. List functional alternatives and their potential threats to your success.

Goals	List goals and corresponding measurements for each goal. Goal 1: Metric: Goal 2: Metric: Goal 3: Metric:
Objectives	List objectives or broad steps for achieving the preceding goals.
Target markets	Select your core customer segments. List information from the profiles of these segments that will guide your development of key messages, communications channels, and so on. Customer segment 1: Influencers: Customer segment 2: Influencers: Customer segment 3: Influencers:

Positioning	Define potential market positions that you are uniquely qualified to fill and have a strong likelihood of owning. Select the market position that most reflects your brand's current and desired marketing strengths and position.
Key messages	Identify key messages for each of your core customer segments. These should be part of your customer profile. Customer segment 1: Key messages: Customer segment 2: Key messages: Customer segment 3: Key messages:
Actions	List marketing actions that are appropriate and affordable for you to execute for each of your customer groups.

Measurement	Define metrics for determining success of actions, messages, media purchases, story pitches, and other elements of your plan.
Execution schedule	Create a chart to outline your tasks, due dates, and responsible parties.

12 Conclusion

The Power of Guiding Principles in Building Business Success

Throughout this book I have discussed the power of lifetime marketing practices and principles. Beyond these, business owners, managers, and virtually anyone trying to sell a product or service needs to develop their own set of personal or guiding principles—the values that guide behavior and interactions with customers and define businesses. Without guiding principles, it will be more difficult to maintain lifetime relationships with customers, partners, and employees and to succeed in general.

Guiding principles need to expand beyond professional practices and values such as product quality and customer service standards. They need to include personal values such as trust, integrity, and commitment. Building a business on these and similar values will do more for your business than most anything. Values attract business; values cement loyalty.

A client of mine, Michele Evans of Evans Chaffee Construction Group, has the following quote from Aristotle on her office door and company letterhead to serve as an introduction to the kind of company she owns and operates:

We are what we repeatedly do. Excellence, then, is not an act, but a habit.

Her other motto is, "We do what we say we will do." Michele has built a very successful business by defining company values, practicing them at all levels, and hiring professionals that adhere to these standards in all their business interactions.

The power of integrity—upholding standards of excellence in all you do and delivering on promises—needs to be the foundation of your marketing programs and customer interactions in order for your business to achieve its potential. You can take your business to the pinnacle of your industry through lifetime marketing practices, and you do not even have to be a nice person to make a lot of money. However, if you operate your business on trust, honesty, fairness, and like values, your business will have the potential to soar.

The story of Earl Graves is a classic example of how personal values and relationships contribute to business success. Earl is one of the most successful businessmen in America. He did not inherit millions with which to start a business and did not take over his family's business. He simply worked hard and built strong relationships with businesspeople based on his ability to be trusted and his ability to do what he said he would do with the utmost attention to quality and detail. A child of immigrants to New York City from Barbados, Earl is today the founder and publisher of *Black Enterprise* magazine, a highly successful publication generating revenues of more than $55 million a year in sales and with a readership of more than 4 million.

Graves is one of the most sought-after role models and leaders for African Americans today and has received numerous awards and much recognition for his business achievements and contributions, far too many to mention here. Given all his achievements and accolades, I fully expected to hear profound words of wisdom about relationship marketing strategies essential to succeeding in business when I interviewed him for this book. Instead, when I asked him to describe the foundation of his success, I essentially got one word—*trust*.

"People need to trust you and believe in you," said Graves. "They need to know that what you say and do are going to be the same."

No matter what career he was in—real estate agent, assistant to Robert F. Kennedy, board member for American Airlines or the Boy Scouts of America, publisher, or entrepreneur—Graves has earned people's respect and loyalty because of the trust he establishes from the very beginning. People who work with Graves on a personal level know that his business is run with the same high standard of integrity with which he runs his own life. His values are what attract people to him and ultimately his business. Having values, sharing those values, and standing for them is what Graves preaches to young entrepreneurs.

"People need to know that you stand for something. And that your principles won't be compromised, that you have integrity," Graves tells associates, college graduates, and those who seek his advise. "Trust is critical in a world where a lot of business deals are still closed with a handshake," continues Graves.

Beyond trust, Graves is committed to giving back to his community. Giving to others through community service is not only a good way to meet new people and broaden your business visibility and network; it also helps form who you are and how people perceive your business. Graves puts much of his personal time, energy, and resources into programs that are not revenue generators, such as programs to help teens and children learn business values early on in life, because he wants to give of himself to others in a way that will help them maximize their potential. A big part of how Graves gives back is the large network of relationships he has helped others to build in order to achieve their own personal goals and wealth. He does this by organizing events that bring black entrepreneurs together to mingle and to share ideas, courage, and strengths, and to support one another's businesses. Graves also has developed a comprehensive resource for tools that will help anyone achieve personal wealth and business success through *www.blackenterprise.com.* These tools include the Black Wealth Initiative, which is a wealth-building kit and guidebook, and career-enhancing tips and links to job-related Web sites.

Graves is committed to helping others succeed because he believes in people, he believes in himself as a leader, and most of all, he believes in something. In turn, thousands of people believe in him and have thus supported his businesses for many years. Standing for something of value, of integrity, and of lasting worth to others will do more for your business than anything else possibly can, maintains Graves.

Gordon B. Hinckley, president of the Mormon Church, or Church of Jesus Christ of Latter-day Saints, recently wrote a book entitled, *Standing for Something* (Times Books), in which he said, "There is something reassuring about standing for something, and knowing what we stand for. For men and women who are true to themselves and to the virtues and standards they have personally adopted, it is not difficult to be true to others."

In business, being true to your customers, external and internal, is essential to building personal and professional relationships that result in successful business and lifetime value. Consumers do not want to affiliate with a brand they cannot trust. Look what happened to accounting and management consulting powerhouse Arthur Andersen when the world found out their work for Enron, a collapsed power company, was not based on truth and accuracy. Shortly after its questionable accounting practices were revealed, the company found itself on the brink of collapse, having lost many of its flagship accounts that did not want to be associated with an accounting firm with a reputation of distrust. Guiding principles and values matter, both personally and professionally.

You may be able to secure customers to your brand through innovative lifetime marketing efforts. And you may able to build a strong base of new customers though effective acquisition programs. Yet, if you do not build your brand on your strong values, you will lose critical opportunities for success.

Figure 12-1 lists the values that have helped to make American Express one of the world's most successful businesses and one with a coveted reputation for service excellence.

Figure 12-1 *American Express Blue Box Values*

All our activities and decisions must be based on, and guided by, these values:

- Placing the interests of clients and customers first.
- A continuous quest for quality in everything we do.
- Treating our people with respect and dignity.
- Conduct that reflects the highest standards of integrity.
- Teamwork—from the smallest unit to the enterprise as a whole.
- Being good citizens in the communities in which we live and work.

To the extent we act according to these values, we believe we will provide outstanding service to our clients and customers, earn a leadership position in our businesses, and provide a superior return to our shareholders.

Copyright © American Express.

As you move forward with your lifetime marketing plan, keep your eyes on the big picture, and build a business that has the foundation to succeed for your lifetime and beyond. To do this, define your brand's guiding principles, practice these principles, and integrate these principles into how your company operates. You also must communicate your principles to your customers, employees, and partners to let them know what you stand for. Doing so not only will define your brand positively, but it also will generate a strong brand image that will attract consumers and enhance brand equity among customers.

Assess your commitments now. Establish your commitments and values in the following areas, and communicate your position to all your customer groups. Let them know what your brand stands for and thus what they can expect when doing business with you.

Quality

Are you committed to delivering the best possible products, services, warranties, or guarantees in your given market? Do you compromise quality to increase your profit margins?

Integrity

Professional integrity includes honesty in all communications and upholding all promises. Companies with integrity do not inflate a product's capabilities or benefits, a business's stability or growth, or engage in marketing activities that are misleading in any way. They stand behind the promises they make in promotions and business deals and strive to meet and exceed customers' expectations in every possible way.

Service

Your customer service says a lot about your company's values. Make sure that you and your employees uphold the standards that will result in the desired brand image and reputation. Remember, customers talk. How you treat one customer will have a direct impact on other customers' attitudes.

Ask yourself

- Are your customers treated with respect and understanding?
- Do they leave your place of business feeling like your most important customer of the day?
- Do your employees treat customers in a way that builds trust and positions your company as one with integrity—as one that puts customers needs first and honors all commitments?

Employees who do not embrace your values and treat customers accordingly have no place on your team. One inconsistent experience or failure to uphold the standards you want your brand to symbolize will jeopardize your brand's image and provoke negative word-of-mouth activities. The cost is high.

Employees

One of the first things a new employee learns at American Express is the company's guiding principles, or what the company calls its "Blue Box Values." As noted earlier, these include "treating our people with respect and dignity." Making the fair treatment of employees one of six core values that guide the company gives employees a sense of security and helps build high morale. It also lets them know up front what is expected of them. The company's values are taken very seriously to the point that employees' performance evaluations include their fulfillment of and adherence to the "Blue Box Values."

To ensure that all employees embrace the values you want your brand to stand for, you must make them a top priority in all that they do and hold them accountable. When possible, let them help to define your brand's values. Employees who are treated with respect, dignity, and fairness and who are given opportunities to grow and thrive professionally are most often the same employees who become loyal champions for your brand and treat customers the way you would treat them yourself.

As a company leader, you set the stage for personal conduct and customer service. Defining a core set of values, living them yourself, and demanding that others on your team do so as well will do more for your brand than most other types of activities.

Communities

Participating in community projects, supporting local charitable and civic groups, and sponsoring local events are all activities that show a brand's commitment to its customers. By purchasing your products or accepting employment, the people in your community support your business and enable you to succeed. Giving back to your communities on a local, national, or global basis is an important part of living your values. You can serve your community by serving on local boards, by participating in local projects such as highway and park cleanup projects and fund raisers for charitable groups such as The United Way or Easter Seals, and by sponsoring local groups or activities such as a Boy Scouts troop or a shelter for victims of domestic violence. Identify programs that support your values, and then stand behind them with your time, money, words, and resources. Doing so not only strengthens your brand's image; it also generates visibility and broadens your company network. Giving back always comes back to you.

Regardless of the nature of your business, define your values. Define your priorities, your commitments, and your standards. By doing so, you will be defining your brand and building a foundation on which you can build relationships and profits for a lifetime.

While there are no guarantees or warranties, expressed or implied, for following the lifetime marketing principles or methods set forth in this book, I do know from years of experience, observation, and research that they do work and can significantly impact a company's profitability when executed properly and consistently. The end result is up to you—how hard you are willing to work to succeed and uphold your customers' respect and satisfaction for the long-term.

Now that you have learned how to boost your business's profitability through lifetime marketing, get started today. Do not delay developing your own lifetime marketing plan and securing a strong competitive advantage, one that puts you ahead of your like competitors and enables you to compete with your larger counterparts. Start today by defining your values and commitments, your goals and priorities, your high lifetime value customers, and corresponding messages.

May you and your business enjoy a lifetime of success and lasting profitability.

References

Web Sites

www.1to1.com
www.adweek.com
www.alpinebank.com
www.amazon.com
www.babycenter.com
www.barnesandnoble.com
www.cnn.com—stories about *E. coli* contamination involving Odwalla and Hudson foods
www.crateandbarrel.com
www.crmforum.com
www.dbmarketing.com/articles—Database Marketing Institute, "Using Lifetime Value in Business-to-Business Marketing," by Arthur Middleton Hughes.
www.the-dma.org
www.drillingdown.com
www.factfinder.census.gov
www.harley.davidson.com
www.ivillage.com
www.mra-net.org
www.prsa.org—Silver Anvil Award
www.saturn.com
www.siebel.com
www.sric-future.com
www.yesmail.com

Sources for Research Studies

www.aberdeen.com

www.businesswire.com

www.cfs.purdue.edu/conscirt/quality.html—Center for Customer Driven Quality at Purdue University.

www.customercare.com—for link to Industry News Archives—"Study Confirms Negative Impact of Poor Service," 2002, Customer Care Institute, Mobius Management Systems (*www.mobius.com*).

www.jupitermedia.com—Jupiter Media Metrix consumer survey.

J. D. Power and Associates Reports: "Internet Research Grows as a Valuable Tool for Used-Vehicle Buyers," November 14, 2001; "New eMarketer Report Reveals Online Shopping Continues to Grow, Despite Downturn in U.S. Economy; New Report Shows That Most of the Growth Will Benefit Traditional Retailers," September 20, 2001.

Intermountain Healthcare—consumer categories for purchasers of managed care products.

Books

Gordon B. Hinckley, *Standing for Something* (New York: Times Books, 2000).

Arthur Middleton Hughes, *Strategic Database Marketing* (Chicago: Probus Publishing, 1995).

Regis McKenna, *Relationship Marketing* (Reading, MA: Addison-Wesley, 1991).

Don Peppers and Martha Rogers, *The One-to-One Future: Building Relationships One Customer at a Time* (New York: Bantam Doubleday Dell Publishing Group, 1993).

Merlin Stone, Derek Davies, and Alison Bond, *Direct Hit Marketing* (New York: Pitman, 1995).

Periodicals

Meredith Levinson, "Slices of Lives," *CIO*, August 15, 2000.

Interviews

Harlan Bratcher, Armani Exchange

Ken Burke, Multimedia Live

Ann Cathcart, The Learning Camp
Ann Colvin, Armani Exchange
John Cooper, Alpine Bank
Sandra Genova, Generation21 Learning Systems
Melinda Gladitsch, entrepreneur
Charles Graves, Charles Graves & Associates
Earl Graves, *Black Enterprise* magazine
Rob Griggs, entrepreneur
Mark Jacobson, direct marketing consultant
Kim Matthews, SteamMaster Cleaning and Restoration
John McMurtry, Steadman Hawkins Sports Medicine Foundation
Anita Russell, CA Russell Partners
Susan Sobbott, American Express
John Tedstrom, FFWD
Wojtek Tilbury, Somnyo Consulting
Rennie Truitt, marketing communications consultant
Tom Vitelli, Intermountain Health Care

About the Author

For nearly 20 years, **Jeanette Maw McMurtry, MBA,** has been helping businesses of all sizes develop and execute successful marketing strategies for building brand equity and lifetime sales among key customers. Her experience includes positions at American Express, Ketchum Communications Worldwide, DDB Worldwide Communications, Intermountain Health Care, and a high-tech start-up. Ms. McMurtry has won numerous awards for innovative and results-generating campaigns using direct communications advertising, public relations, and special event strategies and tools.

Currently, Ms. McMurtry is the principal of The McMurtry Group, a marketing firm based in Colorado's Vail Valley, that provides strategic and tactical marketing support to large and small businesses in all industries. She also conducts seminars on lifetime marketing themes and has presented papers at numerous conferences.

Ms. McMurtry holds an MBA with a marketing emphasis and has earned accreditation in public relations from the Public Relations Society of America (PRSA). She lives in Eagle, Colorado, with her husband, John McMurtry, and their three daughters, Jessica Rose, Jenevieve Virginia, and Jordan June, and a Doberman pinscher named Venus.

More information about The McMurtry Group and lifetime marketing resources and events can be found at *www.mcmurtrygroup.com.*

Index